美国科技企业
新近涉诉典型
案 例 选 编

郭海蓝 代霞·编译

MEIGUO KEJI QIYE
XINJIN SHESU DIANXING
ANLI XUANBIAN

知识产权出版社
全国百佳图书出版单位
—北 京—

图书在版编目（CIP）数据

美国科技企业新近涉诉典型案例选编／郭海蓝，代霞编译．—北京：
知识产权出版社，2023.5
ISBN 978－7－5130－8754－4

Ⅰ.①美…　Ⅱ.①郭…②代…　Ⅲ.①高技术企业—民事诉讼—
案例—美国　Ⅳ.①D971.222.9

中国国家版本馆 CIP 数据核字（2023）第 081847 号

责任编辑：彭小华　　　　　　　责任校对：王　岩
封面设计：张国仓　　　　　　　责任印制：孙婷婷

美国科技企业新近涉诉典型案例选编
郭海蓝　代　霞　编译

出版发行：知识产权出版社有限责任公司	网　　址：http：//www.ipph.cn
社　　址：北京市海淀区气象路 50 号院	邮　　编：100081
责编电话：010－82000860 转 8115	责编邮箱：huapxh@sina.com
发行电话：010－82000860 转 8101/8102	发行传真：010－82000893/82005070/82000270
印　　刷：北京建宏印刷有限公司	经　　销：新华书店、各大网上书店及相关专业书店
开　　本：720mm×1000mm　1/16	印　　张：14.25
版　　次：2023 年 5 月第 1 版	印　　次：2023 年 5 月第 1 次印刷
字　　数：260 千字	定　　价：88.00 元

ISBN 978－7－5130－8754－4

序

　　作为科技发展水平领先全球的国家，美国在孕育出一批强劲的科技企业的同时，也发展出了一套与之适配的法律体系。联邦层面有《国家标准技术研究院法》《美国竞争法》《复兴美国制造业与创新法》等综合性法律，以及以《联邦民事诉讼规则》为代表的联邦诉讼法律，科技专项立法有《半导体芯片保护法》《绿色技术促进法》等单行法律，知识产权保护领域包含《专利法》《商标法》《版权法》《反不正当竞争法》等，辅之以数量庞大的判例规则，对加强科技企业的创新引导和技术前沿领域的法律保护起到了重要的规范指引作用。这一套日臻完善的法律体系不仅对其科技进步和经济发展起到了积极的规则塑造作用，为个人和企业的科技创新提供了充足的规则激励动力，也在客观上构建了一套较为稳定的利益平衡机制，在多元主体参与和复杂产业分工的经济形态下妥善协调着各方利益。更重要的是，完善的科技企业法律保护制度维护了美国在国际贸易分工体系中的优势地位，并不时成为其制裁他国的"大棒"。

　　在以知识产权为主干的美国科技企业法律保护体系中，司法保护制度具有举足轻重的地位，长期的司法实践为制度建设和改良积累了丰富的案例经验素材。与高新科技产业相关的诉讼具有技术难度高、实践操作性强、利益主体牵扯性广的特点，以个案解决式的司法审判来调和各方诉求，再以判例、案例进行规则引导，尤其能够起到克服法律僵化、平衡各方利益、回应现实需求的积极作用。

　　相比较而言，我国的科技产业高速发展、科技企业快速涌现的时间虽晚于美国，但伴随着科技实力和综合国力的迅速提升，我国立法对于科技企业的保护和促进水平也迅速发展，核心专利、知名商标、精品版权等数量持续增加，以强化知识产权法律保护为抓手，激励科技创新、引导产业升级、培育"专精特新"企业逐步成为社会共识。习近平总书记深刻指出："知识产权保护工作关系国家治理体系和治理能力现代化，关系高质量发展，关系人民生活幸福，关系国家对外开放大局，关系国家安全。"①2020 年 11 月 30 日，党的十九届五中全会之后中央政治局进行第一次集体学习，主题就是加强我国知识产权保护工作。②随后，党中央、国务院印发了《知识产权强国建设纲要（2021—2035 年）》，详细部署了知识产权强国建设的总体要求和重点任务。③全面加强知识产权的保护工作将成为激发创新、引领发展的直接动力，而完备的法律法规体系、高效的执法司法体系，正是强化科技创新保护和科技企业引导的重要法治保障。

在以知识产权制度为主干的科技促进法治体系之中，司法力量是当之无愧的中流砥柱。当前，一批涉集成电路、计算机软件等高科技领域相关纠纷的妥善处理，在引导企业突破核心技术、带动技术和产业不断升级的同时，显著提升了我国司法体系服务科技创新大局的能力。依托知识产权司法保护这一制度基础，定位司法为科技创新赋能这一战略目标，总结国内外科技企业诉讼实践的有益经验，成为完善我国科技创新司法保护体系的当然之举。

在此背景下，本书从法律全文数据库（Westlaw）的公共案例中选取近 10 年美国法院审理的涉代表性科技企业的 10 个案例进行翻译，并将原文与译文一并出版，方便读者对照。全书以美国代表性科技企业为主体的诉讼案件为主流，考虑到市场上已有类似的美国知识产权诉讼典型案例译集，本书在案例选取上有如下侧重：在时间上，尽量选取近 10 年来发生的案例，紧盯时代潮流，反映最新的科技企业诉讼样态；在内容上，尽量选取与数字经济、互联网经济、高新技术知识产权保护相关的案例。读者会发现，苹果、谷歌、特斯拉等科技巨头将会成为本书中争讼的主角，数字版权管理、软件应用程序、应用商城广告政策等互联网经济下的特有标的将会成为本书中争讼的主要对象。在体例上，本书采用全文翻译的方式对案例进行详细介绍，而不仅局限于"争议焦点—法庭判决"式的宏观叙事，便于读者不仅能够清楚知悉

---

① "习近平主持中央政治局第二十五次集体学习并讲话"，中华人民共和国中央人民政府网，http：//www.gov.cn/xinwen/2020-12/01/content_5566183.htm，最后访问日期：2022 年 12 月 3 日。

② "习近平主持中央政治局第二十五次集体学习并讲话"，中华人民共和国中央人民政府网，http：//www.gov.cn/xinwen/2020-12/01/content_5566183.htm，最后访问日期：2022 年 12 月 3 日。

③ "中共中央　国务院印发《知识产权强国建设纲要（2021—2035 年）》"，中华人民共和国中央人民政府网，http：//www.gov.cn/zhengce/2021-09/content_5638714.htm，最后访问日期：2022 年 12 月 3 日。

相关诉讼主体的请求被支持或者被驳回的详细理由，也能够近距离了解起诉状修改、法庭听证、管辖异议等程序性事项的运作状态，浸入式感受美国科技企业诉讼实践的真实状况。

　　了解他国经验是为了学习和完善，更是为了创新和超越。在坚持对外开放和推动共建"一带一路"高质量发展的东风之下，我国科技企业的技术水平和国际化程度不断提高，在互联网、大数据、云计算、人工智能、区块链等新兴技术领域，我国企业更是和发达国家站在了同一赛道，逐步开始领跑世界。我们比以往任何时候都更需要了解科技企业司法保护的国际实践，需要发挥司法激励创新创造、维护公平竞争的重要作用。洪涛滚滚乘风势，可以预见，中国政府参与全球科技治理的实践会不断丰富，中国科技企业在国际市场上会不断涌现，希望本书能够在我国科技企业国际化的大潮之中贡献一朵浪花。

郭海蓝　代　霞

2022 年 12 月 30 日

目　录
CONTENTS

United States District Court，M. D. Florida，Tampa Division.

I　AMERICAN NAVIGATION SYSTEMS，INC.，Plaintiff，v. APPLE INC.，Defendant.

Case No 8：14-cv-1130-T-36TBM
Signed 12/01/2014

Attorneys and Law Firms

Barry C. Barnett，Susman Godfrey，LLP，Dallas，TX；Joseph S. Grinstein，Max Lalon Tribble，Jr.，Susman Godfrey，LLP，Houston，TX；Patrick C. Bageant，Susman Godfrey，LLP，Seattle，WA；Richard Edson Fee，Kathleen M. Wade，Fee & Jeffries PA，Tampa，FL；for Plaintiff.

Donald William Ward，Michael D. Jay，Boies，Schiller & Flexner LLP，Santa Monica，CA；Pedro M. Allende，Boies，Schiller & Flexner，LLP，Miami，FL；William D. Marsillo，Boies，Schiller & Flexner LLP，Armonk，NY；for Defendant.

ORDER

Charlene Edwards Honeywell，United States District Judge

*1 This cause comes before the Court upon the Defendant Apple Inc.'s Motion to Transfer Pursuant to 28 U. S. C.§ 1404 (Doc. 54). Plaintiff American Navigation Systems，Inc. ("AmNav") filed a response in opposition to the motion (Doc. 64). Apple filed a reply in further support of its motion (Doc. 76). On November 13，2014，the Court held oral argument on the motion. (Doc. 80.) Upon due consideration of the parties' submissions and the oral argument，the Court will now GRANT Defendant's

Motion to Transfer.

I. BACKGROUND

In this patent infringement case, AmNav accuses Apple of infringing U. S. Patent No.5,902,347 (the "'347 Patent"). The '347 Patent, which has four co-inventors, relates to the display of global positioning system ("GPS") data in real time on a portable mapping device. AmNav alleges that certain of Apple's products that include either the Google Maps or Apple Maps applications infringe upon the invention of the '347 Patent. Specifically, AmNav accuses of infringement the iPhone 3G, iPhone 3GS, iPhone 4, iPhone 4S, iPhone 5, iPhone 5C, iPhone 5S, iPad 1st Generation, iPad 2nd Generation, iPad 3rd Generation, iPad 4th Generation, iPad Air, iPad Mini 1st Generation, and iPad Mini 2nd Generation (collectively, the "Accused Devices"). Doc.1 ¶ 16.

Plaintiff AmNav owns the '347 Patent. Doc.64-1 ("Backman Decl.") ¶ 15. It is a Florida corporation whose only place of business is in Florida. Id.¶¶ 10-12. Its business, which is based in Tampa, involves offering the patents that it owns for license to companies that practice the inventions of its patents or wish to do so in the future. Id.¶ 16. Douglas J. Backman, the sole shareholder, director, and officer of AmNav for over ten years, has owned real property and resided primarily in Florida since April 2009. Id.¶¶ 6-9, 13.

Defendant Apple is a California corporation headquartered in Cupertino, California. Doc.55-2 ("Van Dyke Decl.") ¶ 3. Its management, research and development, and marketing are primarily located in or near Cupertino. Id. The Apple Maps application was developed by engineers at Apple's Cupertino campus. Id.¶ 5. With regard to the Google Maps application, Apple has not had, and does not have, any involvement with its design or development. Id.¶ 7. However, the implementation of the Google Maps application in Apple's devices and in its iTunes App Store was primarily developed by engineers at Apple's Cupertino campus. Id.¶ 6.

AmNav brought this action in this Court, the Middle District of Florida. Apple now seeks to transfer the case to the Northern District of California, arguing that such transfer is warranted under 28 U. S. C.§ 1404 (a).

II. DISCUSSION

Although the substantive law of the Federal Circuit governs patent cases, courts apply the law of the regional circuit when evaluating procedural issues. See *In re Bill of Lading*, *681 F.3d 1323*, *1331 (Fed. Cir.2012)*. Accordingly, Eleventh Circuit law applies to a ruling on a motion to transfer pursuant to 28 U. S. C.§ 1404 (a). *See In re Nissim Corp.*, *316 Fed. Appx.991*, *992 (Fed. Cir.2008)*.

*2 A district court may transfer any civil action to any other district or division where it might have been brought " [f] or the convenience of the parties and witnesses, in the interest of justice". 28 U. S. C.§ 1404 (a). Under Section 1404 (a), a district court has the discretion to grant or deny a motion to transfer. See In re Ricoh Corp., 870 F.2d 570, 573 n.5 (11th Cir.1989). Such motions are analyzed according to an "individualized, case-by-case consideration of convenience and fairness". *Stewart Organization*, *Inc. v. Ricoh Corp.*, *487 U. S.22*, *29 (1988)* (quotation marks and citation omitted).

Factors to consider in determining the propriety of transfer include :

(1) the convenience of the witnesses ; (2) the location of relevant documents and the relative ease of access to sources of proof ; (3) the convenience of the parties ; (4) the locus of operative facts ; (5) the availability of process to compel the attendance of unwilling witnesses ; (6) the relative means of the parties ; (7) a forum's familiarity with the governing law ; (8) the weight accorded a plaintiff's choice of forum ; and (9) trial efficiency and the interests of justice, based on the totality of the circumstances.

Manuel v. Convergys Corp., *430 F.3d 1132*, *1135 n.1 (11th Cir.2005)*. The burden is on the movant to establish that the suggested forum is more convenient. See *Ricoh*, *870 F.2d at 573*. Further, the Court must give considerable weight to the plaintiff's choice of forum, and will not disturb it unless it is "clearly outweighed" by considerations of convenience, cost, judicial economy and expeditious discovery and trial process. See *Robinson v. Giarmarco & Bill*, *P. C.*, *74 F.3d 253*, *260 (11th Cir.1996)*.

A. The District Court for the Northern District of California is an Appropriate Transferee Court

Apple resides in the Northern District of California. Accordingly, the Northern District of California is a venue in which this action might have been brought. See 28 U. S. C.§ 1391 (b) (1). Further, the District Court for the Northern District of California would have subject matter jurisdiction over the claims here pursuant to 28 U. S. C.§§ 1331 and 1338 (a) to the same extent as this Court. The District Court for the Northern District of California is therefore an appropriate transferee court. *See 28 U. S. C.§ 1404 (a)* ; *Windmere Corp. v. Remington Prods., Inc., 617 F. Supp.8, 10 (S. D. Fla.1985)*. The Court will proceed to consider each of the Manuel factors.

B. The Convenience of the Witnesses Favors Transfer

The parties disagree as to which forum is more convenient for the witnesses. On the one hand, Apple argues that the Northern District of California is more convenient. In support, it asserts that all of its witnesses with knowledge of the accused "Maps" applications work in or around Cupertino, California. Van Dyke Decl.¶ 5. It asserts also that with regard to Google Maps, non-party Google employees expected to possess relevant information, such as the engineers who designed and developed the application and the engineers who interacted with Apple in connection with the implementation of the application in the Accused Devices, are likely located in the Northern District of California. It adds that all of these witnesses are expected to provide critical testimony relating to infringement. Finally, it points out that with the exception of Mr. Backman, none of the witnesses reside in the Middle District of Florida.

On the other hand, AmNav argues that the Middle District of Florida is more convenient. In support, it notes that Mr. Backman resides in Florida, that the co-inventors of the '347 Patent reside in Massachusetts and New Hampshire, that the lawyers who prosecuted the '347 Patent reside in Massachusetts, and that the principal businessman who authored AmNav's original business plan for manufacturing devices that practice the '347 Patent resides in Massachusetts. Backman Decl.¶¶ 3, 20-21 ; Doc.55-8 ¶¶ 2-3 ; Doc.64-2 ("DeFalco Decl.") ¶ 2. It notes also that travel from Massachusetts and New Hampshire to Tampa, Florida would require only half the time as travel to San Francisco, California. It adds that these witnesses have knowledge of facts relevant to the scope of the patent, as well as to Apple's invalidity and unenforceability defenses.

*3 The Court is persuaded by Apple's arguments. To begin with, only a single witness—Mr. Backman—actually resides in this District, whereas a number of witnesses reside in the Northern District of California. See *Wi-LAN USA, Inc. v. Apple Inc., Case No.12-cv-24318, 2013 WL 1343535, at 3 (S. D. Fla. Apr.2, 2013)*; see also *Jongerius Panoramic Techns., LLC v. Google Inc., Case No.12-cv-308, Doc.69 (hereinafter "Jongerius"), at 5 (M. D. Fla. Jul.13, 2012).* But more importantly, the Court finds that on balance, the Northern District of California is clearly more convenient for the non-party witnesses. Indeed, this Court does not simply "tally the number of witnesses" in each prospective forum, see *Dale v. United States, 846 F. Supp.2d 1256, 1258 (M. D. Fla.2012)*, but rather must give great weight to the convenience of non-party witnesses, see *Trinity Christian Center of Santa Ana, Inc. v. New Frontier Media, Inc., 761 F. Supp.2d 1322, 1327 (M. D. Fla.2010).*

Here, the sole witness that resides in this District is a party to the litigation, whereas the witnesses that reside in the Northern District of California include also critical third party witnesses from Google. The Court finds that it would be significantly more convenient for Google if this action were transferred to the Northern District of California. Indeed, that is where Google is headquartered. Doc.55-4 ("Wagner Decl.") ¶ 3. By contrast, Google's connections to Florida in relation to the accused Google Maps application is nonexistent—it employs only six people in this state, and those employees are not involved with the management, research, design, development, and/or maintenance of the Google Maps application. Id.¶ 4. It is thus clear that, in light of the importance of Google's testimony, maintaining the action in this forum would inevitably impose on Google the significant burdens of cross-country travel.

AmNav does not dispute that Google's principal place of business is in the Northern District of California or that the Google employees with knowledge of the Google Maps application are expected to reside in that district. AmNav also does not dispute that the testimony from Google's employees will be critical to the case. Rather, AmNav appears to suggest that the Court should give Google's convenience less consideration because its interests are aligned with Apple's. The Court disagrees. The fact remains that, interested or not, Google is not a party to this litigation. AmNav has chosen not to sue Google. Google and Apple do not have an agency relationship. And it is clear that, although Google and Apple collaborated for aspects relating to the implementation of the Google Maps application, Apple had no involvement with the actual development or design of the application. Google's interest thus cannot be discounted.

By contrast, the increase in convenience for the Massachusetts and New Hampshire third parties in maintaining the action in this District is far less pronounced. The Court recognizes that at least one of the co-inventors of the '347 Patent is elderly and that the distance from Massachusetts/New Hampshire to Tampa is geographically closer than the distance from Massachusetts/New Hampshire to San Francisco. However, even if this action were not transferred, significant travel by these parties would still be required if they wished to testify at trial. Indeed, regardless of whether this action is in the Middle District of Florida or the Northern District of California, the Massachusetts and New Hampshire witnesses would still have to travel for at least several hours to appear at trial. The Court finds that the marginal increase in convenience to these witnesses by maintaining the action in this District is easily outweighed by the significant increase in convenience to Google by transferring the action, and accordingly concludes that this factor favors transfer.

C. The Location of the Relevant Documents and Relative Ease of Access to Sources of Proof is Neutral

*4 Apple asserts that "relevant documents and sources of proof are concentrated in the Northern District of California", including its documents relating to "sales, licensing, marketing, customer support, and engineering, including source code, for the Accused Devices and accused 'Maps' applications". Doc.54 at 12-13. Apple asserts also that Google's documents are likely to be housed in the Northern District of California. Finally, Apple suggests that it is unlikely that AmNav will have many relevant documents in the Middle District of Florida.

AmNav disputes this characterization, noting that its documents relating to the conception and reduction to practice of the invention claimed in the '347 Patent are located in the Middle District of Florida. AmNav also argues, and Apple concedes, that all of the documents can be produced electronically. Because Apple has not identified any special circumstances tying its sources of proof to the Northern District of California, e. g., sensitive source code that can be viewed only on computer terminals located at its headquarters, the Court finds that this factor is mostly neutral or otherwise insignificant. See *Trinity, 761 F. Supp.2d at*

1327.

D. The Convenience of the Parties Favors Transfer

Both parties contend that their choice of forum is more convenient on balance. On the one hand, Apple argues that it has extensive ties to the Northern District of California, that the Apple engineers knowledgeable about the Accused Devices and Maps applications are located there, and that AmNav's commercial presence in this District appears to be limited to its legal proceedings. On the other hand, AmNav argues that this District is its home, that this District is plainly more convenient for its principal, Mr. Backman, and that, while it has no presence in the Northern District of California, Apple has research facilities in this District through which it can access documents and source code.

The Court agrees with Apple that the convenience of the parties favors transfer. Importantly, AmNav's past and continued presence in this District appears to be a product of Mr. Backman's choice of residence, and any potential inconvenience of transferring the case appears to inure only to Mr. Backman as an individual and not to AmNav as a business. Indeed, AmNav does not dispute that it has at most a limited commercial presence in this District and that its principal place of business is its litigation counsel's mailing address. The possible inconvenience to AmNav's single witness is outweighed by Apple's well-established presence in the Northern District of California, especially in relation to the products and applications at issue here. This factor therefore favors transfer. Accord Jongerius at 6-7.

E. The Locus of Operative Facts Favors Transfer

Apple argues, and the Court agrees, that the locus of operative facts lies in the Northern District of California. "In patent-infringement cases, the locus of operative facts usually lies where the allegedly infringing product was designed, developed, and produced." *Carroll v. Texas Instruments, Inc., 910 F. Supp.2d 1331, 1339-40 (M. D. Ala.2012)* (quotation marks and citations omitted) ; see also *Seal Shield, LLC v. Otter Prods., LLC, Case No.13-cv-967, 2013 WL 6017330, at 3 (M. D. Fla. Nov.13, 2013)* (same). Here, it is undisputed that the Northern District of California is where Apple designed and developed the Accused Devices. It is also undisputed that the Northern District of California is where the accused Maps applications were designed, developed, and implemented.

*5 AmNav argues that facts relating to a number of Apple's affirmative defenses, such as prosecution history estoppel, occurred outside of California. AmNav also apparently suggests that Apple performs work relating to the Accused Devices and/or Maps applications at its two research facilities in Florida. However, the Court finds these arguments unpersuasive. First, although certain facts relating to Apple's affirmative defenses may have occurred outside of California, these issues are peripheral to the "center of gravity" of the accused activity. Further, even if the Court were to give weight to these considerations, the fact remains that the vast majority of these events did not occur in this District, but rather in Massachusetts and/or New Hampshire, where the invention of the '347 Patent was conceived and reduced to practice, and where the '347 Patent was prosecuted. Second, the deposition testimony makes clear that the employees at the Apple facilities in Florida have not worked, and do not work, on the Accused Devices and/or the accused Maps applications. Apple's presence in Florida is therefore irrelevant with regard to the locus of operative facts factor.

In sum, the secondary considerations raised by AmNav do not alter the fundamental locus of operative facts for this case, which is where the allegedly infringing products and applications were "designed, developed, and produced". The Court therefore finds that this factor strongly favors transfer.

F. The Availability of Process to Compel the Attendance of Unwilling Witnesses is Neutral

This factor is relevant only if a party demonstrates, as a threshold matter, that a particular witness would otherwise be unwilling to testify at trial. See *F. T. C. v. Direct Benefits Grp., LLC*, Case No.11-cv-1186, 2012 WL 3715191, at 4 (*M. D. Fla. Aug.7, 2012*). Apple asserts that the testimony of third party Google will likely be necessary for its defense of this litigation, and that process will be available in the Northern District of California to compel such testimony. However, Apple has failed to demonstrate that Google would be unwilling to testify in the absence of process ; indeed, it does not dispute that Google is an interested party, see, e. g., Doc.79 ¶ 8. Likewise, although AmNav asserts that the Massachusetts and New Hampshire witnesses are "less likely" to testify in California than in Florida, it has not made any showing that these witnesses would be unwilling to do so without process.[1] Accordingly, as neither party has demonstrated the necessity of process to compel the attendance of any witness, this factor is neutral.

G. The Relative Means of the Parties is Neutral

It is unquestionable that Apple is larger and wealthier than AmNav. However, Apple argues, and AmNav does not dispute, that AmNav can litigate this case in the Northern District of California without suffering undue financial burden. Indeed, this is not a situation where one of the parties is an individual, and the other is a corporation. Compare, e. g., *Baker v. Major League Baseball Properties, Inc., Case No.08-cv-114, 2009 WL 1098482, at 3 (N. D. Fla. Apr.22, 2009)*. The Court therefore finds that this factor is neutral. Accord Operating Sys. Solns., LLC v. Apple Inc., Case No.11-cv-1754, Doc.37, at 6-7 (M. D. Fla. Jan.30, 2012).

H. The Forum's Familiarity with the Governing Law is Neutral

The Court agrees with both parties that the Northern District of California and the Middle District of Florida are equivalently well-versed in the applicable federal law of patents. This factor is therefore neutral.

I. Lesser Weight is to be Accorded the Plaintiff's Choice of Forum

" [W] here the operative facts underlying the cause of action did not occur within the forum chosen by the plaintiff, the choice of forum is entitled to less consideration." See *Garay v. BRK Elecs., 755 F. Supp.1010, 1011 (M. D. Fla.1991)*. Here, it is undisputed that none of the underlying facts giving rise to AmNav's claims arose in the Middle District of Florida—the invention was conceived and reduced to practice in Massachusetts and/or New Hampshire, the '347 Patent was prosecuted by attorneys in Massachusetts, and the Accused Devices and Maps applications were designed and developed in California. The Court therefore discounts some of the weight that would normally be afforded this factor.

*6 At the same time, a plaintiff's choice of forum must be afforded "considerable deference" when the plaintiff has elected to bring suit in the district in which he resides. *Mason v. Smithkline Beecham Clinical Labs., 146 F. Supp.2d 1355, 1360 (S. D. Fla.2001)*. Here, it is undisputed that AmNav is a Florida corporation. Apple argues that the Court should nevertheless discount this fact because AmNav's presence here is merely "recent, ephemeral, and an artifact of litigation." The Court agrees, at least to some extent. Although Mr. Backman may be a bona fide resident of Florida, that does not change the fact that AmNav existed here for less than six weeks prior to the filing of the Complaint. AmNav's short tenure in this District is further highlighted by the fact that its predecessor entity was located for over a decade in Massachusetts, where it was originally incorporated. Moreover, as stated in AmNav's Articles of Incorporation, its principal office and mailing address is the address of its counsel for this litigation. In sum, although the Court cannot speculate as to each of the particular reasons why Mr. Backman may have desired to incorporate AmNav in Florida in April 2014, it cannot ignore the very reasonable inference that AmNav's presence here is at least in part an artifact of litigation. See *In re Zimmer Hldgs., Inc., 609 F.3d 1378, 1381 (Fed. Cir.2010)*. In conjunction with the fact that none of the underlying facts occurred in this forum, the Court will therefore afford AmNav's choice of forum little weight.

J. Trial Efficiency and the Interests of Justice are Neutral

In evaluating this factor, a court considers, inter alia, judicial economy and the interest in having localized controversies decided at home. See *Silong v. United States, Case No.05-cv-55, 2006 WL 948048, at 3 & n.22 (M. D. Fla. Apr.12, 2006) (citing Gulf Oil Corp. v. Gilbert, 330 U. S.501, 508-09 (1947))*. Here, the Court finds that this factor is neutral. While the Middle District of Florida may have a shorter time to trial than the Northern District of California, AmNav has not set forth any reasons as to why the potential delay would be prejudicial.

Indeed, if Apple were found to infringe the '347 Patent, AmNav may recover for any of Apple's infringing activities during the interim period. Moreover, the controversy is not localized here, where none of the underlying facts giving rise to the claims occurred. By contrast, the locus of operative facts lies in the Northern District of California, which therefore has a greater interest in resolving this dispute. Accord Jongerius at 10.

III. CONCLUSION

The only factor that favors maintaining the case in this District is the plaintiff's choice of forum. However, not only is that factor afforded lesser weight under the particular circumstances of this litigation, other factors to which this Court must afford great weight—the convenience of the witnesses, the convenience of the parties, and the locus of operative facts—favor transferring the case. Ultimately, the "center of gravity" of the accused activity lies not in the Middle District of Florida, but rather in the Northern District of California—which is therefore the "preferred forum for [this] patent infringement suit." *Trace-Wilco, Inc. v. Symantec Corp., Case No.08-cv-80877, 2009 WL 455432, at 2 (S. D. Fla. Feb.23, 2009)*. The Court finds that AmNav's choice of forum is clearly outweighed by these considerations, and accordingly, it is hereby ORDERED :

1. Defendant's Motion to Transfer Pursuant to 28 U. S. C.§ 1404 (Doc.54) is GRANTED.

2. The Clerk is directed to TRANSFER this case to the United States District Court for the Northern District of California for all further proceedings.

3. The Clerk is directed to close this case.

DONE AND ORDERED in Tampa, Florida on December 1, 2014.

All Citations

Not Reported in Fed. Supp., 2014 WL 12769387.

Footnotes

1. The Court does not credit AmNav's bald assertion that Mr. DeFalco would be unwilling to testify in California. To the contrary, Mr. DeFalco actually implies that he would be willing to testify in California, because nowhere does he state that he is unable or otherwise unwilling to fly to California, only that it would be more inconvenient for him to do so. See DeFalco Decl.¶ 8.

美国佛罗里达州中区联邦地区法院，坦帕分院。

1　美国导航系统公司诉苹果公司

案件编号 8：14-cv-1130-T-36TBM
签署时间：2014 年 12 月 1 日

律师及律师事务所

原告代理律师：得克萨斯州达拉斯市 Susman Godfrey 律师事务所的巴里·巴内特；得克萨斯州休斯顿市 Susman Godfrey 律师事务所的约瑟夫·格林斯坦、小马克斯·拉隆·特里布尔；华盛顿州西雅图市 Susman Godfrey 律师事务所的帕特里克·C. 巴根特；佛罗里达州坦帕市的理查德·埃德森·费、凯瑟琳·M. 韦德、费和杰弗里斯 PA。

被告代理律师：加利福尼亚州圣莫尼卡市 Boies，Schiller & Flexner 律师事务所的唐纳德·威廉·沃德、迈克尔·D. 杰伊；佛罗里达州迈阿密市 Boies，Schiller & Flexner 律师事务所的佩德罗·M. 阿连德；纽约州阿蒙克市 Boies，Schiller & Flexner 律师事务所的威廉·D. 马西洛。

裁定书

夏琳·爱德华兹·霍尼韦尔，美国地区法院法官

*1 根据《美国法典》第 28 卷第 1404 节规定，被告苹果公司提出诉讼地转移动议后，本案被提交至法院（第 54 号文件）。原告美国导航系统公司对该动议提出了反对意见（第 64 号文件）。苹果公司提交了答辩状，以进一步支持其动议（第 76 号文件）。2014 年 11 月 13 日，法院对该动议组织双方进行了口头辩论（第 80 号文件）。在适当考虑了双方的陈述和口头辩论之后，法院现在将批准被告的诉讼地转移动议。

一、背景

在本专利侵权案中，美国导航系统公司指控苹果公司侵犯了美国第 5902347 号专利（′347 专利）。′347 专利有四位共同发明人，该专利技术主要是在便携式测绘设备上实时显示全球定位系统（"GPS"）数据。美国导航系统公司声称，包含谷歌地图或苹果地图应用程序在内的某些苹果公司产品侵犯了′347 专利的发明。具体而言，美国导航系统公司指控 iPhone 3G、iPhone 3GS、iPhone 4、iPhone 4S、iPhone 5、iPhone 5C、iPhone 5S、iPad 一代、iPad 二代、iPad 三代、iPad 四代、iPad Air、iPad Mini 一代和 iPad Mini 二代等设备（统称为"涉诉设备"）侵权。（第 1 号文件第 16 段）

原告美国导航系统公司拥有′347 专利。[第 64-1 号文件（"贝克曼声明"），第 15 段]美国导航系统公司位于佛罗里达州，其唯一的营业地点也位于佛罗里达州。（同上，第 10—12 段）公司业务总部设在坦帕，业务内容包括将其拥有的专利授权给应用该专利发明或希望在将来应用该专利发明的公司。（同上，第 16 段）道格拉斯·J.贝克曼是美国导航系统公司十余年来唯一的股东、董事和高级管理人员，他自 2009 年 4 月起就在佛罗里达州拥有房产，并主要居住于此。（同上，第 6—9 段、第 13 段）

被告苹果公司位于加利福尼亚州，其总部位于加利福尼亚州库比蒂诺。[第 55-2 号文件（"范戴克声明"），第 3 段]其管理、研发和市场营销主要集中在库比蒂诺及其附近区域。苹果地图应用程序由苹果公司库比蒂诺园区的工程师开发。（同上，第 5 段）苹果公司未参与过谷歌地图应用程序的设计和开发。（同上，第 7 段）但是，在苹果公司设备产品及其 iTunes 应用商店中上架的谷歌地图应用程序主要是由苹果公司库比蒂诺园区的工程师开发的。（同上，第 6 段）

美国导航系统公司向佛罗里达州中区联邦地区法院提起诉讼。苹果公司现在申请将此案移交给加利福尼亚州北区联邦地区法院，并称根据《美国法典》第 28 卷第 1404 节第 1 分节，这种移交是合法的。

二、讨论

虽然联邦巡回法院适用实体法管辖专利案件，但是法院在审理程序问题时适用地区巡回法院的法律。参见"提单案"，《美国联邦法院判例集》第三辑第 681 卷第 1323—1331 页（联邦巡回法院，2012 年）。因此，第十一巡回法院根据《美国法典》第 28 卷第 1404 节第 1 分节，对诉讼地转移申请作出裁定。参见"尼西莫公司案"，《美国联邦法院判例集》附录第 316 卷第

991—992 页（联邦巡回法院，2008 年）。

*2 根据《美国法典》第 28 卷第 1404 节第 1 分节，基于司法公正的考量，考虑到诉讼当事人和证人的便利性，地区法院可以将民事诉讼案件移交至其他可以审理该案的地区法院或者分支法院。地区法院有权决定批准或驳回转移案件管辖的申请。参见"理光集团案"，《美国联邦法院判例集》第二辑第 870 卷第 570—573 页（第十一巡回法院，1989 年）。法院会基于"个案的便利性和公正性考量"分析诉讼请求。参见"斯图尔特公司诉理光公司案"，《联邦最高法院判例》第 487 卷第 22—29 页，1988 年（省略引号和引用）。

转移管辖正当性需要考量的因素包括：

（1）证人作证的便利性；（2）相关文件存放地点及获取证据来源的难易程度；（3）诉讼双方参加诉讼的便利性；（4）有效事实发生地（或行为发生地点）；（5）强制不愿出庭的证人出庭的可行性；（6）诉讼双方的可用资源；（7）法院对该案适用法律的熟悉程度；（8）赋予原告选择起诉地的权重；以及（9）基于案件综合考量的审判效率和司法利益。

参见"曼纽尔诉 Convergys 公司案"，《美国联邦法院判例集》第三辑第 430 卷第 1132—1135 页（第十一巡回法院，2005 年）。原告承担证明起诉的法院更便于诉讼进行的责任。参见"理光集团案"，《美国联邦法院判例集》第二辑第 870 卷第 573 页。而且，法院必须充分考虑原告对管辖法院的选择。除非诉讼便利性、诉讼费用、司法经济性、能否快速有效进行证据开示和判决程序等因素"明显超过"原告对管辖法院的选择，否则法院不得干预原告的自由选择权利。参见"鲁滨孙诉贾马尔科和比尔案"，《美国联邦法院判例集》第三辑第 74 卷第 253—260 页（第十一巡回法院，1996 年）。

A. 加利福尼亚州北区联邦地区法院是合适的受转移管辖法院

苹果公司所在地为加利福尼亚州北部地区。因此，根据《美国法典》第 28 卷第 1391 节第 2 分节第 1 款，加利福尼亚州北部地区是本次诉讼的发生地。此外，根据《美国法典》第 28 卷第 1331 节和 1338 节第 1 分节的规定，加利福尼亚州北区联邦地区法院对本案诉讼请求享有和受诉法院同等的属事管辖权。因此，加利福尼亚州北区联邦地区法院是合适的受转移管辖法院。参见《美国法典》第 28 卷第 1404 节第 1 分节；"温德米尔公司诉雷明顿公司案"，《联邦判例补编》第 617 卷第 8—10 页（佛罗里达州南区联邦地区法院，1985 年）。加利福尼亚州北区联邦地区法院将继续考察该案的各个相关因素。

B. 证人作证的便利性有利于案件移交

诉讼双方对于哪个法院更方便证人作证这一问题没有达成一致。一方面，苹果公司认为加利福尼亚州北区联邦地区法院更便于证人作证，其指出己方了解涉诉地图应用程序的证人都在加利福尼亚州库比蒂诺或者库比蒂诺附近工作。［第 55-2 号文件（"范戴克声明"），第 5 段］而且，苹果公司还宣称在谷歌地图方面，可能了解相关信息的非谷歌当事人雇员，如设计和开发该应用程序的工程师以及与苹果公司就在涉诉设备产品上使用该应用程序而进行合作的工程师，可能住在加利福尼亚州北部地区。苹果公司还补充提出所有上述证人都可能提供与侵权行为相关的关键证言。最后，苹果公司指出，除巴克曼先生以外，其他证人都不在佛罗里达州中区。

另一方面，美国导航系统公司认为佛罗里达州中区更为方便。其指出，巴克曼先生住在佛罗里达州，'347 号专利的共同发明人分别住在马萨诸塞州和新罕布什尔州，起诉'347 号专利的律师住在马萨诸塞州，而撰写美国导航系统公司制造实施'347 号专利设备的原始商业计划书的主要商人也住在马萨诸塞州。［第 64-1 号文件（"巴克曼声明"），第 3 段、第 20—21 段；第 55-8 号文件，第 2—3 段；第 64-2 号文件（"德法尔科声明"），第 2 段］美国导航系统公司还指出，从马萨诸塞州和新罕布什尔州到佛罗里达州坦帕市所需时间只有到加利福尼亚州旧金山市的一半。此外，这些证人了解与专利范围以及与苹果公司提出的专利无效和不可执行性抗辩有关的事实。

*3 苹果公司的论点说服了法院。首先，本案证人中，只有巴克曼先生实际居住在佛罗里达州，其他证人都居住在加利福尼亚州北部地区。参见"美国 Wi-LAN 公司诉苹果公司案"，案件编号 12-cv-24318，2013 WL 1343535，at 3（佛罗里达州南区联邦地区法院，2013 年 4 月 2 日）；另见"琼格里乌斯全景技术有限责任公司诉谷歌公司案"，案件编号 12-cv-308，Doc.69（以下简称"琼格里乌斯案"），at 5（佛罗里达州中区联邦地区法院，2012 年 7 月 13 日）。但更重要的是，法院认为综合来看加利福尼亚州北区显然对非诉讼方证人更为便利。事实上，法院并不是简单地通过"统计可能出庭的证人人数"来决定管辖，参见"戴尔诉美国案"，《联邦判例补编》第二辑第 846 卷第 1256—1258 页（佛罗里达州中区联邦地区法院，2012 年）；也高度重视非诉讼方证人的便利性，参见"圣安娜三一基督教中心诉新前沿传媒公司案"，《联邦判例补编》第二辑第 761 卷第 1322—1327 页（佛罗里达州中区联邦地区法院，2010 年）。

本案中，居住在佛罗里达州的唯一证人是诉讼一方当事人，而居住在加利福尼亚州北区的证人还包括来自谷歌公司的第三方关键证人，且谷歌总部就在加利福尼亚州北部地区。法院认为，如果将这一诉讼转移至加利福尼亚州北部地区，对谷歌公司来说会更加方便。[第55-4号文件（"瓦格纳声明"），第3段]相比之下，谷歌公司与涉诉谷歌地图应用程序在佛罗里达州不存在关联性，因为谷歌公司在佛罗里达州只雇用了6名员工，且这些员工并未参与谷歌地图应用程序的管理、研究、设计、开发和/或维护。（同上，第4段）但因此，很明显，鉴于谷歌公司证词的重要性，在佛罗里达州诉讼必然会给谷歌带来沉重的跨州负担。

美国导航系统公司对于谷歌公司的主要营业地点在加利福尼亚州北部地区、了解谷歌地图应用程序的谷歌员工居住在加利福尼亚州北部地区以及谷歌员工的证词对此案至关重要均不否认。但相反，美国导航系统公司建议法院应该较少考虑谷歌公司的便利性，因为其利益与苹果公司的利益一致。法院对此表示不予赞同。事实上，无论是否存在利益关连，谷歌公司都不是这场诉讼的当事人。美国导航系统公司选择不起诉谷歌公司。谷歌公司和苹果公司之间也不存在代理关系。虽然谷歌公司和苹果公司在谷歌地图应用程序的使用方面进行合作，但苹果公司并未参与该应用程序的实际研发或设计，因此谷歌公司的利益不容小觑。

相比之下，在佛罗里达州诉讼给马萨诸塞州和新罕布什尔州的第三方证人带来的便利远远没有那么明显。法院确认，'347号专利的共同发明人中至少有一位是老年人，并且从马萨诸塞州/新罕布什尔州到坦帕的地理距离比到旧金山的距离更近。但是，即使不移交该诉讼，如果这些当事方希望在审判中作证，也仍然需要耗费大量行程。事实上，无论此诉讼是在佛罗里达州中部地区还是在加利福尼亚州北部地区进行，马萨诸塞州和新罕布什尔州的证人都要奔波至少几个小时才能出庭。法院认为，移交该诉讼给谷歌公司带来的显著便利要远远超过不移交该诉讼给马萨诸塞州和新罕布什尔州的证人带来的微弱便利，因此，该因素有利于案件移交。

C. 相关法律文件所在地和获取证据资源的相对容易程度是中立因素

*4 苹果公司声称，"相关法律文件和证据来源集中在加利福尼亚州北部地区"，包括与"涉诉设备和地图应用程序的销售、许可、营销、客户支持和工程（包括源代码）"有关的文件。（第54号文件，第12—13段）苹果公司还声称谷歌公司的文件很可能存于加利福尼亚州北部地区。最后，苹果公司表明美国导航系统公司在佛罗里达州中部地区不太可能存有大量相关文件。

美国导航系统公司对此提出异议，并指出其与'347号专利所要求保护的发明的概念和与实践有关的文件位于佛罗里达州中部地区。美国导航系统公司还主张所有文件都可以通过电子形式生成，苹果公司表示认同。由于苹果公司尚未发现任何将其证据来源与加利福尼亚州北部地区相关联的特殊情况，例如只能在位于其总部的计算机终端上查看的敏感源代码，因此法院认为该因素很大程度上是中立的或无关紧要的。参见"崔尼蒂公司案"，《美国联邦法院判例集》副刊第二辑第 761 卷第 1327 页。

D. 当事人便利性有利于案件移交

双方都认为，权衡之下，其各自对法院地的选择更为便利。一方面，苹果公司辩称其与加利福尼亚州北部地区有着广泛的关联，熟悉涉诉设备和地图应用程序的工程师即在此处；而美国导航系统公司在该地区的商业活动似乎仅限于其法律诉讼。另一方面，美国导航系统公司认为其本部位于佛罗里达州，对于公司负责人贝克曼先生来说该地区显然更方便；尽管美国导航系统公司不位于加利福尼亚州北部地区，但苹果公司在佛罗里达州拥有研究设备，可以通过这些设备获得文件和源代码。

法院认同苹果公司的观点，即当事方的便利性有利于案件移交。重要的是，美国导航系统公司过去以及未来在加利福尼亚州北部地区经营是基于贝克曼先生对居住地的选择，移交案件的任何潜在不便似乎只对贝克曼先生个人产生影响，而对美国导航系统公司没有影响。实际上，美国导航系统公司并不否认它在该地区只有有限的商业业务，其主要营业地点是其诉讼律师的通信地址。苹果公司在加利福尼亚州北部地区稳定经营，尤其是涉案产品和应用程序都在此处，在此地诉讼远远超过了给美国导航系统公司单一证人可能带来的不便。因此，该因素有利于案件移交。参见"琼格里乌斯案"，第 6—7 点。

E. 有效事实的发生地有利于案件移交

苹果公司辩称有效事实发生地在加利福尼亚州北部地区。法院也对此观点表示同意。"在专利侵权案件中，有效事实的发生地通常是被控侵权产品的设计、开发和生产地。"参见"卡罗尔诉得克萨斯仪器公司案"，《联邦判例补编》第二辑第 910 卷第 1331—1340 页（亚拉巴马州中区法院，2012 年）（引号和引文略）；另参见"Seal Shield 公司诉 Otter Prods 公司案"，案件编号 13-cv-967，2013 WL 6017330，at 3（佛罗里达州中区联邦地区法院，2013 年 11 月 13 日）（同上）。因此，加利福尼亚州北部地区是苹果公司设计和开发涉诉设备产品的地方，也是设计、开发和使用涉诉地图应用程序的地方。

*5 美国导航系统公司辩称，与苹果公司的积极抗辩有关的事实，如禁止反悔原则①，发生在加利福尼亚州以外。美国导航系统公司还明确表示，苹果公司在佛罗里达州有两个研究机构从事与涉诉设备产品和／或地图应用程序相关的工作。然而，法院认为这些论点不具有说服力。首先，尽管某些与苹果公司的积极抗辩有关的事实可能发生在加利福尼亚州以外，但这些事项与被控活动的"重心"无关。此外，即使法院对这些事项给予重视，事实仍然是绝大多数事件不是发生在加利福尼亚州，而是发生在马萨诸塞州和／或新罕布什尔州。而 '347 号专利的发明诞生和投入实践，以及被起诉的地方正是在马萨诸塞州和／或新罕布什尔州。其次，证词表明，在佛罗里达州苹果公司的员工过去和现在都未参与涉诉设备产品和／或涉诉地图应用程序相关的工作。因此，苹果公司是否在佛罗里达州与有效事实的所在地因素无关。

总而言之，美国导航系统公司提出的次要考虑因素并没有改变本案有效事实的基本发生地，即所谓的侵权产品和应用程序的"设计、开发和生产地"。因此，法院认为这一因素极有利于案件移交。

F. 强制不愿出庭的证人出庭的可行性是中立因素

作为一个基本问题，这一因素只有在一方当事人证明某一证人不愿出庭作证的情况下才具有相关性。参见"联邦贸易委员会诉直接利益集团公司案"，案件编号 11-cv-1186，2012 WL 3715191，at 4（佛罗里达州中区联邦地区法院，2012 年 8 月 7 日）。苹果公司声称，第三方谷歌公司的证词可能是其诉讼辩护所必需的，并且加利福尼亚州北区有强制提供此类证词的程序。但苹果公司未能证明谷歌公司在没有诉讼程序的情况下不愿意出庭作证；事实上，苹果公司并不否认谷歌公司是利益相关方。（参见，如第 79 号文件，第 8 段）同样，尽管美国导航系统公司声称马萨诸塞州和新罕布什尔州的证人在加利福尼亚州作证的可能性"小于"在佛罗里达州作证的可能性，但目前没有任何证据表明这些证人在没有法律程序的情况下不愿出庭作证。[1] 因此，由于双方都没有证明有必要采取程序强迫任何证人出庭，故该因素是中立的。

G. 诉讼双方的可用资源是中立因素

不可否认的是，与美国导航系统公司相比，苹果公司规模更大、资金也

---

① 译者注：专利侵权诉讼中的一种法律规则，指专利法上的审批过程禁反言，即专利权人如果在专利审批过程中，为了满足法定授权要求而对权利要求的范围进行了限缩，则在主张专利权时，不得将通过该限缩而放弃的内容纳入专利权的保护范围。在美国，禁止反悔原则的适用要求专利权人对权利要求的限缩必须以书面方式进行，并记录在档。相关判例可见 Festo Corporation v. Shoketsu Kinzoku Kogyo Kabushiki。

更雄厚。但是苹果公司辩称，美国导航系统公司在加利福尼亚州北区提起诉讼无须承受过度的经济负担，对此，美国导航系统公司没有提出异议。事实上，这并不符合一方当事人是个人而另一方当事人是公司的情况。参见"贝克诉美国职业棒球大联盟资产公司案"，案件编号 08-cv-114，2009 WL 1098482，at 3（佛罗里达州北区联邦地区法院，2009 年 4 月 22 日）。因此，法院认定这一因素是中立的。参见"Accord Operating Sys. Solns 公司诉苹果公司案"，案件编号 11-cv-1754，Doc.37，at 6-7（佛罗里达州中区联邦地区法院，2012 年 1 月 30 日）。

H. 法院对该案适用法律的熟悉程度为中立因素

法院认可双方的陈述，即加利福尼亚州北区和佛罗里达州中区的联邦地区法院都同样精通可适用于本案的联邦专利法。因此，法院认定这两个地区的法院对管辖法律的熟悉程度为中立因素。

I. 降低原告选择起诉地的权重

"如果构成诉因的有效事实未发生在原告选择的法院管辖区，那么原告对法院的选择权将被削弱。"参见"加雷诉 BRK 电子案"，《联邦判例补编》第 755 卷第 1010—1011 页（佛罗里达州中区联邦地区法院，1991 年）。本案中，毫无争议的一点是，美国导航系统公司提起诉讼所依据的有效事实发生地都不在佛罗里达州中部地区，这些有效事实包括：该发明诞生和实践于马萨诸塞州和 / 或新罕布什尔州；起诉苹果公司侵犯了美国′347 号专利的律师位于马萨诸塞州；涉诉设备产品和地图应用程序的设计地和开发地在加利福尼亚州。因此，法院降低了通常赋予这一因素的权重。

*6 但与此同时，如果原告选择向其居住地的法院提起诉讼，法院必须给予原告对法院管辖地选择的"充分尊重"。参见"梅森诉史克必成公司临床实验室案"，《联邦判例补编》第二辑第 146 卷第 1355—1360 页（佛罗里达州南区法院，2001 年）。本案中，美国导航系统公司是一家佛罗里达州的公司是无可争议的。苹果公司辩称法院不应忽视这一因素，因为美国导航系统公司"最近才于佛罗里达州成立，其短暂的成立不过是为了方便诉讼"。法院对此表示一定程度的认同。即使巴克曼先生的确居住于佛罗里达州，但这也不能改变美国导航系统公司在提交起诉状之前，在此处的存续时间不足六周的事实。美国导航系统公司在该地区的短暂存续，进一步突出了该公司此前已在注册地马萨诸塞州存在十多年的事实。此外，正如美国导航系统公司章程所述，其主要办公地址和通信地址就是本次诉讼的律师地址。总而言之，尽管

法院无法推测巴克曼先生于 2014 年 4 月在佛罗里达州成立美国导航系统公司的具体原因，但法院可以非常合理地推断，美国导航系统公司在佛罗里达州的成立至少在一定程度上是为了诉讼。参见"Zimmer Hldgs 公司案"，《美国联邦法院判例集》第三辑第 609 卷第 1378—1381 页（联邦巡回法院，2010 年）。因此，鉴于没有有效事实发生在本法院的管辖区域，故法院不会给予美国导航系统公司对于法院管辖地的选择以过大权重。

J. 审判效率与司法利益为中立因素

在评估这一因素时，法院充分考虑了司法经济性以及在本地审理地方性争议的利益。参见"斯隆诉美国案"，案件编号 05-cv-55，2006 WL 948048，at 3 & n.22（佛罗里达州中区法院，2006 年 4 月 12 日）（援引"海湾石油公司诉吉尔伯特案"，《联邦最高法院判例》第 330 卷第 501—509 页，1947 年）。本案中，法院认为这一因素是中立因素。尽管佛罗里达州中区法院的审理时间可能比加利福尼亚州北区法院的审理时间更短，但美国导航系统公司并未提出任何理由来说明潜在的延迟会造成损害。

实际上，如果苹果公司被认定侵犯了'347 号专利，美国导航系统公司可以就苹果公司在过渡期内的任何侵权行为进行追偿。此外，争议并不局限于此，因为引起诉讼的有效事实均未发生于此。有效事实的发生地在加利福尼亚州北区，因此该地区对解决这一争端具有更大的利益相关性。参见"琼格里乌斯案"第 10 点。

三、结论

唯一有利于在该地区维持本案管辖的因素是原告对起诉地（法院）的选择。然而，基于一些特殊情况，这一因素在本案的权重较小，而法院必须给予这些特殊情况——证人的便利、当事人的便利和有效事实的发生地等，以较大的权重，这些特殊情况都有利于转移案件管辖。最终，由于被控行为的"重心"不在佛罗里达州中部地区，而在加利福尼亚州北部地区，加利福尼亚州北区法院是"专利侵权诉讼的首选法庭"。参见"威尔科痕迹公司诉赛门铁克公司案"，案件编号 08-cv-80877，2009 WL 455432，at 2（佛罗里达州南区联邦地区法院，2009 年 2 月 23 日）。法院认为，美国导航系统公司对起诉地的选择显然与这些考虑因素相抵消，因此，判决如下：

1. 批准被告根据《美国法典》第 28 卷第 1404 节（第 54 号文件）提出的诉讼地转移动议。

2. 书记官受命将此案移交至加利福尼亚州北区联邦地区法院进行进一步的诉讼程序。

3. 书记官受命结案。

本案于 2014 年 12 月 1 日在佛罗里达州坦帕市结案和裁定。

所有引用

在《联邦判例补编》，2014 年 WL 12769387 中未见报道。

脚注

1. 美国导航系统公司直截了当地声称德法尔科先生不愿意在加利福尼亚州作证，法院并不认同这一说法。相反，德法尔科先生实际上暗示他愿意在加利福尼亚州作证，因为他没有说他不能或不愿飞往加利福尼亚州，只是说他这样做会更不方便。（参见"德法尔科声明"第 8 段）

United States District Court, N. D. California.

II APPLE INC., Plaintiff, v. MOBILE STAR LLC, et al., Defendants.

Case No.16-cv-06001-WHO
Signed 09/12/2017

Attorneys and Law Firms

Joseph Edward Petersen, Kilpatrick Townsend and Stockton LLP ; Vickie L. Feeman, Thomas H. Zellerbach, Diana Rutowski, Frances Cheever, Orrick Herrington & Sutcliffe LLP, Menlo Park, CA ; Nathan D. Shaffer, Orrick, Herrington & Sutcliffe LLP, San Francisco, CA ; Cathy Ching Shyong ; for Plaintiff.

Aaron Joseph Moss, Greenberg Glusker Fields Claman & Machtinger LLP ; Brian K. Brookey, Steven Erick Lauridsen, Tucker Ellis LLP ; Joshua Michael Geller, Greenberg Glusker LLP, Los Angeles, CA ; Andrew Levine, John Tobias Rowe, Jonas Noah Hagey, Braunhagey & Borden LLP ; Walter Christian Pfeffer, Singer Bea LLP, San Francisco, CA ; for Defendants.

ORDER GRANTING MOTION FOR LEAVE

Re : Dkt. No.148
William H. Orrick, United States District Judge

INTRODUCTION

*1 Apple seeks leave to take a second deposition of non-party Amazon on issues not covered at the first deposition. It argues that the scope of the first deposition was limited by the stipulated order permitting early discovery prior to its motion for a preliminary injunction. Amazon objects to the request because a second deposition would be unduly burdensome, the information requested is not necessary for Apple's case, and the issues could have been covered at the first deposition. As a compromise, to avoid the expense and burden of appearing for a deposition, Amazon offers to respond to a deposition by written questions. Apple rejects that offer. Because the burden here is not undue and the information requested cannot be secured solely through document productions and is more effectively secured from a live deposition (as opposed to a deposition by written questions) , I GRANT Apple's motion for leave to take a second Rule 30 (b) (6) deposition of Amazon. The September 20, 2017 hearing is VACATED. Civ. L. R.7-1 (b).

BACKGROUND

On October 17, 2016, Apple filed this case alleging Mobile Star supplied Amazon and Groupon with counterfeit Apple-branded products. Complaint ¶ 1 (Dkt. No.1). Apple moved for expedited discovery. Following the hearing on that motion, Apple and Mobile Star agreed to a stipulated order for expedited discovery in support of Apple's then-pending motion for a preliminary injunction. Stipulated Order (Dkt. No.43).

That agreement limited the discovery Apple could seek from Mobile Star, and allowed the parties to serve discovery subpoenas on Amazon but did not limit the scope of discovery that could be sought. Id. at 2-3. Apple then subpoenaed Amazon requesting documents and Rule 30 (b) (6) deposition testimony on two topics : Amazon's purchase of Apple-branded products from Mobile Star and the origin of other counterfeit Apple-branded products. Ex. A to the Declaration of Thomas H. Zellerbach [Dkt. No.148](Subpoena).

More specifically, the Subpoena sought deposition testimony (1) on the identity and quantity of all Apple-branded products that Mobile Star sold Amazon over the previous three years and (2) linking twelve Amazon order numbers to the sources who provided Amazon with the product. Subpoena at 7. The Subpoena also required Amazon to produce documents that (1) identified all Apple-marked products acquired from Mobile Star by any means within the past three years and

(2) showed the source of twelve products identified by their Amazon Standard Identification Number and Amazon Order Number. Subpoena at 6.

According to Apple, Amazon did not fully comply with the Subpoena. Apple complains that Amazon produced only 38 documents requested by Apple (and other documents responsive to Mobile Star's request). Zellerbach Decl., ¶ 3. Apple contends that Amazon's witness was only prepared to testify to the origin of the counterfeit products purchased by Apple on the Amazon website. Motion for Leave [Dkt. No.148] at 2-4 ; Zellerbach Decl., ¶ 4.1.[1]

*2 In order to secure the discovery Apple contends it needs for the merits of this case, on May 1, 2017, Apple served Amazon a second subpoena identifying additional topics not covered in the first deposition and additional document requests. Second Subpoena [Dkt. No.159, Ex.1], Zellerbach Decl., ¶ 6. After discussions with Amazon, where Amazon objected only to the proposed date of deposition, Apple served a final amended subpoena on June 28, 2017, setting July 7, 2017 as the deposition date. Zellerbach Decl., Ex. B (Amended Subpoena).[2]

Amazon objected to the second deposition request because Apple did not seek leave to take a second deposition, and informed Apple that it would not appear for the deposition. Zellerbach Decl., ¶ 7. Amazon continued to produce responsive documents, however, providing 113 supplemental documents on July 5, July 21, and August 18, 2017. Declaration of Brian Buckley ¶ 7 [Dkt 160] . Apple moved to compel Amazon to appear at the second deposition in the U. S. District Court in Western District of Washington. On August 4, 2017, Judge Jones denied Apple's Motion to Compel, concluding that Apple needed to seek leave from me before a second deposition could be compelled. Zellerbach Decl., Ex. C. Accordingly, Apple now seeks leave from me to take the second Rule 30 (b) (6) deposition of Amazon.[3] Motion for Leave [Dkt. No.148] at 2.[4]

LEGAL STANDARD

*3 A party requesting multiple depositions of a deponent must obtain leave of court. *Fed. R. Civ. P.30 (a) (2) (A) (ii)*. A deposition is limited to one day consisting of seven hours unless ordered by the court or stipulated by the parties. *Fed. R. Civ. P.30 (d) (1)*.[5] *Rule 30 (a) (2) provides that a "court must grant leave to the extent* consistent with Rule 26 (b) (2) ".

Rule 26 (b) (2) in turn provides that a court must limit discovery where "the discovery sought is unreasonably cumulative or duplicative", "the party seeking discovery has had ample opportunity to obtain the information by discovery in the action", or "the burden or expense of the proposed discovery outweighs its likely benefit, considering the needs of the case, the amount in controversy, the parties' resources, the importance of the issues at stake in the action, and the importance of the discovery in resolving the issues".

The parties dispute whether Apple must show good cause for seeking the second Amazon deposition. Compare cases cited at Apple Reply at 3 with Amazon Oppo. at 7-8. For purposes of ruling on this motion I will assume the good cause standard applies and under that standard GRANT Apple's motion for leave to serve its deposition subpoena. Zellerbach Decl., Ex. D.

DISCUSSION

Apple argues that the deposition it wants, seeking discovery on seven topics, is key to proving its willful infringement cases against Mobile Star and, as shown by documents recently produced by Amazon, can only be secured through deposition. Amazon opposes on the bases of burden and relevance, that Apple already had the opportunity to secure this information, and that the less burdensome and more convenient method of deposition by written questions is sufficient to meet Apple's needs.

Amazon contends that the burden required to prepare for and attend the second deposition is outweighed by the minimal relevance of the information sought to Apple's claims against Mobile Star. Oppo. at 9-13. While courts must be especially cautious not to burden non-parties (who typically deserve extra protection from the courts) with discovery obligations, Amazon played a central role in the underlying dispute and has information solely within its deponent's knowledge relevant to Apple's claim of willful infringement against Mobile Star. See Apple Reply at 5-7. Apple has explained why the information sought about Amazon's procedures and steps with respect to verifying the authenticity of Apple-branded products Amazon purchased from Mobile Star is directly relevant to its willful infringement claims against Mobile Star. Amazon's complaint that Apple may be attempting to secure confidential discovery from it—an Apple competitor—is blunted by the fact that the only procedures and steps that must be discussed at the deposition are those that Amazon took with respect to the purchases from and investigations related to Mobile Star.[6]

*4 While it is true that nothing in the Stipulated Order restricted Apple from taking full blown discovery from Amazon, my purpose in allowing expedited discovery was so that Apple could secure enough discovery to support its motion for a Preliminary Injunction, not to be ready for trial. That explains why Apple's initial document requests and deposition topics were so limited. Transcripts of Proceedings Held on 11-9-16 [Dkt. No.45] at 7-8. I recognize that Amazon had no control over or input into that process as a third-party and that the second deposition places an additional burden on it. However, because of the central role it played in the underlying events, I find that there is good cause for a second deposition.

As to the argument that a second deposition would be unduly cumulative, duplicative, and obtainable through written deposition testimony, Apple has shown that the discovery it seeks is implicated by but not answered by the documents produced by Amazon. Reply at 5-7. Amazon's offer of a deposition by written questions under Rule 31 is not an effective solution given the complex issues in this case, the central role Amazon played in the underlying events, and Amazon's apparent knowledge regarding the Mobile Star's sale of counterfeit items to it.

CONCLUSION

There is good cause for leave to take a second Amazon deposition. Apple's motion for leave is GRANTED.

IT IS SO ORDERED.

All Citations

Not Reported in Fed. Supp., 2017 WL 4005468.

Footnotes

1. Amazon contends that it produced 585 documents and the deposition witness was prepared and qualified on both topics listed in the deposition and testified for a full day on January 11, 2017. Opposition/Response [Dkt. No.158]

3-4. According to Apple over 90 percent of Amazon's document production consists of documents that were responsive to Mobile Star's subpoena including communications between Apple and Amazon. Apple's Reply〔Dkt. No.170〕at 2.

2. The seven new deposition topics are (1) how and when Mobile Star began selling Apple-branded products to Amazon ; (2) the process and criteria Amazon used to qualify Mobile Star to sell the Apple-branded products ; (3) Amazon's procedures for ordering and buying products from Mobile Star ; (4) Amazon's steps to authenticate the Apple-branded products Mobile Star sold ; (5) the investigative procedures Amazon followed in June 2016 when responding to complaints and concerns that the Mobile Star products were counterfeit ; (6) all complaints and counterfeit allegations made to Amazon regarding Mobile Star Apple-branded products and any investigatory procedures followed by Amazon ; and (7) the quantity and identity of all Apple-branded products Mobile Star distributed to Amazon since October 17, 2012.

3. In support of its Reply, Apple relies on information Mobile Star and Amazon have marked as confidential and, in accordance with the Northern District's Local Rules, filed an administrative motion to conditionally file under seal the portions of its pleadings referencing those materials. Dkt. No.169. In support of continued sealing, Mobile Star filed a declaration from its CEO Jack Braha〔Dkt. No.183〕stating that good cause exists to seal Ex. G to the Shaffer Declaration〔Dkt. No.169-9〕and page 7 : 17 in Apple's Reply because the information relates "to Mobile Star's confidential business information and trade secrets, including the prices and quantities of goods purchased by Mobile Star's customers. The materials also include confidential correspondence between Mobile Star and its customers, which reveal sensitive and proprietary information about Mobile Star's business operations and finances". Braha Decl.¶ 5. I agree that good cause exists to seal Ex. G to the Shaffer Declaration because the attached email discloses Mobile Star's pricing. However, good cause has not been shown to seal the text at page 7, line 17 of the Reply, disclosing Amazon's belief that unidentified products supplied by Mobile Star were counterfeit. Amazon filed a declaration from Brian Buckley in support of continued sealing of its information, asserting materials "relate to Amazon's proprietary systems and processes, including those that assist Amazon in preventing counterfeit goods from being sold on the Amazon marketplace and for identifying the source of a specific product

shipped through an Amazon facility". Dkt. No.180, ¶ 7. I agree and GRANT the motion to seal as to Shaffer Exs. C, D, and E as the information discloses details about Apple's inventory, sales, and investigatory processes. However the motion is DENIED as to Exhibit B, and Reply Br. at 5 : 22-27, 6 : 11-12, 6 : 15-19, 6 : 23-26, 7 : 24-25 as that information merely references Amazon requiring samples and conducting investigations but does not disclose any confidential details of processes or procedures, as well as general information regarding Amazon's beliefs about source of Mobile Star's goods. Dkt. Nos.169-4 & 169-5 shall be UNSEALED by the clerk.

4. Apple objected and continues to object to Amazon's standing to appear in this Court to oppose Apple's motion for leave. However, as described in my August 17, 2017 Order Regarding Request to Shorten Time and Briefing on Motion for Leave, it makes sense for purposes of judicial efficiency to allow Amazon to explain its objections now. August 17, 2017 Order [Dkt. No.153].

5. The parties dispute whether leave of court is required before a party may take a second Rule 30 (b) (6) deposition and there are cases on both sides of that issue. See, e. g., Blackwell v. City & Cty. of San Francisco, No. C-07-4629 SBA (EMC), 2010 WL 2608330, at 1 (N. D. Cal. June 25, 2010) (recognizing split in opinions). However, I need not reach this question because Apple has sought leave, if not in the first instance then at least in the second, after Judge Jones ruled leave was required.

6. Amazon argues that the deposition topics seeking seek testimony about Amazon's conduct, internal procedures, and investigatory techniques would not help Apple build its case against Mobile Star. Oppo. at 13. Apple disagrees, provides a short explanation of each topic's necessity, and notes that even if Amazon had reason to be concerned, the Protective Order in this case permits Amazon to restrict use of its confidential information to this case. Reply at 8.

美国加利福尼亚州北区联邦地区法院

2 苹果公司诉 MOBILE STAR 有限责任公司等

案件编号：16-cv-06001-WHO
签署时间：2017 年 9 月 12 日

律师及律师事务所

原告代理律师：凯拓国际律师事务所的约瑟夫·爱德华·彼得森；加利福尼亚州门洛帕克市奥睿律师事务所的薇琪·费里曼、托马斯·泽勒巴赫、戴安娜·鲁托夫斯基和弗朗西斯·奇弗；加利福尼亚州旧金山市奥睿律师事务所的内森·谢弗；熊琪。

被告代理律师：Greenberg Glusker Fields Claman & Machtinger 律师事务所的亚伦·约瑟夫·莫斯；塔克埃利斯律师事务所的布莱恩·布鲁克和史蒂文·埃里克·劳里德森；加利福尼亚州洛杉矶市 Greenberg Glusker 律师事务所的约书亚·迈克尔·盖勒；Braunhagey & Borden 律师事务所的安德鲁·莱文、约翰·托拜厄斯·罗威和乔纳斯·诺亚·哈吉；加利福尼亚州旧金山市 Singer Bea 律师事务所的沃尔特·克里斯蒂安·费弗尔。

许可动议批准

关于第 148 份案卷
威廉·H. 奥瑞克，美国地区法官

引言

*1 苹果公司请求就第一次取证未涉及的问题向非诉讼方亚马逊公司进行

第二次取证。苹果公司认为，允许在申请预先禁令动议之前进行证据开示的规定对第一次取证的范围造成了限制。亚马逊公司反对这一请求，因为第二次取证过于烦琐，所要求提供的信息对苹果公司案件而言并非必要，且这些问题原本在第一次取证时即可涉及。为了避免出庭作证的费用和负担，作为折中方案，亚马逊公司表示可以通过书面证词进行作证。苹果公司拒绝了这一提议，并提出二次作证费用负担并不过分，且苹果公司所要求提供的信息不能仅通过出示文件获取，通过现场证词（相对于通过书面方式得到证词而言）的方式可以得到更有效的确认。本庭批准苹果公司的动议，允许按照第30（b）（6）条的规定对亚马逊公司进行第二次取证。2017 年 9 月 20 日的听证会取消。《民事诉讼地方规则》第 7–1 条（b）款。

背景

2016 年 10 月 17 日，苹果公司提起诉讼，指控 Mobile Star 公司向亚马逊公司和高朋网提供假冒苹果品牌的产品。起诉状第 1 段（待审案件目录第 1 号）。苹果公司请求加快证据开示。在该动议的听证会之后，苹果公司和 Mobile Star 公司达成关于加快证据开示的协议，以支持苹果公司的（当时悬而未决的）预先禁令动议。[和解令（待审案件目录第 43 号）]

该协议限制了苹果公司向 Mobile Star 公司寻求证据开示，并允许双方请求法院向亚马逊公司送达证据开示传票，但没有限制可以要求的证据开示范围。（和解令待审案件目录第 43 号第 2—3 页）苹果公司随后请求法院向亚马逊公司发出传票。要求亚马逊公司提供相关文件和第 30（b）（6）条规定的证词，内容涉及以下两点：亚马逊从 Mobile Star 公司购买苹果品牌产品的情况，以及其他假冒苹果品牌产品的来源。如 A 出示给托马斯·H. 泽勒巴赫的声明示例（待审案件目录第 148 号）（传票）。

具体而言，传票要求提供的证词包括：（1）说明过去三年中 Mobile Star 公司向亚马逊公司出售的所有苹果品牌产品的标识和数量；（2）将 12 个亚马逊订单号与向亚马逊公司提供产品的来源相匹配。（传票第 7 页）传票还要求亚马逊公司出示文件证明：（1）验明过去 3 年内以任何方式从 Mobile Star 公司获得的所有标有苹果标志的产品；（2）说明亚马逊标准标识号和亚马逊订单号确定的 12 种产品的来源。（传票第 6 页）

苹果公司称亚马逊公司并未完全遵守传票的规定，只提供了苹果公司要求的 38 项文件（以及应 Mobile Star 公司要求作出回应的其他文件）。（"泽勒巴赫声明"第 3 段）苹果公司称亚马逊公司的证人只准备证明苹果公司在亚马逊网站上购买的假冒伪劣产品的来源。[许可动议（待审案件目录第148号）第2—4段；"泽勒巴赫声明"第4.1段][1]

*2 为了证据开示，苹果公司要求了解本案的案情实质，并于2017年5月1日向亚马逊公司发送了第二份传票，明确第一次证据开示中未涉及的其他事项以及额外的文件要求。[第二份传票（待审案件目录第159号，附件1"泽勒巴赫声明"第6段]。经与亚马逊公司协商，亚马逊公司仅对拟议的证据开示日期表示反对，苹果公司于2017年6月28日送达了经修改的最终传票，将2017年7月7日定为证据开示日期。"泽勒巴赫声明"，Ex.B（修正传票）][2]

亚马逊公司反对第二次取证请求，理由是苹果公司没有得到第二次取证许可，并且告知苹果公司其将不会出席第二次取证。（"泽勒巴赫声明"第7段）然而，亚马逊公司继续提供答复性文件，并且于2017年7月5日、7月21日以及8月18日提供了113份补充文件。["布赖恩·巴克利宣言"第7段（待审案件目录第160号）]苹果公司提出强制动议，要求亚马逊公司出席在美国华盛顿西区地区法院的第二次取证。2017年8月4日，琼斯法官驳回了苹果公司要求亚马逊公司出席的强制动议，裁定苹果公司在强制进行第二次证据开示前需要从法官处获得许可。（"泽勒巴赫声明"，附件C）因此，苹果公司现在向本庭请求获批第二次取证许可。[3][许可动议（待审案件目录第148号）第2点][4]

法律标准

*3 要求同一证人多次宣誓作证的一方必须获得法院的许可。《联邦民事诉讼规则》第30（a）（2）（A）（ii）条。除非法院命令或双方另有约定，否则宣誓作证的时间以1天以内且不超过7小时为限。《联邦民事诉讼规则》第30（d）（1）条。[5]《联邦民事诉讼规则》第30（a）（2）条规定："法庭应当在符合《联邦民事诉讼规则》第26（b）（2）条的范围内授予许可。"

《联邦民事诉讼规则》第26（b）（2）条规定了在"请求的证据开示存在不合理重复"、"请求证据开示的一方有充分机会通过诉讼中的证据披露获得信息"或者"考虑到案件需要、争议金额、双方资源、诉讼中案件争点的重要性以及证据开示在解决争点中的重要性，进行证据开示的负担会超过其可能带来的利益"的情况下，法庭应当对证据开示进行限制。

双方对苹果公司是否必须出示第二次寻求亚马逊公司宣誓作证的正当理由存在争议。本庭对苹果公司在答辩状第3点中引用的案例与亚马逊公司异议答辩状中的第 7—8 点进行了对比。为对该动议作出裁决，本庭将假设正当理由标准在本案中可以适用，并根据该标准对苹果公司关于允许其送达宣誓作证传票的动议予以批准。（"泽勒巴赫声明"，附件 D）

讨论

苹果公司辩称，其希望获得的 7 个取证内容是证明 Mobile Star 公司故意侵权的关键，正如亚马逊公司最近提供的文件所示，该等取证内容只能通过宣誓作证获得保全。亚马逊公司基于举证责任和关联性两方面提出反对，认为苹果公司已经有机会保全这些信息，并且通过书面证词取证这种负担更轻且更为便捷的方式足以满足苹果公司的需求。

亚马逊公司称，苹果公司请求开示的信息与其对 Mobile Star 公司主张的权利关联性极小，超过了准备和参加第二次取证所造成的负担。（"异议答辩状"第 9—13 点）尽管法院特别谨慎地避免向非当事方施加证据披露义务的负担（非当事方通常应获得法院的额外保护），但亚马逊公司在潜在争议中发挥了核心作用，并且其作为证人所掌握的信息完全与苹果公司针对 Mobile Star 公司所提出的故意侵权的权利主张相关信息有关。（参阅"苹果公司的答辩状"第 5—7 点）苹果公司解释，其所寻求的用于验证亚马逊公司从 Mobile Star 公司购买的苹果品牌产品的真实性方面的程序和步骤的信息，与其针对 Mobile Star 公司所提出的故意侵权指控直接相关。由于亚马逊公司从 Mobile Star 公司购买和调查相关产品的程序和步骤是作证时必须讨论的，因此，亚马逊公司所提出的关于苹果公司可能试图从其（苹果公司的竞争对手）处获得机密证据开示的申诉无效。[5]

*4 虽然和解令中确实没有对苹果公司从亚马逊公司获取全面的证据开示进行限制，但本庭允许加快证据开示是为了让苹果公司能够获得足够的证据开示来支持其申请预先禁令的动议，而不是为了审判。这也解释了苹果公司最初的文件请求和强制作证请求受到限制的原因。［2016 年 11 月 9 日的诉讼记录（待审案件目录）第 45 号第 7—8 点］本庭承认亚马逊公司作为第三方无法控制或参与该过程，并且第二次取证给其造成了额外的负担。但由于亚马逊公司在案件中发挥的核心作用，本庭认为有充分的理由进行第二次取证。

至于第二次取证将会带来的过度累加、重复取证以及可以通过书面证词获取证据的问题，苹果公司表明自己所寻求的证据开示在亚马逊公司提供的文件中有所涉及，但是并没有得到明确回复。（见"答辩状"第 5—7 点）鉴于本案问题复杂、亚马逊公司在该案件中起到关键作用以及亚马逊公司对

Mobile Star 公司销售假冒产品明显知情，根据《联邦民事诉讼规则》第 31 条规定，亚马逊公司提供书面证词无法有效解决问题。

结论

苹果公司有充分的理由要求对亚马逊公司进行第二次取证。苹果公司的请求动议获得法院许可。

判决如上。

所有引文

未在《联邦判例补编》2017 年 WL 4005468 中报告。

脚注

1. 亚马逊公司辩称其提供了 585 份文件，宣誓作证证人对证词中所列的两个问题都进行了准备且符合条件，并且在 2017 年 1 月 11 日进行了一整天的质证。[反对/答辩（待审案件目录第 158 号）第 3—4 点] 据苹果公司称，亚马逊公司所提供的文件 90% 以上是在对 Mobile Star 公司的传票作出应答，其中包括苹果公司与亚马逊公司之间的通信。[苹果公司答辩状（待审案件目录第 170 号）第 2 点]

2. 七项新的取证内容包括：

（1）Mobile Star 公司是如何以及何时开始向亚马逊公司销售苹果品牌产品的；

（2）亚马逊公司用于确认 Mobile Star 公司销售苹果品牌产品资格的流程和标准；

（3）亚马逊公司从 Mobile Star 公司订购和购买产品的流程；

（4）亚马逊公司对 Mobile Star 公司销售的苹果品牌产品进行认证的步骤；

（5）亚马逊公司在 2016 年 6 月回应有关 Mobile Star 公司产品系假冒产品的投诉时所遵循的调查程序；

（6）向亚马逊公司提出的所有关于 Mobile Star 公司的苹果品牌产品的所有投诉和假冒指控，以及亚马逊公司遵循的所有调查程序；

（7）自 2012 年 10 月 17 日以来，Mobile Star 公司向亚马逊公司销售的所有苹果品牌产品的数量和标识。

3. 为了支持其答辩状，苹果公司将从 Mobile Star 公司和亚马逊公司获取的信息标记为机密信息，并根据北区地方法规，提交了一项行政动议，要求有条件地将引用这些材料的诉状部分封存归档。（待审案件目录第169号）为了支持继续封存，Mobile Star 公司提交了其首席执行官杰克·布拉哈的声明（待审案件目录第183号），该声明指出有充分的理由封存沙弗声明附件 G（待审案件目录第169-9号）和苹果公司答辩状的第7页第17行，因为这些信息涉及"Mobile Star 公司的机密商业信息和商业秘密，包括 Mobile Star 公司客户购买商品的价格和数量。这些材料还包括 Mobile Star 公司与其客户之间的机密通信，这些通信披露了有关 Mobile Star 公司业务运营和财务的敏感信息和专有信息"。（"布拉哈声明"第5段）本庭同意封存沙弗声明附件 G 有充分理由，因为所附的电子邮件披露了 Mobile Star 公司的定价；然而没有充分理由封存答辩状中第7页第17行的文字，该文字披露了亚马逊公司认为 Mobile Star 公司提供的不明产品是假冒商品。亚马逊公司提交了一份布赖恩·巴克利的声明，以支持继续封存其信息，该声明声称材料"涉及亚马逊公司的专有系统和流程，包括帮助亚马逊公司防止假冒商品在亚马逊市场上销售，以及用于识别通过亚马逊设施运输的特定产品来源的系统和流程"。（待审案件目录第180号第7段）本庭同意并批准封存沙弗声明附件 C、附件 D 以及附件 E 的动议，因为这些信息披露了苹果公司的库存、销售和调查过程的细节。然而，本庭驳回关于封存附件 B 以及布赖恩答辩状中第5点（第22—27页）、第6点（第11—12页、第15—19页、第23—26页）以及第7点（第24—25页）的动议，因为这些信息仅提及亚马逊公司要求样品和进行调查，但未披露任何流程或程序的机密细节和亚马逊公司关于 Mobile Star 公司商品来源的一般信息。待审案件目录第169-4号文件和第169-5号文件应由书记员启封。

4. 苹果公司持续反对亚马逊公司出庭反对苹果公司申请许可的动议。然而，正如本庭在2017年8月17日发布的《关于要求缩短申请许可时间并简要说明的命令》中所述，为提高司法效率，目前允许亚马逊公司解释其异议答辩状是合理的。[2017年8月17日的命令（待审案件目录第153号）]

5. 当事方就一方依据《联邦民诉规则》第30（b）（6）条进行第二次取证之前是否需要法院许可存在争议，但该问题双方都有案例可以参考。例如布莱克威尔诉旧金山 City & Cty 案，案件编号 C-07-4629 SBA（EMC），2010 WL 2608330, at 1（加利福尼亚州北区法院，2010年6月25日，承认判决意见存在分歧）。但是，本庭无须提及该问题，因为琼斯法官裁定需要许可后，苹果公司已经申请了许可，即使一审未解决，二审也会解决。

6. 亚马逊公司辩称，寻求证明亚马逊公司行为、内部程序和调查技术的证词无助于苹果公司起诉 Mobile Star 公司一案。（"异议答辩状"第 13 点）苹果公司表示不予认同，并对每个问题的必要性作了简短的解释，指出亚马逊公司无须担心，因为本案中的保护令已经批准对于亚马逊公司机密信息的使用仅限于本案中。（"答辩状"第 8 点）

United States District Court, E. D. Texas, Marshall Division.

III CONTENTGUARD HOLDINGS, INC., Plaintiff, v. GOOGLE INC., Defendant. Contentguard Holdings, Inc., Plaintiff, v. Amazon. com, Inc., et al., Defendants.

Civil Action No.2 : 14-cv-00061-JRG
Civil Action Nos 2 : 13-cv-01112-JRG
Signed 04/15/2014

Attorneys and Law Firms

Holly Elin Engelmann, Craig John Donahue, McKool Smith PC, Dallas, TX ; Radu A. Lelutiu ; Robert A. Cote, Jr., Angela Vorpahl, David R. Dehoney, McKool Smith PC, New York, NY ; Samuel Franklin Baxter, McKool Smith, Marshall, TX ; Seth Raymond Hasenour, McKool SmithPC, Austin, TX ; for Plaintiff.

Gregory Blake Thompson, James Mark Mann, Mann Tindel & Thompson, Henderson, TX ; Glen Eric Summers, Alison G. Wheeler, Katherine Hacker, Bartlit Beck Herman Palenchar & Scott, Denver, CO ; Jennifer Haltom Doan, Joshua Reed Thane, Haltom & Doan, Texarkana, TX ; Abby M. Mollen, Bartlit Beck Herman Palenchar & Scott LLP ; David T. Pritikin, Richard A. Cederoth, Sidley Austin ; Mairead Schwab, Skadden Arps Slate Meagher & Flom ; Robert W. Unikel, Kaye Scholer LLP, Chicago, IL ; Bryan K. Anderson, Nathan Greenblatt, Sidley Austin LLP ; James Joseph Elacqua, Ian Chen, William Jerry Casey, Skadden Arps Slate Meagher & Florn ; Michael

J. Malecek, Timothy K. Chao, Kaye Scholer LLP, Palo Alto, CA ; Kelly A. Krellner, Sidley Austin LLP, San Francisco, CA ; Melissa Richards Smith, Gillam & Smith, LLP, Marshall, TX ; John Steven Torkelson, Sheria Dranise Smith, Carter Scholer Arnett Hamada & Mockler PLLC, Dallas, TX ; Scott F. Partridge, Bradley Bowling, Lisa Catherine Kelly, Baker Botts LLP, Houston, TX ; KD Shull, Huawei Technologies USA Inc., Plano, TX ; Eric Hugh Findlay, Roger Brian Craft, Findlay Craft PC, Allen Franklin Gardner, Michael E. Jones, Potter Minton, Tyler, TX ; Jay C. Chiu, Peter J. Wied, Terrence D. Garnett, Vincent K. Yip, Goodwin Procter LLP, Los Angeles, CA ; Michael Joseph Barta, Baker Botts LLP, Washington, DC ; Neil Phillip Sirota, Robert Lawrence Maier, Baker Botts, New York, NY, for Defendants.

MEMORANDUM OPINION AND ORDER

RODNEY GILSTRAP, UNITED STATES DISTRICT JUDGE

*1 Before the Court are three related motions in two related cases—Google, Inc.'s ("Google") Motion to Stay (Dkt. No.15) in Civil Action No.2 : 14-cv-00061 (the "Google Action") ; [1] ContentGuard Holdings, Inc.'s ("ContentGuard") Motion for Consolidation (Dkt. No.14) in the Google Action ; and Motorola Mobility LLC's ("Motorola") Motion to Sever Plaintiff's Claims Against Motorola (Dkt. No.55) in Civil Action No.2 : 13-cv-01112 (the "Amazon Action"). Given that the three motions involve common questions of underlying fact, the Court deems it proper to address all three motions jointly. Having considered the parties' written submissions and for the reasons set forth below, the Court DENIES Google's Motion to Stay ; DENIES ContentGuard's Motion for Consolidation ; and CARRIES Motorola›s Motion to Sever.

I. BACKGROUND

ContentGuard filed the Amazon Action against Amazon. com, Inc., Apple Inc., BlackBerry Corporation, Huawei Device USA, Inc., and Motorola Mobility LLC on December 18, 2013, alleging patent infringement. On January 17, 2014, ContentGuard amended its complaint in the Amazon Action, joining HTC Corporation, Samsung Electronics Co., Ltd. and their respective affiliates as additional defendants.

The technology at issue relates to digital rights management ("DRM") and digital content distribution. Defendants in the Amazon Action are portable device manufacturers (the "Manufacturer Defendants"), who are accused of, among other things, "provid [ing] hardware and software components required by the claims of the ContentGuard DRM patents to enable the [Amazon] Kindle DRM solution to operate on their devices"; using Google Play Books, Google Play Movies and Google Play Music (collectively, the "Google Play apps") on their respective devices to practice ContentGuard's DRM patents; and implementing one or more versions of the Unique Identifier Technology Solution ("UITS") on their devices. (Amazon Action, Amd. Compl.¶¶ 50, 52, 54.) While the Google Play apps form the basis for some of ContentGuard's infringement claims against the Manufacturer Defendants, ContentGuard did not name Google as a defendant in the Amazon Action, in either its original or amended complaint.

On January 31, 2014, Google filed a declaratory judgment action in the Northern District of California, seeking a declaration that Google Play Books, Google Play Music and/or Google Play Movies do not infringe ContentGuard's DRM patents (the "NDCA Action"). (See Google Action, Dkt. No.15-2.) Five days later, on February 5, 2014, ContentGuard sued Google in this Court for allegedly infringing, both directly and indirectly, the same set of patents as asserted in the Amazon Action. Specifically, ContentGuard accuses Google of providing access to content and apps that use the ContentGuard DRM solutions, providing instructions and advertisings for using such content and apps, and providing hardware and software components required by the claims of ContentGuard's DRM patents. (Google Action, Compl.¶ 39.)

*2 On March 20, 2014, the U. S. District Court for the Northern District of California issued an Order addressing Google's request to enjoin ContentGuard from proceeding with its later-filed Google Action before this Court. (See Google Action, Dkt. No.24-1.) The California court denied the injunction sought by Google on the ground of comity and judicial efficiency, and invited this Court to decide whether we should stay the Google Action or transfer it. (See id. at 4.)

On April 7, 2014, this Court held a scheduling conference in the Amazon Action setting various case management schedules including the dates for a claim construction hearing and jury selection. There are no motions to stay or transfer venue currently pending in the Amazon Action.

II. GOOGLE'S MOTION TO STAY

By the instant motion, Google seeks a stay of the Google Action pending the resolution of the NDCA Action under the "first-to-file" rule. While the Amazon Action is the earliest-filed case in the trilogy, Google argues that the NDCA action should be deemed first-filed as between ContentGuard and Google, thereby taking precedence over the later-filed Google Action before this Court. ContentGuard, on the other hand, contends that the Amazon Action is the first-filed case, which takes precedence over Google's DJ action in California.

The "first-to-file" rule "is a doctrine of federal comity, intended to avoid conflicting decisions and promote judicial efficiency, that generally favors pursuing only the first-filed action when multiple lawsuits involving the same claims are filed in different jurisdiction". *Merial Ltd. v. Cipla Ltd.*, *681 F.3d 1283, 1299 (Fed. Cir.2012)*. "When two actions that sufficiently overlap are filed in different federal district courts, one for infringement and the other for declaratory relief, the declaratory judgment action, if filed later, generally is to be stayed, dismissed, or transferred to the forum of the infringement action." *Futurewei Technologies, Inc. v. Acacia Research Corp.*, *737 F.3d 704, 708 (Fed. Cir.2013)*. The first-to-file rule, however, "is not rigidly or mechanically applied—an ample degree of discretion, appropriate for disciplined and experienced judges, must be left to the lower courts". *Merial*, *681 F.3d at 1299*. Exceptions may be made if justified by "considerations of judicial and litigant economy, and the just and effective disposition of disputes". *Futurewei*, *737 F.3d at 708*. Resolution of whether the second-filed action should proceed presents a question sufficiently tied to patent law that the question is governed by the law of the Federal Circuit. Id.

Here, Google's declaratory judgment action in California admittedly is not a mirror image of the Amazon case. Google itself is not a party to the Amazon Action. Although the Google Play apps do form the basis for some of ContentGuard's claims against the Manufacturer Defendants, both Google and ContentGuard seem to agree that the patented technology includes a hardware component, the infringement of which may depend on the different devices supplied by individual Manufacturer Defendant. (See *Google Action*, *Dkt. Nos.15 at 5*, *Dkt. No.19 at 5*.) To invoke the "first-to-file" rule, however, the Federal Circuit does not require the original and the follow-up actions to be identical. It instead instructs lower courts to focus on whether the two actions "substantially overlap, " in light of "considerations of judicial and litigant economy, and the just and effective disposition of disputes". See *Futurewei, 737 F.3d at 708*; accord *Save Power Ltd. v. Syntek Fin. Corp., 121 F.3d 947, 950 (5th Cir.1997)* (" [Defendant] argues that the "first to file" rule does not apply in this case because neither the issues nor the parties are identical to those in the Original Action. The rule does not, however, require that cases be identical. The crucial inquiry is one of 'substantial overlap'[of issues] .") ; see also *Intersearch Worldwide, Ltd. v. Intersearch Group, Inc., 544 F. Supp.2d 949, 959 (N. D. Cal.2008)* (" [E] xact identity [of parties] is not required to satisfy the first-to-file rule") ; *ProofPoint, Inc. v. Innova Patent Licensing, LLC, No.5 : 11-cv-02288, 2011 WL 4915847, at 7 (N. D. Cal. Oct.17, 2011)* (holding that the focus on judicial efficiency underlying the first-to-file rule supported declining jurisdiction in the later-filed declaratory judgment action, even though the plaintiff to the DJ action—supplier of the accused technology—had not been named as defendant in the original patent infringement suit).

*3 Here, the Amazon Action and the NDCA Action substantially overlap as to whether the Google Play apps infringe a set of ContentGuard's DRM patents, which are asserted in both cases. In the Amazon Action, each Manufacturer Defendant is accused of "providing products and methods that use one or more of the Google Play apps to practice the claimed invention." (See Amazon Action, Amd. Compl.¶ 52.) While infringement of the hardware component of the patented technology may vary with individual device manufacturer, adjudicating the Amazon Action would inevitably require a determination of whether the Google Play apps practice the claimed invention as alleged. However, such a determination is the very subject of the NDCA Action, where Google seeks a declaration that these apps do not infringe any of the asserted patents. (See NDCA Action, Compl.) Allowing the NDCA Action to proceed in parallel with the

Amazon Action would involve two district courts making independent decisions regarding whether the same accused technology infringes the same set of patents. Such runs directly counter to the principles of judicial efficiency and comity underlying the first-to-file rule. Therefore, although the NDCA Action is not a mirror image of the Amazon Action, the Court finds that the two cases "substantially overlap" such that the Amazon Action should be deemed first-filed and accordingly take precedence over the NDCA Action. See *Futurewei*, *737 F.3d at 708.*

Google next contends that, under the "customer-suit" exception to the first-to-file rule, the NDCA Action still takes precedence because the Amazon Action is a customer suit peripheral to ContentGuard's infringement claims against Google. The Court disagrees. The "customer-suit" exception applies "where the first suit is filed against a customer who is simply a reseller of the accused goods, while the second suit is a declaratory action brought by the manufacturer of the accused goods". *Kahn v. Gen. Motors Corp.*, *889 F.2d 1078*, *1081 (Fed. Cir.1989).* Under such circumstances, the first-to-file rule gives way to the "manufacturer's presumed greater interest in defending its actions against charges of patent infringement". Id. In evaluating the customer-suit exception, "the primary question is whether the issues and parties are such that the disposition of one case would be dispositive of the other". *Proofpoint*, *2011 WL 4915847 at 7 n.5* (citing *Katz v. Siegler*, *909 F.2d 1459*, *1463 (Fed. Cir.1990)*).

In this case, resolution of Google's declaratory judgment action would not be dispositive of the Amazon Action. First, Google is not the only supplier of allegedly infringing technology in the Amazon case. The Manufacturer Defendants are accused of using two other features unrelated to Google, namely, the Amazon Kindle DRM and the Unique Identifier Technology Solution ("UITS"). Second, even the Google-related claims in the Amazon Action would not be necessarily resolved upon the complete adjudication of Google's declaratory judgment action, as Google itself admits that "the issues of infringement [in the Amazon Action] could vary depending on each customer's accused use of Google's technology on the customer's various accused devices". (See Google Action, Dkt. No.15 at 5.) Resolution of the NDCA Action therefore would not resolve all charges against the Manufacturer Defendants in the first-filed Amazon Action.[2] Permitting the NDCA Action to take precedence over the Amazon Case would not support the best interest of efficiency or judicial economy.

Google rests its argument primarily on *Adobe Sys. Inc. v. Select Retrieval*, *No.12-2342, 2014 WL 497441 (S. D. Cal. Feb.6, 2014)*, where the court assumed jurisdiction in Adobe System Incorporated's ("Adobe") later-filed declaratory judgment action of non-infringement, despite earlier infringement actions filed against Adobe's customers. The Adobe case, however, is distinguishable from the present situation. The asserted patents in Adobe do not include a hardware component, the infringement of which depends on each customer's individually accused device. The patentee's allegations against each of Adobe's customers were "essentially the same, varying only to the extent that each Adobe customer maintained its own website". *Adobe, 2014 WL 497441 at 2*. There, unlike here, the adjudication of Adobe's declaratory judgment claim of non-infringement would squarely resolve the patentee's infringement claims against each of Adobe's customers. See id. at 4. Moreover, the patentee in Adobe filed multiple lawsuits against Adobe's customers in various district courts including the courts in Delaware, Maine and Illinois. See id. at 5. There, the court declining to exercise jurisdiction in Adobe's declaratory judgment action would subject Adobe (through its customers) to "potentially inconsistent judgments regarding whether its technology infringes the patent". Id. In this case, however, ContentGuard did not file suits in various district courts against different device manufacturers who use Google's technology. This Court's best understanding is that all device manufacturers currently being accused by ContentGuard are before this Court in the Amazon Action. ContentGuard's infringement claims against Google are also before this Court. Having the infringement claims asserted against the device manufacturers and those asserted against Google adjudicated in one court would ensure judicial consistency—the very result that the Adobe court sought to achieve.

*4 Given the substantial overlapping of key infringement issues between the Amazon Action and the NDCA Action, this Court is persuaded that the Amazon Action is the first-filed case, and, as such, takes precedence over Google's later-filed declaratory judgment action in California. Accordingly, Google's request to stay the Google Action before this Court pending the resolution of the NDCA Action, based on the first-to-file rule, is hereby DENIED.

III. CONTENTGUARD'S MOTION FOR CONSOLIDATION

In addition to opposing Google's Motion to Stay, ContentGuard further moves this Court to consolidate the Google Action with the Amazon Action for discovery and case management purposes, which motion Google opposes. (See Google Action, Dkt. Nos.14, 20.)

Under Federal Rule of Civil Procedure 42 (a), "[i]f actions before the court involve a common question of law or fact, the court may...consolidate the actions". Fed. R. Civ. P.42 (a) (emphasis added). This rule providing for the consolidation of actions is "permissive and vests a purely discretionary power in the district court". *Whiteman v. Pitrie, 220 F.2d 914, 918 (5th Cir.1955)*. However, when prejudice to rights of the parties "obviously results from the order of consolidation", the action of the trial court may be held to be reversible error. See id.

Here, as noted above, despite two features unrelated to Google which are also accused in the Amazon Action, the Amazon and the Google Actions substantially overlap as to whether the Google Play apps infringe ContentGuard's DRM patents. Such would ordinarily justify consolidation at least for certain pretrial purposes. That said, this Court shares the view of our sister court in California that ContentGuard appears to have gone to "considerable effort to avoid suing Google in Texas, evidently fearing a motion to transfer, until its hand was forced" by Google filing the NDCA Action. (See Dkt. No.24-1 at 4.) From the beginning, ContentGuard was well aware that Google's technology is involved in the accused infringing products. The original complaint of the Amazon Action specifically identified the Google Play apps as being used to practice the asserted patents. ContentGuard could have named Google as a defendant in the Amazon Action, both in its original complaint and in the amended complaint, but elected not to do so. To now grant ContentGuard's request and have the Amazon and Google Actions proceed on a consolidated basis might be deemed by future litigants as an invitation to follow a similar path. Such is not an invitation this Court wishes to issue. Therefore, given that ContentGuard has voluntarily forgone the opportunity to sue Google together with the Manufacturer Defendants, this Court elects not to exercise its discretion to consolidate the

Google Action into the Amazon Action. ContentGuard's Motion for Consolidation is hereby DENIED.

IV. MOTOROLA'S MOTION TO SEVER

By the instant motion Motorola seeks to sever ContentGuard's claims against it from the Amazon Action, alleging that joinder is improper under 35 U. S. C.§ 299 and Fed. R. Civ. P 20. (See Amazon Action, Dkt. No.55.)

Under Rule 20, joinder is proper where : (1) the claims against the defendants arise out of the "same transaction, occurrence, or series of transactions or occurrences", and (2) there is a "question of law or fact common to all defendants". Fed. R. Civ. P.20 (a) (2) ; In re EMC Corp., 677 F.3d 1351, 1356 (Fed. Cir.2012) ("In re EMC I"). In In re EMC I, the Federal Circuit clarified the standard for joinder by holding that " [c] laims against independent defendants (i. e., situations in which the defendants are not acting in concert) cannot be joined under Rule 20's transaction-or-occurrence test unless the facts underlying the claim of infringement asserted against each defendant share an aggregate of operative facts". Id. at 1359. In addition, "joinder is not appropriate where different products or processes are involved." Id. "Unless there is an actual link between the facts underlying each claim of infringement, independently developed products using differently sourced parts are not part of the same transaction, even if they are otherwise coincidentally identical." Id.

*5 Here, the Manufacturer Defendants are each accused of using three software applications on their devices to practice ContentGuard's DRM patents, i. e., the Amazon Kindle app, the Google Play apps, and the UITS specification. The claims against the Manufacturer Defendants therefore share at least a set of common facts regarding these three software applications. Despite the existence of a hardware component, the infringement of which may depend on the different devices supplied by individual Manufacturer Defendant, the accused instrumentality in this case—the use of the three common software applications on each Defendant's device—is not clearly based on "independently developed products using differently sourced parts", and the common facts regarding the accused software may well constitute "an actual link between the facts underlying each claim of infringement". See *In re EMC Corp., 677 F.3d at 1359.*

That said, "even if a plaintiff's claims arise out of the same transaction and there are questions of law and fact common to all defendants, district courts have the discretion to refuse joinder in the interest of avoiding prejudice and delay, ensuring judicial economy, or safeguarding principles of fundamental fairness". Id. at 1360 (citing *Acevedo v. Allsup's Convenience Stores, Inc., 600 F.3d 516, 521 (5th Cir.2010)*). "In a complicated patent litigation a large number of defendants might prove unwieldy, and a district court would be justified in exercising its discretion to deny joinder when different witnesses and documentary proof would be required." Id. (citations omitted).

Here, a total of nine ContentGuard patents are asserted in the Amazon Action against seven device manufacturers. Each Defendant, except for Amazon, is accused of infringing all nine of the asserted patents, while Amazon is accused of infringing seven of the nine asserted patents. (See Amazon Action, Compl.¶¶ 128-34.) The patents at issue altogether include 27 independent claims and 287 dependent claims, [3] and proving infringement of the hardware component of the patented technology may depend on each Manufacturer Defendant›s individual devices. Clearly, this case is a "complicated patent litigation" with multiple defendants where "different witnesses and documentary proof would be required" from each Defendant. See *In re EMC, 677 F.3d at 1360*. In a case of this complexity, to force all Manufacturer Defendants to share a single trial might prejudice their ability to build an effective defense against ContentGuard's allegations, which counsels against joinder.

Ultimately, however, this Court finds the record has not been sufficiently developed at this point in time for it to determine with clarity whether or not joinder is proper in this case.

While ContentGuard's claims against each Manufacturer Defendant share the common facts underlying the three accused software applications and may depend on each Defendant's individually accused devices, no evidence has been proffered regarding how the accused software-hardware combination corresponds to claims of the asserted patents. If, for instance, ContentGuard's claims are predominantly software-based, then the common facts underlying such claims may constitute "an actual link" connecting all Defendants sufficient to support joinder in this case. See id. at 1359. On the other hand, if the hardware component turns out to play the dominant role in determining how the three software applications are used specifically on each Defendant's device, then the claims against each Defendant may be sufficiently distinguished such that keeping them jointly in one case would be improper. Given that the case is still in its early stage and discovery has barely started, the Court deems it prudent to carry the joinder issue and let the parties further develop the record to resolve, among other things, the relative significance of the software and hardware components of ContentGuard's claims. Accordingly, Motorola's Motion to Sever is hereby CARRIED by the Court. Motorola is directed to file with the Court, within the next sixty (60) days, a supplemental brief of no more than ten (10) pages excluding supporting attachments, to more clearly establish the facts as to such software-hardware correlation as discussed above. ContentGuard shall file any opposition brief, subject to the same page limit, within fifteen (15) days thereafter.

V. CONCLUSION

*6 For the reasons stated above, the Court hereby DENIES Google's Motion to Stay ; DENIES ContentGuard's Motion for Consolidation ; and CARRIES Motorola›s Motion to Sever.

So ORDERED and SIGNED this 15th day of April, 2014.

All Citations

Not Reported in Fed. Supp., 2014 WL 1477670.

Footnotes

1. In the alternative to its Motion to Stay, Google seeks to transfer the Google Action to the Northern District of California. (SeeDkt. No.15 at 9-16.) The Court will address Google's Alternative Motion to Transfer in a separate opinion.

2. Indeed, resolution of the NDCA Action, as it is currently pled, would not be dispositive of even the Google Action before this Court. Google sought a declaration in the NDCA Action that the Google Play apps do not infringe any of ContentGuard's asserted patents. (See NDCA Action, Compl. at 22.) In the Google Action, however, Google is accused not only of providing the Google Play apps, but also as a device manufacturer based on its Android devices marketed under

the trademark "Nexus". (See Google Action, Compl.¶ 16.) While the two Google actions are clearly related, resolution of the NDCA Action would not address the hardware component of the patented technology, which allegedly is infringed by Google's Nexus devices.

3. To date, ContentGuard has not indicated which claims are asserted against which Manufacturer Defendant specifically.

美国得克萨斯州东部联邦地区法院，马歇尔分院。

3　CONTENTGUARD 控股有限公司诉谷歌股份有限公司；CONTENTGUARD 控股有限公司诉亚马逊公司等

案件编号 2：14-cv-00061 JRG；
案件编号 2：13-cv-01112-JRG
签署时间：2014 年 4 月 15 日

律师和律所事务所

　　原告代理律师：得克萨斯州达拉斯 McKool Smith 律师事务所的霍莉·艾琳·英格曼和克雷格·约翰·唐纳修；纽约州纽约 McKool Smith 律师事务所的拉杜·勒鲁图、小罗伯特·科特、安吉拉·沃帕尔和大卫·德奥尼；得克萨斯州马歇尔 McKool Smith 律师事务所的塞缪尔·富兰克林·巴克斯特；得克萨斯州奥斯汀 McKool Smith 律师事务所的赛斯·雷蒙德·哈塞努尔。

　　被告代理律师：得克萨斯州亨德森 Mann Tindel & Thompson 律师事务所的格利高里·布莱克·汤普森和詹姆斯·马克·曼恩；科罗拉多州丹佛 Bartlit Beck Herman Palenchar & Scott 律师事务所的格伦·埃瑞克·萨默斯、艾丽森·惠勒和凯瑟琳·哈克；得克萨斯州得克萨卡纳 Haltom & Doan 律师事务所的詹妮弗·霍尔托姆·多恩和约书亚·里德·塞恩；Bartlit Beck Herman Palenchar & Scott 律师事务所的艾比·莫伦；盛德律师事务所的大卫·普里蒂金和理查德·赛德罗斯；世达律师事务所的梅雷亚德·施瓦布；伊利诺伊州芝加哥凯寿律师事务所的罗伯特·乌尼克；盛德律师事务所的布莱恩·安德森和内森·格林布拉特；世达律师事务所的詹姆斯·约瑟夫·埃拉库亚、陈伊恩和威廉·杰瑞·凯希；加利福尼亚州帕洛阿托凯寿律师事务所的迈克尔·马莱切克和蒂莫西·赵；加利福尼亚州旧金山盛德律师事务所的凯利·克莱尔纳；得克萨斯州马歇尔 Gillam & Smith 律师事务所的玛丽莎·理查兹·史密斯；得克萨斯州达拉斯 Carter Scholer Arnett Hamada & Mockler 律师事务所的约翰·史蒂文·托克尔森和谢里亚·德拉尼斯·史密斯；得克萨斯州休斯顿贝克博茨律师事务所、KD Shull 律师事务所、得克萨斯州普莱诺华为美国研发公司的斯科特·帕特里奇、布拉德利·鲍林和莉莎·凯瑟琳·凯利；得克萨斯州泰勒 Potter Minton 律师事务所的埃里克·休·芬德利、罗杰·布莱恩·克拉夫、芬德利·克拉夫特·PC、艾伦·富兰克林·加德纳和迈克尔 琼斯；加利福尼亚州洛杉矶古德温律师事务所的杰·邱、彼得·威德、特伦斯·加内特和文森特·伊普；哥伦比亚特区华盛顿贝克博茨律师事务所的迈克尔·约瑟夫·鲍尔托；纽约州纽约贝克博茨律师事务所的尼尔·菲利普·西罗塔和罗伯特·劳伦斯·梅尔。

备忘录意见和命令

罗德尼·吉尔斯特拉普，美国地区法官

*1 法院收到了两个相关案件的三项相关动议：谷歌股份有限公司（以下简称"谷歌公司"）在第 2：14-cv-00061 号民事诉讼案（以下简称"谷歌诉讼"）中提出的"中止动议"①（待审案件目录第 15 号）；[1]ContentGuard 控股有限公司（以下简称"ContentGuard 公司"）在谷歌诉讼中提出的"合并动议"②（待审案件目录第 14 号）；摩托罗拉移动有限责任公司（以下简称"摩托罗拉公司"）在第 2:13-cv-01112 号民事诉讼案（"亚马逊诉讼"）中提出"分离动议"③（待审案件目录第 55 号）。鉴于这三项动议涉及共同的基本事实问题，本院认为合并处理这三项动议更为恰当。在考虑各方当事人提交的书面陈述之后，并基于下述理由，本院驳回谷歌公司提出的"中止动议"；驳回 ContentGuard 公司提出的"合并动议"；执行摩托罗拉公司提出的"分离动议"。

一、背景

2013 年 12 月 18 日，ContentGuard 公司针对亚马逊公司、苹果公司、黑莓公司、华为终端美国公司和摩托罗拉公司提起了指控专利侵权的亚马逊诉

---

① 译者注：在 NDHC 诉讼判决之前，中止谷歌诉讼的进行。

② 译者注：合并审理谷歌诉讼与亚马逊诉讼。

③ 译者注：将原告 ContentGuard 公司针对摩托罗拉公司的指控从亚马逊诉讼中分离出来。

讼。2014 年 1 月 17 日，ContentGuard 公司修改了其诉状，将 HTC 公司、三星电子株式会社及其关联公司追加为被告。

涉案技术涉及数字版权管理（以下简称"DRM"）和数字内容分发。亚马逊诉讼的被告是便携式设备制造商（以下简称"制造商被告"），其指控内容为："提供 ContentGuard 公司 DRM 专利所要求的硬件和软件组件，使得亚马逊 Kindle 的 DRM 解决方案可以在其设备上运行"；在其各自的设备上使用谷歌图书、谷歌电影和谷歌音乐（以下统称为"谷歌商城应用程序"）来运用 ContentGuard 公司 DRM 专利；在其设备上应用一个或多个版本的唯一标识符技术解决方案（"UITS"）。（亚马逊诉讼，修改版起诉状，第 50 段、第 52 段、第 54 段）尽管谷歌商城应用程序构成 ContentGuard 公司对制造商被告提出侵权指控的部分依据，但是 ContentGuard 公司在其最初或者修改后的起诉状中均未将谷歌公司列为亚马逊诉讼的被告。

2014 年 1 月 31 日，谷歌公司向加利福尼亚州北区联邦地区法院提起确认之诉，要求法院确认谷歌图书、谷歌音乐以及谷歌电影并未侵犯 ContentGuard 公司的 DRM 知识产权（简称"NDCA 诉讼"）。（谷歌诉讼，待审案件目录第 15–2 号）5 天后，即 2014 年 2 月 5 日，ContentGuard 公司在同一法院起诉谷歌公司，指控其直接和间接地侵犯了 ContentGuard 公司在亚马逊诉讼中主张的相同专利。具体而言，ContentGuard 公司控诉谷歌公司向使用 ContentGuard 公司 DRM 解决方案的内容和应用程序提供了权限，提供了使用此类内容和应用程序的说明和广告，并提供了 ContentGuard 公司 DRM 专利要求所需的硬件和软件组件。（谷歌诉讼，起诉状，第 39 段）

*2 2014 年 3 月 20 日，美国加利福尼亚州北区联邦地区法院颁布命令，处理了谷歌公司的请求，即禁止 ContentGuard 公司在该法院继续其后来提起的谷歌诉讼。（谷歌诉讼，待审案件目录第 24–1 号）加利福尼亚州法院以礼让原则和司法效率为由驳回了谷歌公司申请的禁止令，并请本院自行决定是否中止谷歌诉讼或移送处理。（同上，第 4 页）

2014 年 4 月 7 日，本院就亚马逊诉讼召开了日程安排会议，确定了各案件管理的时间安排，包括释义听证会和陪审团选择的日期。亚马逊诉讼中目前还没有中止或者移送的动议。

二、谷歌的中止动议

通过即时动议，谷歌公司寻求在 NDCA 诉讼得到解决之前根据"先申请原则"暂停谷歌诉讼的执行。虽然亚马逊诉讼是"三部曲"中最早申请的案件，但是谷歌公司辩称 NDCA 诉讼应被视为 ContentGuard 公司和谷歌公司之间最早提起诉讼的案件，因此优先于后来在本院申请的谷歌诉讼。而 ContentGuard 公司辩称，亚马逊诉讼是第一个申请的案件，应优先于谷歌公司在加利福尼亚州法院的确认之诉。

"先申请原则"，"是一项联邦（法院）礼让原则，旨在避免判决冲突并提高司法效率，当涉及相同诉求的多起诉讼在不同司法管辖区提起时，通常倾向于只先审理最先申请的诉讼"。参见"梅里亚有限公司诉西普拉有限公司案"，《美国联邦法院判例集》第三辑第 681 卷第 1283—1299 页（联邦巡回法院，2012 年）。"如有两个充分重叠的诉讼在不同的联邦地区法院申请，一个提起侵权诉讼，另一个提起确认性救济诉讼，确认之诉如果在后提起，通常会被中止、驳回或转移到提起侵权诉讼的法院。"参见"华为美国研发公司诉阿卡西亚研究公司案"，《美国联邦法院判例集》第三辑第 737 卷第 704—708 页（联邦巡回法院，2013 年）。然而，"先申请原则"，"并不能死板或机械地适用——应当给下级法院纪律严明和经验丰富的法官留出足够程度的自由裁量权"。参见"梅里亚案"，《美国联邦法院判例集》第三辑第 681 卷第 1299 页。如果"考虑司法和诉讼经济性，以及公正有效地处理争议的必要性"，则可以有例外。参见"华为美国研发公司诉阿卡西亚研究公司案"，《美国联邦法院判例集》第三辑第 737 卷第 708 页。第二次提起的诉讼是否应当继续受理的前提是要与专利法密切相关，且受联邦巡回法院的法律管辖。（参见，同上）

本案中，谷歌公司在加利福尼亚州的确认之诉与亚马逊诉讼并不完全相同。谷歌公司本身并非亚马逊诉讼的当事方。尽管谷歌应用程序确实构成 ContentGuard 公司对制造商被告提出的相关诉讼的基础，但谷歌公司和 ContentGuard 公司似乎都同意包括硬件组件在内的专利技术是否构成侵权可能取决于个别制造商被告提供的不同设备。参见"谷歌诉讼"，待审案件目录第 15 号第 5 页，待审案件目录第 19 号第 5 页。但是，为了援引"先申请原则"，联邦巡回法院并不要求原始诉讼和后续诉讼完全一致。相反，联邦巡回法院指示下级法院根据"考虑司法和诉讼经济性，以及公正有效地处理争议的必要性"，重点关注这两项诉讼是否"实质上重叠"。参见"华为美国研发公司案"，《美国联邦法院判例集》第三辑第 737 卷第 708 页；根据"节能有限责任公司诉 Syntek Fin 公司案"，《美国联邦法院判例集》第三辑第 121 卷第 947—950 页（第五巡回法院，1997 年）（"被告辩称，'先申请原则'在本案中不适用，因为争点和当事人与原始诉讼中的争点和当事人都不相同。但是，该原则并不要求案件完全相同。关键的调查在于［争点］是否构成'实质性重叠'的要素之一"）；另参见"Intersearch Worldwide 有限责任公司诉 Intersearch 集团公司案"，《联邦判例补编》第二辑第 544 卷第 949—959 页（加利福尼亚州北区联邦地区法院，2008 年）（"'先申请原则'无须［当事人］的确切身份"）；参见"美国网络安全公司诉英诺华专利实施许可有限责任公司案"，案件编号 5∶11-cv-02288，2011 WL 4915847，at 7（加利福尼亚州北区法院，2011 年 10 月 17 日）（裁定在"先申请原则"的基础上强调司法效率，并在随后的确认之诉中弱化司法管辖权，即便确认之诉的原告，即该被指控技术的供应商，尚未在最初的专利侵权诉讼中被列为被告）。

*3 本案中，亚马逊诉讼和 NDCA 诉讼在谷歌商城应用程序是否侵犯了 ContentGuard 公司的 DRM 专利方面，其诉求实质上是一致的，这一点在两个案件中都得以确认。亚马逊诉讼中，所有制造商被告都被指控"提供使用一个或多个谷歌商城应用程序的产品和方法来运用所声称的发明"。（详见亚马逊诉讼，修改版起诉状，第 52 段）尽管专利技术的硬件组件侵权情况可能因设备制造商的不同而有所不同，但对亚马逊诉讼的判决将不可避免地需要确定谷歌商城应用程序是否运用了所声称的发明。而这正是 NDCA 诉讼的实质问题，谷歌公司要求声明这些应用程序不侵犯任何所主张的专利。（详见于 NDCA 诉讼，起诉状）允许 NDCA 诉讼与亚马逊诉讼并行将涉及两个地区法院就同一被控技术是否侵犯同一组专利作出独立裁决，这直接违反"先申请原则"的司法效率和礼让原则。因此，尽管 NDCA 诉讼并不是亚马逊诉讼的镜像案件，但法院认为这两个案件"实质上重叠"，故亚马逊诉讼理应作为首先提起的案件，并因此优先于 NDCA 诉讼。参见"华为美国研发公司案"，《美国联邦法院判例集》第三辑第 737 卷第 708 页。

谷歌公司接着辩称，根据"先申请原则"的"客户诉讼"例外，NDCA 诉讼仍然具有优先权，因为亚马逊诉讼是 ContentGuard 公司针对谷歌公司的侵权指控的外围客户诉讼。本院不认同这一观点。"客户诉讼"例外情况适用的"第一种诉讼仅针对涉诉商品的转销客户，而第二种诉讼是涉诉商品的制造商提起的确权诉讼"。参见"卡恩诉通用汽车公司案"，《美国联邦法院判例集》第二辑第 889 卷第 1078—1081 页（联邦巡回法院，1989 年）。在这种情况下，"先申请原则"让位于"被推定的制造商对其针对专利侵权指控的诉讼进行辩护的更大利益"。（同上）在评估客户诉讼例外时，"首要的问题是，争点和当事人是否会使一个案件的处理结果将另一个案件产生决定性影响"。参见"美国网络安全公司诉英诺华专利实施许可有限责任公司案"，2011 WL 4915847，at 7 n.5［引用"卡茨诉西格勒案"，《美国联邦法院判例集》第二辑第 909 卷第 1459—1463 页（联邦巡回法院，1990 年）］。

本案中，谷歌公司确认之诉的解决不会对亚马逊诉讼产生决定性影响。首先，谷歌公司并不是亚马逊案中被控侵权技术的唯一供应商。制造商被告被指控使用了另外两个与谷歌公司无关的功能，即亚马逊 Kindle DRM 和 UITS（唯一标识技术解决方案）。其次，即使是亚马逊诉讼中与谷歌公司相关的指控，也不一定能在谷歌公司的确认之诉完全裁决后得到解决，因为谷歌公司本身承认亚马逊诉讼中的侵权问题可能会因每个客户在其各种被控设备上使用谷歌技术的情况而有所不同。（谷歌诉讼，待审案件目录第 15 号第 5 页）因此，NDCA 诉讼的解决无法消除先申请的亚马逊诉讼中针对制造商被告的任何指控。[2] 允许 NDCA 诉讼优先于亚马逊案件并不会有利于获得最大审判效率和司法利益。

谷歌公司的论点主要基于"Adobe 公司（以下简称"Adobe"）诉 Select Retrieval 案"，案件编号 12-2342，2014 WL 497441（加利福尼亚州南区联邦地区法院，2014 年 2 月 6 日），该案中，法院判决支持 Adobe 后来提交的确认之诉为非侵权，尽管存在早先支持 Adobe 的客户已经提起了侵权诉讼。然而，Adobe 案与本案情况是有区别的。Adobe 案中声称的专利不包括硬件组件，其侵权取决于每个客户自己的涉诉设备。专利权人对 Adobe 的每个客户的指控"基本上相同，不同之处仅在于 Adobe 各客户自行维护自己的网站"。"Adobe案"，2014 WL 497441，at 2。与本案不同的是，对 Adobe 的非侵权确认之诉的裁决将直接解决专利权人针对 Adobe 的每个客户的侵权诉讼。（Adobe 案，第 4 页）此外，Adobe 的专利权人在各个地区法院（包括特拉华州、缅因州和伊利诺伊州的法院）针对 Adobe 的客户提起了多项诉讼。（Adobe 案，第 5 页）在这些地区，拒绝对 Adobe 的声明性判决行使管辖权的法院将使 Adobe（通过其客户）面临"关于其技术是否侵犯专利存在可能不一致的判决"。（Adobe 案）然而本案中，ContentGuard 公司并未在各个地区法院对使用谷歌技术的不同设备制造商提起诉讼。本院认为，目前被 ContentGuard 公司指控的所有设备制造商在亚马逊诉讼中都在本院受审。ContentGuard 公司对谷歌公司的侵权指控也在本院审理。对设备制造商的侵权指控和对谷歌的侵权指控在一个法院受审将确保司法的一致性——这正是 Adobe 案中法院希望看到的结果。

*4 鉴于亚马逊诉讼和 NDCA 诉讼之间的关键侵权争点存在实质性重叠，本院认为亚马逊诉讼是先申请的案件，因此该诉讼优先于谷歌公司后续在加利福尼亚州提起的确认之诉。因此，基于先申请原则，谷歌公司提出在 NDCA 诉讼解决之前暂停在本院审理谷歌诉讼的请求在此被驳回。

三、ContentGuard 公司的合并动议

除了反对谷歌公司的中止动议，出于证据开示和案件管理的目的，ContentGuard 公司还进一步向本院提出将谷歌诉讼与亚马逊诉讼合并的动议，谷歌公司对此表示反对。（参见谷歌诉讼，待审案件目录第 14 号、第 20 号）

根据《联邦民事诉讼规则》第 42 节第 1 分节，"如果向法院提起的诉讼涉及共同的法律问题或事实问题，法院可以……合并诉讼"。《联邦民事诉讼规则》第 42 节第 1 分节（额外强调）。这条规则明确合并诉讼需要"受到许可，并赋予地区法院绝对的自由裁量权"。参见"怀特曼诉皮特里案"，《美国联邦法院判例集》第二辑第 220 卷第 914—918 页（第五巡回法院，1955 年）。但是，当"明显因为合并诉讼"而造成当事人双方的权利受损时，初审法院的行为理应视为可撤销的错误行为。（同上）

本案中，如上所述，尽管在亚马逊诉讼中也指控了两项与谷歌公司无关的功能，但亚马逊诉讼和谷歌诉讼在谷歌商城应用程序是否侵犯 ContentGuard 公司的 DRM 专利方面存在内容上的实质性重叠。这通常证明合并诉讼是合理的，至少在审前目的的证明上是合理的。因此，本院同意加利福尼亚州法院的观点，即 ContentGuard 公司似乎已经"竭尽全力避免在得克萨斯州起诉谷歌，显然是担心谷歌的转移动议，直到谷歌在 NDCA 诉讼中被迫采取行动"。（待审案件目录第 24-1 号第 4 页）从一开始，ContentGuard 公司就很清楚谷歌公司的技术与涉诉侵权产品有关。亚马逊诉讼的原始起诉书明确指出，谷歌商城应用程序实际应用了所声明的专利。ContentGuard 公司本可以在其原始起诉书和修改后的起诉书中将谷歌公司列为亚马逊诉讼的被告，但它选择了不这样做。现在批准 ContentGuard 公司的请求，并将亚马逊诉讼和谷歌诉讼合并进行，这可能会被未来的诉讼当事人视为类似路径可遵循的信号。但本院并不想释放出这样的信号。因此，鉴于 ContentGuard 公司自愿放弃了将谷歌公司和制造商被告一起起诉的机会，本院决定不予行使自由裁量权将谷歌诉讼与亚马逊诉讼合并。在此驳回 ContentGuard 公司的合并动议。

四、摩托罗拉公司的分离动议

摩托罗拉公司试图通过这一即时动议，将 ContentGuard 公司针对其提出的指控从亚马逊诉讼中分离出来，称根据《美国法典》第 35 卷第 299 节和《联邦民事诉讼规则》第 20 条规定，合并诉讼是不适当的。（见亚马逊诉讼，待审案件目录第 55 号）

　　根据《联邦民事诉讼规则》第 20 条规定，在以下情况下，适用合并：
（1）针对被告的权利主张源自"同一交易、事件或一系列交易或事件"，（2）存
在"所有被告共同的法律或事实问题"。《联邦民事诉讼规则》第 20 节第 1
分节第 2 款；"易安信公司案"，《美国联邦法院判例集》第三辑第 677 卷第
1351—356 页（联邦巡回法院，2012 年）。易安信公司案中，联邦巡回法院厘
清了共同诉讼的标准，认为"根据第 20 节的交易或事件标准，针对独立被告（即
被告并非一致行动的情形）的诉讼不能合并，除非针对每个被告的侵权主张
所依据的事实具有共同的事实集合"。（同上，第 1359 页）此外，"在涉及不
同产品或程序的情况下，合并诉讼是不适当的"。（同上）"除非每项侵权主张
所依据的事实之间存在实际联系，否则使用不同来源零件的独立开发产品不
属于同一交易，无论它们在其他方面有多少巧合的相同。"（同上）

　　*5 本案中，被告制造商均被指控在其设备上使用三个应用软件程序来运
用 ContentGuard 公司的 DRM 专利，即亚马逊 Kindle 应用程序、谷歌商城应
用程序和 UITS 规范。因此，针对被告的权利主张至少在这三种软件应用程
序方面包含一系列共同事实。尽管存在硬件组件，其侵权行为可能依赖于个
别制造商被告提供的不同设备，但本案中的被控工具（即在每个被告设备上
使用三种共同的软件应用程序）显然不是基于"使用不同来源零件的独立开
发产品"，而关于被控软件的事实很有可能构成"每项侵权主张所依据的事实
之间存在实际联系"。参见"易安信公司案"，《美国联邦法院判例集》第三辑
第 677 卷第 1359 页。

　　也就是说，"即使原告的诉讼请求来自同一交易，并且存在所有被告共
同面对的法律和事实问题，为了避免损害和延误，确保司法的经济性，或者
维护基本的公平原则，地区法院可以自由裁量拒绝追加诉讼"。[同上，第
1360 页；另见"阿塞维多诉奥赛普便利店公司案"，《美国联邦法院判例集》
第三辑第 600 卷第 516—521 页（第五巡回法庭，2010 年）]"复杂的专利诉
讼中，大量的被告可能难以处理，当需要不同的证人和书证时，地区法院有
理由行使自由裁量权拒绝追加诉讼。"（同上，引言省略）

　　本案中，针对 7 家设备制造商提出的亚马逊诉讼中，共涉及 9 项
ContentGuard 公司专利。除亚马逊公司以外，每个被告均被控侵犯了全部 9
项涉案专利，而亚马逊公司被控侵犯其中 7 项专利。（参见"亚马逊案"，起
诉状，第 128—34 段）涉案专利包括 27 项独立权利要求和 287 项从属权利
要求，[3] 并且专利技术硬件部分的侵权可能取决于每一制造商被告的单独设备。
显然，这是一个有大量被告，并且每个被告"需要不同的证人和书证"的"复
杂专利诉讼"案件。参见"易安信公司案"，《美国联邦法院判例集》第三

辑第 677 卷第 1360 页。在这样复杂的案件中，强迫所有制造商被告共同参加一次审判可能会损害其针对 ContentGuard 公司的指控形成有效抗辩的能力，从而不利于追加诉讼。

然而，最终法院认为该证据就目前而言并不充足，因此无法准确地裁决本案合并审理是否恰当。

虽然 ContentGuard 公司针对每一制造商被告的主张与三个被控软件应用程序具有共同事实基础，并且可能依赖于每一被告各自的被控设备，但是没有证据表明被控软件和硬件的组合如何与涉案专利的主张相对应。例如：一方面，如果 ContentGuard 公司的主张主要基于软件，那么这些主张所依据的共同事实可能构成关联所有被告的"实际链接"，而这种链接足以支持本案合并审理。（同上，第 1359 页）另一方面，如果硬件部分对于确定在每个被告的设备上如何具体使用三个软件应用程序方面起决定性作用，那么每个被告的主张可能存在较大差异，因此将这些主张合并审理并不合适。鉴于本案仍处于早期阶段，证据开示阶段才刚刚开始，法院认为谨慎的做法是搁置合并审理问题，让双方当事人进一步完善证据，以解决 ContentGuard 公司诉讼的软硬件组成部分的相对重要性等问题。因此，法院支持了摩托罗拉公司的分离动议，并要求摩托罗拉公司在 60 天内内向法院提出不超过 10 页（不含辅助附件）的补充辩论意见，以更清楚地确定上述软硬件相关性的事实。ContentGuard 公司应在 15 天内提交异议答辩状，并遵守相同的页数限制。

五、结论

*6 基于上述理由，法院驳回谷歌公司的中止动议，驳回 ContentGuard 公司的合并动议；执行摩托罗拉公司的分离动议。

于 2014 年 4 月 15 日裁决并签署所有条款。

在《联邦判例补编》2014 年 WL 1477670 中未见报道。

脚注

1. 谷歌公司试图将谷歌诉讼转移至加利福尼亚州北区联邦地区法院，以替代其中止动议。（见待审案件目录第 15 号，第 9—16 页）本院将在另一份意见书中处理谷歌公司的替代性诉讼地转移动议。

2. 事实上，按照目前情况，解决 NDCA 诉讼甚至不会对提交给本院的谷歌诉讼产生决定性的影响。谷歌公司在 NDCA 诉讼中要求声明谷歌商城应用程序没有侵犯 ContentGuard 公司声称的任何专利。（见 NDCA 诉讼，起诉状，第 22 段）然而，在谷歌诉讼中，谷歌公司不仅被指控提供谷歌商城应用程序，还被指控是一家基于以"Nexus"商标销售的安卓设备的设备制造商。（见谷歌诉讼，起诉状，第 16 段）虽然这两项谷歌诉讼明显相关，但解决 NDCA 诉讼并不能解决专利技术硬件部分的问题，同时，据称谷歌公司的 Nexus 设备侵犯了这项专利技术。

3. 到目前为止，ContentGuard 公司还没有明确指出哪些权利主张是针对哪家制造商提出的。

United States District Court, W. D. Texas, Austin Division.

IV DataQuill, Limited, Plaintiff, v. APPLE INC., Defendant.

No. A-13-CA-706-SS.
Signed June 13, 2014.

Attorneys and Law Firms

Andres Healy, Floyd G. Short, Parker C. Folse, III, Susman Godfrey LLP, Seattle, WA ; Blaine A. Larson, Leslie V. Payne, Michael F. Heim, Nathan J. Davis, Robert Allan Bullwinkel, Heim Payne and Chorush LLP ; Joseph S. Grinstein, Susman Godfrey LLP, Houston, TX ; Douglas R. Wilson, Heim Payne & Chorush, LLP, Austin, TX ; for Plaintiff.

Adam M. Greenfield, Matthew J. Moore, Timothy J. O'Brien, Latham & Watkins LLP, Washington, DC ; Alan D. Albright, Sutherland Asbill & Brennan LLP, Austin, TX ; Dale Chang, Latham & Watkins LLP, Chicago, IL ; Douglas Ethan Lumish, Gabriel Simeone Gross, Michelle R. MA, Latham & Watkins LLP, Menlo Park, CA ; Philip X. Wang, Latham & Watkins LLP, Los Angeles, CA ; for Defendant.

ORDER

SAM SPARKS, District Judge

*1 BE IT REMEMBERED on this day the Court reviewed the file in the above-styled cause, and specifically Defendant Apple Inc.'s Motion to Transfer Venue [# 48], Plaintiff DataQuill, Ltd.'s Sealed Response [# 60], and Apple's

Reply [# 65] ; DataQuill's Sealed Motion to Compel [# 61], Apple's Response [# 67], and DataQuill's Sealed Reply [# 74] ; DataQuill's post-hearing Notice [# 77] ; and Apple's post-hearing Sealed Notice [# 80] . Having reviewed the documents, the governing law, the arguments of counsel at the hearing held May 2, 2014, and the file as a whole, the Court now enters the following opinion and orders GRANTING the motion to transfer and transferring this case to the United States District Court for the Northern District of California.

BACKGROUND

DataQuill is a British Virgin Islands-based company and the owner of five patents sharing a specification and describing a pen-or quill-like handheld device capable of scanning items and transmitting data wirelessly.[1] Apple, headquartered in Cupertino, California, makes a variety of products, including the smartphone branded the "iPhone". DataQuill alleges a series of Apple products—several iterations of the iPhone and its App Store, iTunes, and iBooks software programs—infringes these patents. DataQuill therefore filed suit against Apple in Austin, Texas.

Apple has moved to transfer this case to its home turf : the United States District Court for the Northern District of California, which encompasses California's Silicon Valley generally and Cupertino specifically. Apple does not deny having connections to this district. Apple has two campuses in Austin and employs some 3, 500 people here. Both Apple and the City of Austin have plans to increase Apple's footprint in Austin over the next decade, including expansion plans and additional tax incentives on top of those already given to the tech giant. And the processors at the heart of many iPhones, including the most recent generation of the product, are manufactured for Apple in Austin by South Korean conglomerate Samsung. But Apple maintains the information relevant to this dispute is centered in and around Cupertino, where Apple's engineers have developed each and every product accused of infringing DataQuill's patents.

DataQuill disagrees and contends Austin is a fine venue for a patent infringement suit against Apple. DataQuill plays up Apple's "substantial presence in Austin", and makes a largely burden-focused argument against transfer to the Northern District of California. Amidst accusations of discovery gamesmanship and a high-rhetoric motion to compel, DataQuill insists it should not be forced to litigate against Apple in Apple's backyard.

The Court held a hearing on these pending motions on May 2, 2014. After listening to the parties' arguments, the Court ordered the parties to confer on their primary discovery dispute and further ordered Apple to file with the Court an additional pleading setting forth additional, potentially relevant contacts in the Austin area. With that process now complete, the Court turns to the merits of the transfer motion and concludes the Northern District of California is clearly the more convenient venue for the trial of this lawsuit.

ANALYSIS

A. Legal Standard

*2 "For the convenience of the parties and witnesses, in the interest of justice, a district court may transfer any civil action to any other district or division where it might have been brought." 28 U. S. C.§ 1404 (a). Section 1404 (a) "is intended to place discretion in the district court to adjudicate motions for transfer according to an 'individualized, case-by-case consideration of convenience and fairness'". *Stewart Org., Inc. v. Ricoh Corp..., 487 U. S. 22, 29, 108 S. Ct. 2239, 101 L. Ed.2d 22 (1988)* (quoting *Van Dusen v. Barrack, 376 U. S. 612, 622, 84 S. Ct. 805, 11 L. Ed.2d 945 (1964)*). "There can be no question but that the district courts have broad discretion in deciding whether to order a transfer" under § 1404 (a). *In re Volkswagen of Am., Inc., 545 F.3d 304, 313-15 (5th Cir.2008)* (internal quotation marks omitted).

The preliminary question in a motion for transfer of venue is whether the suit could have originally been filed in the destination venue. Id. at 312. If it could have, the focus shifts to whether the party requesting the transfer has demonstrated the "convenience of parties and witnesses" requires transfer of the action, considering various private and public interests. See *Gulf Oil Corp. v. Gilbert, 330 U. S.501, 508, 67 S. Ct. 839, 91 L. Ed. 1055 (1974)*.[2]

The private interest factors are : " (1) the relative ease of access to sources of proof ; (2) the availability of compulsory process to secure the attendance of witnesses ; (3) the cost of attendance for willing witnesses ; and (4) all other practical problems that make trial of a case easy, expeditious and inexpensive ." *In re Volkswagen AG*, *371 F.3d 201, 203 (5th Cir.2004)* (*citing Piper Aircraft Co. v. Reyno, 454 U. S.235, 241 n.6, 102 S. Ct.252, 70 L. Ed.2d 419 (1981)*). The public interest factors are : " (1) the administrative difficulties flowing from court congestion ; (2) the local interest in having localized interests decided at home ; (3) the familiarity of the forum with the law that will govern the case ; and (4) the avoidance of unnecessary problems of conflict of laws [or in] the application of foreign law." Id. Although the Gilbert factors are "appropriate for most transfer cases, they are not necessarily exhaustive or exclusive" ; indeed, the Fifth Circuit has noted "none...can be said to be of dispositive weight". *In re Volkswagen of Am.*, *545 F.3d at 313-15* (quoting *Action Indus.*, *Inc. v. U. S. Fid.& Guar. Corp.*, *358 F.3d 337, 340 (5th Cir.2004)*). Despite the wide array of private and public concerns, a court must engage in a "flexible and individualized analysis" in ruling on a motion to transfer venue. Stewart, 487 U. S. at 29.

Though the above is similar to the standard in the forum non conveniens context, § 1404 (a) requires a lesser showing of inconvenience. *In re Volkswagen of Am.*, *545 F.3d at 314*. As such, the movant need not show the Gilbert factors substantially outweigh the plaintiff's choice of venue—it is enough to show the new venue is clearly more convenient than the original one. See id. Nonetheless, as the Supreme Court has cautioned, while the movant's burden is lessened, the plaintiff's choice of venue is still to be considered. See *Norwood v. Kirkpatrick, 349 U. S.29, 32, 75 S. Ct.544, 99 L. Ed.789 (1955)*. Accordingly, the Fifth Circuit's rule is that while the plaintiff's choice of venue is not a factor under Gilbert, it places a "significant" burden of proof upon the movant to "show good cause for the transfer". *In re Volkswagen of Am.*, *545 F.3d at 314 n.10*. "Thus, when the transferee venue is not clearly more convenient than the venue chosen by the plaintiff, the plaintiff's choice should be respected." Id. at 315.

B. Application

*3 There is no dispute this case "might have been brought" in the Northern District of California, where Apple is headquartered, so the preliminary hurdle in the § 1404 (a) analysis is easily cleared. See id. The Court therefore turns to the numerous Gilbert factors, beginning with the private interest factors and concluding with the public interest factors.

The first private interest factor is the relative ease of access to sources of proof. Id. The Fifth Circuit has cautioned this factor remains relevant despite technological advances having made electronic document production commonplace. Id. at 316. The Federal Circuit has observed that " [i] n patent infringement cases, the bulk of the relevant evidence usually comes from the accused infringer", and therefore the location of the defendant's documents tends to be the more convenient venue. *In re Genentech, Inc., 566 F.3d 1338, 1345 (Fed. Cir.2009)*. Apple has designed each of the accused products at its headquarters in Cupertino. Accordingly, documents relevant to the development and creation of Apple's products are likely to be found in Cupertino, even if some of the documents may be equally accessible electronically from Austin. Additionally, DataQuill has failed to demonstrate the existence of any meaningful documents at Apple's Austin campuses, which do not perform design work and primarily house customer service functions for the company. Although Samsung manufacturers chips for Apple in Austin, the manufacturing of those chips is not at issue in this case, and Samsung has not been sued. Instead, the focus of the infringement story appears to be on the way Apple products use software such as iTunes or the App Store to remotely access information.[3] Solving that puzzle requires information from Apple's software and hardware engineers in Cupertino, not its third-party processor manufacturer in Austin. The evidence also demonstrates whatever limited amount of relevant information exists in Austin is likely to be significantly outweighed by the amount of relevant information present in Cupertino. This factor weighs in favor of transfer.

The second private interest factor is the availability of compulsory process to secure the attendance of witnesses. *In re Volkswagen of Am., 545 F.3d at 316*. Apple has identified eight former employees who helped develop some of the accused products and who presently reside in the Northern District of California. Similarly, Apple has identified a handful of inventors whose prior art was cited by the Patent Office in the examination of the patents-in-suit and who presently reside in the Northern District of California. The California court's absolute subpoena power over these numerous witnesses weighs in favor of transfer. Id. at 316 ; *In re Genentech, 566 F.3d at 1345*. DataQuill primarily faults Apple for failing to provide details as to these named individuals' proposed testimony, but Apple need not provide such concrete information at this stage of the litigation.

Cf. *In re Volkswagen of Am.*, *545 F.3d at 317 n.12* (noting, in the forum non convenienscontext, affidavits of specific testimony are not required) ; see also In re Genentech, 566 F.3d at 1343-44 (when conducting a § 1404 (a) analysis, identification of witnesses relevant to issues which might arise at trial is sufficient ; district courts "need not evaluate the significance of the identified witnesses' testimony"). Additionally, there is nothing to counterbalance the weight of these California witnesses in this district. Although DataQuill suggests (with far less specificity[4]) there may be prior art inventors in Texas, too, the maj ority of relevant non-party witnesses appear to reside in and around Silicon Valley. This factor weighs in favor of transfer.

*4 The third private interest factor is the cost of attendance for willing witnesses. *In re Volkswagen of Am.*, *545 F.3d at 317*. Apple has identified a number of Cupertino-based witnesses who are likely to possess specific knowledge relevant to the accused products, in addition to any of the former Apple designers who may willingly appear to testify. Inconvenience to these witnesses increases as the distance they must travel increases, and traveling to a local court is far more convenient than traveling to Texas. See id. at 317 (discussing the "100-mile" rule). DataQuill has not identified any willing witnesses residing in this district. This factor weighs in favor of transfer.

The fourth private interest factor looks to practical concerns in the expedient and inexpensive trial of the case. Id. at 315. This is a lawsuit between a foreign plaintiff and a defendant with longstanding and significant ties to the Northern District of California, both generally and specifically with regard to the issues in this case. Most of the witnesses are in California. DataQuill has no presence in Austin. There can be no question it will be more practical to try this case in California than in Texas. This factor weighs in favor of transfer.

Turning to the public interest factors, the first is administrative difficulties related to court congestion. Id. Attempting to accurately understand another court's docket from the outside is always a difficult task. DataQuill relies on publicly available data concerning the average time to trial in each district to suggest this Court can get these parties to trial first. It is unclear whether that is true. As the parties should know, they will not receive a trial setting in this Court until their Markman order is entered. The Court is already setting cases in early 2016, and thus even two parties on an expedited and agreed Markman schedule are unlikely to receive a trial setting less than two years from now. On top of that, this case has already been pending since August of 2013, and the resolution of this motion was delayed by a complex criminal trial, which occupied the Court's docket for the entire month of May 2014. The Northern District of California no doubt has its troubles, too, and they likely are not visible from bland statistics such as average time to trial. This factor is neutral.[5]

The second public interest factor is the local interest in resolution of the case. Id. at 317. Apple has decades of history with the people of Cupertino (where it employs over 16,000 workers) and with the Northern District of California. Apple has smaller, much more recent connections with this district given Apple's presence here and expansion plans for the future. But this case is about Apple's actions in designing and developing the iPhone and some of its software products, all of which happened in Cupertino. Whether those developers willfully infringed DataQuill's patents "calls into question the work and reputation" of residents of the Northern District of California, not the Western District of Texas. See *In re Hoffmann-La Roche Inc., 587 F.3d 1333, 1336 (Fed. Cir.2009)*. The fact iPhones are sold to Austin residents is largely irrelevant, as the mere presence of accused products in a district does not create a local interest. See *In re Volkswagen of Am., 545 F.3d at 318* (holding such a rationale "stretches logic in a manner that eviscerates the public interest that this factor attempts to capture"). This factor weighs in favor of transfer.

*5 The third and fourth public interest factors concern the familiarity of the forum with the governing law and the avoidance of conflict of laws problems. Id. at 315. Neither factor is particularly relevant here, as neither district has a demonstrated advantage in applying federal patent law and the parties have not raised any potential conflict of laws issues. These factors are neutral.[6]

CONCLUSION

Because most of the Gilbert factors weigh in favor of transfer to the Northern District of California and none weigh in favor of retaining the case in the Western District of Texas, the Court concludes transfer is appropriate. There is no dispute Apple has a presence in this district, but that presence is unrelated to this litigation. The egg is here, but the yolk is not. The Northern District of California is clearly the more convenient venue.

Accordingly,

IT IS ORDERED that Defendant Apple Inc.'s Motion to Transfer Venue 〔#48〕is GRANTED ;

IT IS FURTHER ORDERED that DataQuill's Sealed Motion to Compel 〔#61〕is DENIED ;

IT IS FINALLY ORDERED that this case is TRANSFERRED to the United States District Court for the Northern District of California.

All Citations

Not Reported in F. Supp.3d, 2014 WL 2722201.

Footnotes

1. The five patents are United States Patent Numbers 6058304 ("Data Entry System"), 7139591 ("Hand Held Telecommunications And Data Entry Device"), 7505785 ("Data Entry Systems"), 7920898 ("Data Entry Systems"), and 8290538 ("Data Entry Systems").

2. Although Gilbert dealt with forum non conveniens, the Fifth Circuit applies the "Gilbert factors" in the 1404 (a) context. See In re Volkswagen of Am., 545 F.3d at 314 n.9.

3. For example, DataQuill notes many of its claims include the presence of a "controller", an element it believes satisfied by the Samsung-manufacturedprocessor. At this early stage, it is unclear whether the absence of a "controller" will be part of Apple's defense. However, the controller itself is at best tangential to the core dispute over how the iPhone uses software to interact with remote data sources. This may explain why Apple represents DataQuill did not mention the controller—or any of the other basic hardware characteristics contained in the claims, such as a "display", a "reading sensor", "memory", a "speaker, " or a "camera" —in its discovery requests, and instead focused on "Acquisition Functionality", a term DataQuill defined in terms of the use of iTunes, App Store, and iBooks software. Def.'s Reply 〔#65-2〕, Ex.2.

4. DataQuill provides a list of names of "Texas inventors", but no information as to their present whereabouts or whether they would be subject to compulsory process in this district.

5. Any additional delay caused by the transfer itself is irrelevant. The Fifth Circuit recently held "garden-variety delay associated with transfer is not to be taken into consideration when ruling on a § 1404 (a) motion to transfer". *In re Radmax, Ltd., 720 F.3d 285, 289 (5th Cir.2013).*

6. Apple suggests the courts in the Northern District of California are "uncommonly familiar" with the iPhone given Apple's extensive litigation history there. Assuming familiarity with the parties or products can be relevant to the transfer analysis, Apple has not identified any specific knowledge likely to be relevant to DataQuill's patent infringement claims, and thus this consideration would be neutral as well.

美国得克萨斯州西区联邦地区法院，奥斯汀分院。

4　DataQuill 有限责任公司诉苹果公司

案件编号：A-13-CA-706-SS
签署时间：2014 年 6 月 13 日

律师和律所事务所

原告代理律师：华盛顿州西雅图 Susman Godfrey 律师事务所的安德列斯·希利、弗洛伊德·肖特和帕克·福尔斯三世；Heim Payne and Chorush 律师事务所的布莱恩·拉森、莱斯利·佩恩、迈克尔·海姆、内森·戴维斯和罗伯特·艾伦·布尔温克尔；得克萨斯州休斯顿 Susman Godfrey 律师事务所的约瑟夫·格林斯坦；得克萨斯州奥斯汀 Heim Payne & Chorush 律师事务所的道格拉斯·威尔逊。

被告代理律师：华盛顿哥伦比亚特区瑞生律师事务所的亚当·格林菲尔德、马修·摩尔和蒂莫西·奥布莱恩；得克萨斯州奥斯汀顺德伦律师事务所的艾伦·阿尔布莱特；伊利诺伊州芝加哥瑞生律师事务所的戴尔·Chang；加利福尼亚州门洛帕克瑞生律师事务所（有限责任合伙公司）的道格拉斯·伊森·卢米什、加布里埃尔·西蒙尼·格罗斯和米歇尔·马；加利福尼亚州洛杉矶瑞生律师事务所的菲利普·王。

裁定书

萨姆·斯帕克斯，地区法院法官

*1 当日，法院以上述理由对文件进行了审查，特别是被告苹果公司诉讼地转移的动议［# 48］、原告 DataQuill 公司的密封答复［# 60］和苹果公司的答辩状［# 65］；DataQuill 公司的强制执行动议［#61］、苹果公司的答复

［#67］和 DataQuill 公司的密封答复［#74］；DataQuill 公司的庭后通知［#77］、苹果公司的庭后密封通知［#80］。法院在审查了文件、管辖法、2014 年 5 月 2 日举行的听证会上律师的论点以及整个案卷之后，现批准将本案移交美国加利福尼亚州北区联邦地区法院的动议，并作出判决意见和命令。

背景

　　DataQuill 公司位于英属维尔京群岛，该公司拥有 5 项专利，这 5 项专利共享一份说明书，描述了一种能够扫描物品并无线传输数据的类似笔或羽毛笔的手持设备。[1] 苹果公司总部位于加利福尼亚州库比蒂诺，其生产的众多产品中包括名为 "iPhone" 的智能手机。

　　DataQuill 公司指控苹果公司包括 iPhone 的几个迭代产品及其应用程序商店、iTunes 和 iBooks 软件程序等在内的一系列产品侵犯了这 5 项专利。因此，DataQuill 公司在得克萨斯州奥斯汀对苹果公司提起诉讼。

　　苹果公司提出将案件转移到其所在地的加利福尼亚州北区法院的动议，该法院辖区包括加利福尼亚州的硅谷和库比蒂诺。苹果公司不否认与奥斯汀有联系。其在奥斯汀拥有两个园区，雇用了约 3 500 名员工。苹果公司和奥斯汀市政府计划在未来 10 年内增加苹果公司在奥斯汀的业务，制定扩张计划并在已给予该科技巨头的税收优惠基础上增加额外的税收优惠。而且，包括最新一代产品在内的许多 iPhone 核心处理器都是由韩国企业集团三星集团在奥斯汀为苹果公司代工的。但是，苹果公司坚持认为与诉讼有关的信息集中在库比蒂诺及其附近地区，被指控侵犯 DataQuill 公司专利的所有产品都是由苹果公司的工程师在那里开发的。

　　DataQuill 公司对此表示异议，并辩称奥斯汀是对苹果公司提起专利侵权诉讼的最佳地点。DataQuill 公司以苹果公司实际存在于奥斯汀，转移动议会在很大程度上对诉讼造成负担为由，反对将案件转移到加利福尼亚州北区法院。DataQuill 公司指责苹果公司在证据开示中耍花招，并高调地提出了对苹果公司的强制执行动议，坚持认为其不应该被迫在苹果公司总部对苹果公司提起诉讼。

　　2014 年 5 月 2 日，法院对这些未决的动议组织了听证。在听取双方辩论后，法院命令当事方就其最初的证据开示争议进行商讨，并进一步命令苹果公司向法院提交一份补充答辩状，列明其与奥斯汀地区的其他潜在联系。随着这一过程的结束，法院倾向于诉讼地转移动议的优点，并作出裁定，加利福尼亚州北区地区法院显然是审理这一诉讼更为便利的诉讼地。

分析

A. 法律标准

*2 "为方便当事人及证人，维护司法公正，地区法院可将任何民事诉讼移交至其他可以审理民事诉讼的地区法院或分支法院。"《美国法典》第 28 卷第 1404 节第 1 分节。第 1404 节第 1 分节 "赋予地区法院自由裁量权，即根据案件的'独特性，及个案的便利性和公平性考量'等要素来对诉讼地转移动议作出裁决"。参见 "美国斯图尔特公司诉理光公司案"，《联邦最高法院判例》第 487 卷第 22—29 页；《联邦最高法院判例汇编》第 108 卷第 2239 页；《联邦最高法院判例汇编律师版》第二辑第 101 卷第 22 页（1988 年）[引用 "范杜森起诉巴拉克案"，《联邦最高法院判例》第 376 卷第 612—622 页；《联邦最高法院判例汇编》第 84 卷第 805 页；《联邦最高法院判例汇编律师版》第二辑第 11 卷第 945 页（1964 年）]。根据《美国法典》第 28 卷第 1404 节第 1 分节，"毫无疑问，地区法院在决定是否移交案件时具有很大的自由裁量权"。"美国大众汽车公司案"，《美国联邦法院判例集》第三辑第 545 卷第 304 页、第 313—315 页（第五巡回法院，2008 年）（内部引语省略）。

诉讼地转移动议的首要问题在于该诉讼最初是否可以在转移地提起。（《美国联邦法院判例集》第三辑第 545 卷第 312 页）如果可以，考虑到各种私人和公共利益，重点就转移到请求移交的一方能否证明因 "当事人和证人便利性" 而要求转移。参见 "海湾石油公司诉吉尔伯特案"，《美国案例汇编》第 330 卷第 501—508 页；《联邦最高法院判例汇编》第 67 卷 839 页；《联邦最高法院判例汇编律师版》第 91 卷第 1055 页（1974 年）。[2]

私人利益因素包括："（1）获取证据来源的相对难易度；（2）确保证人出庭的强制程序的可行性；（3）愿意作证的证人的出庭费用；（4）所有其他可以促使案件审判便利、快速和节约成本的实际问题。"参见 "德国大众汽车公司案"，《美国联邦法院判例集》第三辑第 371 卷第 201—203 页（第五巡回法院，2004 年）（引用 "派珀飞机公司诉雷诺案"，《美国案例汇编》第 454 卷第 235—241 页；《最高法院判例汇编》第 102 卷第 252 页；《最高法院判例汇编律师版》第二辑第 70 卷第 419 页（1981 年）。公共利益因素包括："（1）法院案件众多导致的行政管理困难；（2）在国内对当地利益进行裁决的地方利益；（3）诉讼地对管辖案件适用法律的熟悉程度；（4）避免不必要的法律冲突问题（或）适用外国法律的问题。"（引语同上）虽然吉尔伯特因素（私人和公共利益因素）"适用于大多数转移案件，但其不一定是详尽或唯一的因素"；事实上，第五巡回法院也表明 "没有任何因素……可以视为决定性的重

要因素"。参见"美国大众汽车公司案",《美国联邦法院判例集》第三辑第
545 卷第 313—315 页［引用"马佩斯工业公司诉美国富达担保公司案",《美
国联邦法院判例集》第三辑第 358 卷第 337—340 页（第五巡回法院,2004 年）]。
因涉及大量私人和公共问题,法院在裁决诉讼地转移动议时必须进行"灵活、
个性化的分析"。（参见"斯图尔特案",《联邦最高法院判例》第 487 卷第 29 页）

尽管上述内容类似于"不方便法院原则"的标准,但是《美国法典》第
1404 节第 1 分节要求较少体现不便之处的陈述。（参见"美国大众汽车公司
案",《美国联邦法院判例集》第三辑第 545 卷第 314 页）因此,本案中原告
无须证明吉尔伯特因素实质上超过原告的诉讼地选择权,只要证明新的诉讼
地明显比原来的诉讼地更便利足矣。（同上）尽管如此,正如联邦最高法院所
称,虽然申请人的举证责任减轻了,但原告对诉讼地的选择仍应予以考虑［参
见"诺伍德诉柯克帕特里克案",《美国案例汇编》第 349 卷第 29 页、第 32 页;
《联邦最高法院判例汇编》第 75 卷第 544 页;《联邦最高法院判例汇编律师版》
第 99 卷第 789 页（1955 年）]因此,第五巡回法院的规则是,尽管原告对诉
讼地的选择不是"吉尔伯特案"中的考虑因素,但它给申请人施加了"重大"
的举证责任,要求其"提供充分的转移理由"。（参见"美国大众汽车公司案",
《美国联邦法院判例集》第三辑第 545 卷第 314 页）"因此,如果转移的诉讼
地并不明显比原告选择的诉讼地更方便,即应尊重原告的选择。"（《美国联邦
法院判例集》第三辑第 545 卷第 315 页）

B. 申请

*3 毫无疑问,这一案件"本应在"苹果公司总部所在的加利福尼亚州北
区提起诉讼,因此《美国法典》第 1404 节第 1 分节分析中的初步障碍很容易
消除。（同上）故法院将焦点转向众多的吉尔伯特因素,即私人利益因素和公
共利益因素。

第一个私人利益因素是获取证据来源的相对难易度。（参见"美国大众
汽车公司案",《美国联邦法院判例集》第三辑第 545 卷第 314 页）第五巡回
法院注意到,虽然技术进步已经使得电子文档制作非常普遍,但这一因素仍
然很重要。（同上,第 316 页）。联邦巡回法院注意到,"在专利侵权案件中,
相关证据通常大部分来自被控侵权人",故被控侵权人文件存放地往往是更
方便的证据收集地点。参见"美国基因科技公司案",《美国联邦法院判例集》
第三辑第 566 卷第 1338—1345 页（联邦巡回法院,2009 年）。本案中每种
涉诉产品都是苹果公司在其位于库比蒂诺的总部设计的。因此,即使其中一
些文件同样可以电子方式在奥斯汀获取,但与苹果公司产品的开发和创造有

关的文件更可能在库比蒂诺找到。此外，DataQuill 公司未能证明苹果公司奥斯汀园区中存在任何有意义的文档，这些园区并不负责设计工作，主要负责公司的客户服务工作。尽管三星集团在奥斯汀为苹果公司生产芯片，但芯片生产在本案中并不存在争议，三星集团也未被起诉。相反，侵权重点在于苹果公司产品使用苹果音乐软件或苹果应用商店之类的软件远程访问信息的方式。[3] 要解决这一难题，需要来自苹果公司位于库比蒂诺的软件和硬件工程师的信息，而不是位于奥斯汀的第三方处理器制造商。还有证据表明，位于库比蒂诺的相关信息的数量可能会大大超过存在于奥斯汀的有限相关信息的数量。该因素有利于案件转移。

　　第二个私人利益因素是确保证人出庭的强制程序的可行性。参见"美国大众汽车公司案"，《美国联邦法院判例集》第三辑第 545 卷第 316 页。苹果公司已经确认了有 8 名目前居住在加利福尼亚州北部地区的前雇员帮助其开发了部分涉诉产品。同样，苹果公司确认了少数发明者的现有技术被专利局在诉讼专利审查中引用过，这些发明者目前居住在加利福尼亚州北部地区。加利福尼亚州法院对这些证人的绝对传唤权有利于案件转移。参见"美国大众汽车公司案"，《美国联邦法院判例集》第三辑第 545 卷第 316 页；"美国基因科技公司案"，《美国联邦法院判例集》第三辑第 566 卷第 1345 页。DataQuill 公司指责苹果公司没有提供以上证人的拟议证词细节，但在现阶段，苹果公司不需要提供具体信息。参见"美国大众汽车公司案"，《美国联邦法院判例集》第三辑第 545 卷第 317 页（在不方便法院情况下，不需要提供具体证词）；另见"美国基因科技公司案"，《美国联邦法院判例集》第三辑第 566 卷第 1343—1344 页（在依据《美国法典》第 1404 节第 1 分节进行分析时，若对庭审可能出现的事实问题的相关证人的鉴定是充分的，地区法院"无须评估已鉴定的证人证词的重要性"）。此外，任何事实都无法抵消前述加利福尼亚州证人在这个地区的重要性。尽管 DataQuill 公司认为（没有那么具体 [4]），得克萨斯州可能也有一些现有技术的发明者，但大多数相关的非当事人证人似乎居住在硅谷及其周边地区。该因素有利于案件转移。

　　*4 第三个私人利益因素是愿意作证的证人的出庭费用。参见"美国大众汽车公司案"，《美国联邦法院判例集》第三辑第 545 卷第 317 页。除了愿意出庭作证的前苹果公司设计师，苹果公司确认了可能拥有与涉诉产品相关的专门知识的部分证人在库比蒂诺。地理距离增加给这些证人带来更多的不便，去当地法院比去得克萨斯州要方便得多。（同上，第 317 页，讨论"100 英里"规则）。DataQuill 公司没有发现任何居住在本地区的愿意作证的证人。该因素有利于案件转移。

第四个私人利益因素是便利案件审理和降低诉讼费用的实际考虑。(同上，第315页)。本案中原告来自国外，而被告与加利福尼亚州北部地区有着长期且重要的联系，无论从总体上还是具体上看，这一事实都与本案的争点密切相关。而且大部分证人都在加利福尼亚州。DataQuill 公司在奥斯汀没有业务实体。毫无疑问，在加利福尼亚州审理这个案件比在得克萨斯州更切合实际。该因素有利于案件转移。

公共利益因素方面，首先是法院案件众多导致的行政管理困难。(同上)试图从外部准确理解另一法院积压的案件数量向来是一件难事。DataQuill 公司依据公开获取的各个地区平均审判时间的数据，建议本院可以首先审判这些当事人。目前还不清楚这是否属实。各方当事人应该知道，在马克曼命令生效之前，他们不会收到本院的审判安排。本院已经在2016年年初作好了案件审判安排，因此，即使是加急且商定好的马克曼流程上的双方当事人，也不太可能在2年内收到审判安排。此外，本案自2013年8月以来一直悬而未决。在此期间，因复杂的刑事审判进程，本案不断推迟审理。2014年5月，法院的审判资源都集中在该刑事案件上。加利福尼亚州北部地区无疑也有它自身的麻烦，而这些问题可能难以从平平无奇的统计数据(如平均审判时间)中得以窥见。该因素是中性的。[5]

第二个关于公共利益的因素是案件解决过程中的地方利益。(同上，第317页)苹果公司与库比蒂诺的居民(苹果公司在库比蒂诺招募了超过16 000名员工)以及加利福尼亚州北区法院相处已有数十年。相较于加利福尼亚州北部地区，苹果公司与本地区的关联更小，其与本地区的关联因苹果公司实体所在地和未来扩张计划才于近期得以建立。但本案涉及的是苹果在设计和开发 iPhone 及其某些软件产品方面的行为，而所有这些行为都发生在库比蒂诺。这些开发者是否故意侵犯 DataQuill 的专利而"让人对加利福尼亚州北区(而非得克萨斯州西区)居民的工作和声誉产生了疑问"。参见"霍夫曼－拉·洛克有限公司案"，《美国联邦法院判例集》第三辑第587卷第1333—1336页(联邦巡回法院，2009年)苹果公司生产的 iphone 卖给奥斯汀居民的事实在很大程度上是无关紧要的，因为仅凭涉诉产品在某地的存在并不能创造地方利益。参见"美国大众汽车公司案"，《美国联邦法院判例集》第三辑第545卷第318页(该案例认为"通过破坏该因素试图维护的公共利益，来延伸逻辑")。该因素有利于案件转移。

*5 第三项和第四项公共利益因素分别是法院对适用法律的熟悉程度和避免法律冲突问题。(同上，第315页)这两个因素在本案中不是特别重要，因为这两个地区法院在适用联邦专利法方面均未体现出特别优势，且双方当事

人均未提出潜在的法律冲突问题。这两个因素均属中性。[6]

结论

由于吉尔伯特案中的大多数因素都有利于将案件转移至加利福尼亚州北区法院管辖，而没有一个因素有利于将案件保留在得克萨斯州西部地区，本法院裁定将案件转移至加利福尼亚州北区法院是合适的。苹果公司在本地区的存在是没有争议的，但这种存在与本案无关。所谓"鸡蛋在这里，但蛋黄不在"。加利福尼亚州北区法院显然是更方便的诉讼地。

据此，本案裁决如下：

批准被告苹果公司关于诉讼地转移的动议［＃48］；

驳回 DataQuill 公司的强制执行动议［＃61］；

将此案移交至美国加利福尼亚州北区联邦地区法院。

所有引用

在《美国联邦法院判例集》第三辑，2014 年 WL 2722201 中未见报道。

脚注

1. 这 5 项专利的美国专利号分别是 6058304（"数据输入系统"）、7139591（"手持电信和数据输入设备"）、7505785（"数据输入系统"）、7920898（"数据输入系统"）和 8290538（"数据输入系统"）。

2. 虽然吉尔伯特因素处理的是法院不方便的情况，但第五巡回法院在《美国法典》第 1404 节第 1 分节的情境下适用了"吉尔伯特因素"。参见"美国大众汽车公司案"，《美国联邦法院判例集》第三辑第 545 卷第 314 页。

3. 例如，DataQuill 公司指出，其许多主张都包含"控制器"的存在，并认为三星制造的处理器满足了这一要求。在本案早期阶段，尚不清楚缺少"控制器"是否会成为苹果公司辩护的一部分。然而，控制器本身充其量只是与 iPhone 如何使用软件与远程数据源交互这一核心争议沾边，并非核心争议本身。这也许可以解释为什么苹果公司提出异议称 DataQuill 公司在其证据开示请求中没有提到控制器和诉请中提到的其他基本硬件，如"显示器"、"读取传感器"、"存储器"、"扬声器"或"摄像头"，而是将焦点集中在"获取功能"上，"获取功能"是 DataQuill 公司在苹果音乐软件、苹果应用程序商店和苹果图书软件的使用中定义的术语。（被告答辩状［＃65-2］，Ex.2）。

4. DataQuill 公司提供了一份"得克萨斯州发明者"的名单，但没有关于他们现居地或者他们是否会在这个地区被强制到庭的信息。

5. 任何由案件移交本身引起的额外延迟都无关紧要。第五巡回法院最近裁定,"在审理依据《美国法典》第 1404 节第 1 分节提出的诉讼地转移动议时,不予考虑与移交相关的普通延迟"。参见"Radmax 公司案",《美国联邦法院判例集》第三辑第 720 卷第 285—289 页(第五巡回法院,2013 年)。

6. 苹果公司表示,鉴于苹果公司在加利福尼亚州北区法院已有相当丰富的诉讼经验,该地区的法院对 iPhone "非常熟悉"。假设对各方或产品的熟悉程度与案件移交分析有关,苹果公司尚未确定任何可能与 DataQuill 公司专利侵权诉讼相关的专业知识。因此,这种考虑也是中立的。

United States District Court, N. D. California, San Jose Division.

V　Free Range Content, Inc., et al., Plaintiffs, v. Google Inc., Defendant.

Case No.14-cv-02329-BLF
Signed 05/13/2016

ORDER GRANTING IN PART AND DENYING IN PART MOTION TO DISMISS

[Re : ECF 94]

BETH LABSON FREEMAN, United States District Judge

*1 Plaintiffs, former AdSense publishers, bring this purported class action to challenge Google for allegedly terminating their accounts without cause and unlawfully withholding revenue they had accrued over their last one to two months as publishers. The Court previously dismissed the case with leave to amend. See First Dismissal Order, ECF 66. Defendant now asks the Court to dismiss the action with prejudice. Mot., ECF 94. For the reasons stated below, the Court GRANTS IN PART and DENIES IN PART the Motion to Dismiss without leave to amend.

I. BACKGROUND

Through Google's AdSense for Content program ("AdSense") , Google contracts with website operators who publish ads on their websites in exchange for a percentage of the money advertisers pay to place the ads. Third Am. Compl. ("TAC") ¶ 23, ECF 92. Plaintiffs are former AdSense publishers who allege that

Google terminated each of them without cause and withheld the entirety of the earnings they had accrued but had not yet been paid upon termination. Id.¶¶ 14-17, 50, 63, 73, 85, 134. Plaintiffs seek to represent a class of former publishers in 40 countries whose balances Google withheld in their entirety upon termination. Id.¶ 115.[1]

A. AdSense Terms

The AdSense Terms ("Terms") constitute the contract between Google and U. S. publishers. Id.¶ 27. Plaintiffs allege that the Terms took numerous forms over the years that they were publishers, id. n.27 : 10 pages of "Terms and Conditions" until mid-2013, id. Exh. B ("T&C"), ECF 92-2, when they were replaced by a 5-page "Terms of Service, " id. Exhs. A, C ("TOS"), ECF 92-1, 92-3. Both were non-negotiable and linked to non-negotiable "Program Policies" and "Branding Guidelines". TAC ¶ 27. Plaintiffs allege that the Payment and Termination Terms central to this litigation ("Challenged Terms") remained substantially similar between the contracts. Id.¶¶ 23-25, 29-31. The Court identifies the relevant portions of each below.

1. Payment Term

The Payment Term states, " [Y] ou will receive a payment related to the number of valid clicks…valid impressions…or other valid events performed in connection with the display of Ads on your Properties, in each case as determined by Google". TOS ¶ 5 ; see also T&C ¶ 11. Plaintiffs allege that this constitutes a promise by Google to pay publishers for interactions with the ads they publish. TAC ¶ 23.

At the same time, Plaintiffs allege that the Payment Term purports to allow Google, in its sole discretion, to withhold earnings from a publisher for invalid activity. TAC ¶ 25. The TOS provide, "Payments will be calculated solely based on our accounting. Payments to you may be withheld to reflect or adjusted to exclude…any amounts arising from invalid activity, as determined by Google in its sole discretion". TOS ¶ 5. The T&C stated, "Google shall not be liable for any payment based on [invalid activity] " and that "Google reserves the right to withhold payment…due to any [invalid activity or breach] by You, pending Google's reasonable investigation…" T&C ¶ 11.

*2 As defined in the Payment Term, "invalid activity" includes : (i) spam or invalid clicks "by any person, bot, automated program or similar device"; (ii) clicks solicited by payment, false representation, or request; (iii) ads served to users whose JavaScript is disabled; and (iv) clicks "co-mingled with a significant amount of the activity described...above". See, e. g., TOS ¶ 5. Plaintiffs allege that any invalid activity they did not cause should be excused under the Terms' force majeure provision, see TAC ¶¶ 55, n.16, n.18, 92, which provides, "Neither party will be liable for inadequate performance to the extent caused by a condition (for example, natural disaster, act of war or terrorism, riot, labor condition, governmental action, and Internet disturbance) that was beyond the party's reasonable control". TOS ¶ 14; see alsoT&C ¶ 10.

Finally, the Payment Term also provides, " [i] f you dispute any payment made or withheld relating to the Services, you must notify Google in writing within 30 days of any such payment. If you do not, any claim relating to the disputed payment is waived". TOS ¶ 5; see also T&C ¶ 11.

2. Termination Term

The Termination Term provides, "Google may at any time terminate the Agreement, or suspend or terminate the participation of any Property in the Services for any reason". TOS ¶ 10; T&C ¶ 6. The TOS also states, "If we terminate the Agreement due to your breach or due to invalid activity, we may withhold unpaid amounts..." TOS ¶ 10.

Plaintiffs allege that the Terms require Google to apply discretion when withholding funds for invalid activity but that Google instead imposes a blanket policy of withholding all of a publisher's unpaid earnings upon termination for invalid activity. TAC ¶¶ 31-32. Plaintiffs contend that this blanket withholding occurs regardless of how many ads a publisher legitimately served and notwithstanding Google's alleged ability to distinguish between valid and invalid activity. Id.¶¶ 32-33. Plaintiffs also allege that the withholding does not translate to refunds for advertisers. Id. n.8, ¶¶ 46, 48.

In addition, Plaintiffs allege that the Challenged Terms are unenforceable because they constitute an unreasonable liquidated damages provision and are unconscionable. Id.¶¶ 139-142. Regarding unconscionability, Plaintiffs allege that publishers are typically unrepresented individuals or small businesses, who do not and cannot negotiate any of the Terms. Id.¶ 28. Plaintiffs allege that they nevertheless entered into the contract because they "were convinced that there was no real alternative to AdSense for publication of ads on web properties" given AdSense's ability to target ads, leverage Google's search technology, set up accounts quickly and easily, and access the largest global advertiser pool on the web. Id.¶ 20.

B. Plaintiffs

Plaintiffs illustrate Google's alleged practices with their own experiences, as well as online comments by purported former publishers, an anonymous report from a self-described former Google employee, and pleadings in other lawsuits. Id.¶¶ 50-113. The Court summarizes each Plaintiff's alleged experience below.

1. Free Range Content

Free Range Content ("FRC"), a California corporation, was a publisher from approximately July 2012 to March 2014. Id.¶¶ 14, 51. FRC published ads on various websites, which it monitored for compliance with the Terms. Id.¶ 51. In February 2014, FRC's earnings, as estimated by Google, began to increase at a previously unseen rate ; by the end of the month, the earnings had surpassed $40,000. Id.¶¶ 53, 57. FRC reported the increase to Google, asking for help in ascertaining the source and correcting any problem. Id.¶ 54. FRC set up a meeting with a Google representative for March 6, 2014, but Google disabled FRC's account on March 4, 2014 due to "invalid activity" and withheld the entirety of FRC's unpaid earnings. Id.¶ 58. The termination notice identified an internal appeal process, which FRC timely used to seek reinstatement of its account and the earnings Google withheld. Id.¶ 59. On March 6, FRC had its scheduled call and, on March 7, 2014, FRC's appeal was denied. Id.¶ 60.

*3 FRC alleges that, if invalid activity occurred on its sites, FRC did not cause it. Id.¶ 55. FRC contends that any invalid activity should therefore be excused as a force majeure. Id.¶ 55. FRC additionally alleges that it was at least due the earnings from valid activity in its final pay period—perhaps $8,000 to $11,000— but that Google withheld the entirety of its February 2014 earnings without any attempt to limit the withholding to invalid activity. TAC ¶¶ 57, 61.

2. Coconut Island Software

CIS, a Hawaii corporation, was a publisher from March 2005 through November 2012. Id.¶¶ 15, 64. Like FRC, CIS alleges that it successfully served thousands of ads on sites that complied with the Terms. Id.¶¶ 66-68. CIS alleges that its owner spent thousands of dollars in fees for programming, connectivity, and equipment to participate in AdSense, and that the revenue from AdSense constituted a substantial portion of its owner's family income. Id.¶¶ 66, 69.

Notwithstanding CIS' alleged compliance, Google terminated CIS on November 16, 2012, because its specialists had "found that [CIS] was not in compliance with [Google's] policies", including webmaster guidelines and the "spirit" of AdSense policies. Id.¶ 70. That same day, CIS appealed using the same process FRC used, but the appeal was denied three days later. Id.¶ 71. CIS alleges that, at the time of termination, Google owed it earnings for the preceding 1.5 months, which amounted to approximately $2,400. Id.¶¶ 71, 72.

3. Taylor Chose

Ms. Chose, a resident of Minnesota, was a publisher from approximately September 2013 to November 2013. Id.¶¶ 16, 74. Ms. Chose alleges that she complied with the Terms. Id.¶¶ 76-77. Like CIS, Ms. Chose paid hosting fees and for a domain name to participate in AdSense. Id.¶ 78. On November 27, 2013, Google terminated Ms. Chose, stating that it is "important for sites displaying AdSense ads to offer significant value to the user by providing unique and relevant content, and not to place ads on auto-generated pages or pages with little to no content". Id.¶ 79. Ms. Chose alleges that her site was composed of original content and that she did not intentionally violate any Google policy. Id.¶ 79. Ms. Chose estimates that, at the time of termination, she was owed $25,000, which Google withheld in full. Id.¶¶ 80-81. Ms. Chose alleges that she did not appeal the termination because she was not aware that she could. Id.¶ 82. Unlike the termination notices sent to FRC and CIS, the notice sent to Ms. Chose did not mention the appeal process. Id.¶ 82 (citing Exh.11 to Google's First Motion to Dismiss, ECF 39-11).

4. Matthew Simpson

Mr. Simpson, a resident of Canada, was a publisher from approximately February 2012 through mid-June 2013. Id.¶¶ 17, 86. Mr. Simpson alleges that he successfully served thousands of ads and complied with the Terms. Id.¶¶ 88-89, 91. Nevertheless, in June 2013, Google terminated Mr. Simpson's account for invalid activity. Id.¶ 91. At that time, his unpaid earnings amounted to approximately $147, all of which was withheld. Id.¶¶ 93-94. Like FRC, Mr. Simpson contends that any invalid activity on his site should be excused as a force majeurebecause he did not cause it. Id.¶ 92. Mr. Simpson also alleges that he paid for hosting and domain registration to participate in AdSense, as well as for the products he reviewed on his sites. Id.¶ 90. Mr. Simpson did not appeal his termination or dispute the withholding of his unpaid earnings. Id.¶ 95.

*4 Based on these allegations, Plaintiffs seek to bring the following claims on behalf of a class of former publishers from 40 countries not limited to any time frame, id.¶ 115 : (1) violation of California Civil Code § 1671 (b) ; (2) breach of contract ; (3) breach of the implied covenant of good faith and fair dealing, (4) unjust enrichment ; (5) violation of the Unfair Competition Law ("UCL") , Cal. Bus. & Prof. Code §§ 17200 et seq. ; and two requests for declaratory relief, one pursuant to the California Declaratory Judgment Act, Cal. Civ. Pro. Code § 1060, and one pursuant to the Federal Declaratory Judgment Act, 28 U. S. C.§ 2201 (a) , declaring the Challenged Terms unenforceable as unconscionable and unreasonable liquidated damages provisions.

II. LEGAL STANDARD

To survive a Rule 12 (b) (6) motion to dismiss, "a complaint must contain sufficient factual matter, accepted as true, to 'state a claim to relief that is plausible on its face'". *Ashcroft v. Iqbal, 556 U. S.662, 678 (2009)* (quoting *Bell Atlantic Corp. v. Twombly, 550 U. S.544, 570 (2007)*). When considering a motion to dismiss, the Court "accept [s] factual allegations in the complaint as true and construe [s] the pleadings in the light most favorable to the nonmoving party". *Manzarek v. St. Paul Fire & Marine Ins. Co., 519 F.3d 1025, 1031 (9th Cir.2008)*. The Court "need not, however, accept as true allegations that contradict matters properly subject to judicial notice or by exhibit". *Sprewell v. Golden State Warriors, 266 F.3d 979, 988 (9th Cir.2001)*.

III. DISCUSSION

A. Breach of Contract

Defendant argues that Plaintiffs' breach of contract claim fails because, as in their first pleading, they do not sufficiently allege performance or excuse. Mot. at

7-10. Defendant also challenges Plaintiffs' allegations that the Challenged Terms are unenforceable. Id. at 10-17. Finally, Defendant seeks to dismiss Mr. Chose and Ms. Simpson's claims, arguing that they waived their right to assert any payment-related claim by failing to timely dispute the withholding with Google. Id. at 18-19. The Court considers each argument in turn.

1. Performance or Excuse

"In order to plead and prove a successful claim for breach of contract in California, a plaintiff must show : (1) the existence of a contract ; (2) plaintiff's performance or excuse for non-performance ; (3) defendant's breach ; and (4) damage to plaintiff resulting therefrom." *Google, Inc. v. Jackman, No.5 : 10-CV-04264 EJD, 2011 WL 3267907, at 4 (N. D. Cal. July 28, 2011)* (citing *Careau & Co. v. Sec. Pac. Bus. Credit, Inc., 222 Cal. App.3d 1371, 1388 (1990)*).

The Court previously dismissed Plaintiffs' breach of contract claim for failure to adequately allege performance or excuse. First Dismissal Order at 1. The Court granted leave to amend and Plaintiffs now allege that they complied with the Terms. See TAC ¶¶ 51-52, 67-68, 76-77, 79, 88-89, 91, 132 ; n.11, 15, 20, 22. Defendant argues that these additions do not suffice and challenges each Plaintiff separately. Mot. at 7-10.

a. FRC

First, Defendant contends that FRC admitted breach in the original complaint by alleging that it "was due some substantial portion of [its estimated $40,000 earnings] …perhaps in the $8,000 to $11,000 range [   ] for AdSense ads it had dutifully served during that final period…" Mot. at 8 (citing Compl.¶ 22, ECF 1). Defendant reads this as an admission that 75-80 percent of FRC's ad clicks in its final pay period were invalid. Id. In the TAC, Plaintiffs anticipate this argument and allege that FRC made no such admission, but rather referred "in good faith to what it recollected seeing on Google's dashboard before Google terminated its account". TAC ¶ 57.

*5 The Court agrees with Plaintiffs. FRC did not admit breach ; rather FRC alleged, and continues to allege, that activity on its site had spiked and it could not discern why. See, e. g., Compl.¶ 20. Because FRC did not know what caused the spike, it could not have admitted that invalid activity had occurred. Thus, the Court cannot find that FRC has failed to allege performance.

Defendant additionally argues that FRC's allegations of compliance are implausible because of its business model, which Defendant describes as "placing ads on thousands of third-party websites", including "over 100,000 domains". Mot. at 8. The Terms permit publishers to display ads on third-party sites only if the sites are "in compliance with [the AdSense] program policies". See Exh.2 to Gray Decl. at 12, ECF 94-3. Defendant argues that FRC necessarily breached because it could not possibly have continuously reviewed every site on which it displayed ads, nor does the TAC allege that it did so. Mot. at 8.

Plaintiffs respond that they have alleged that "FRC monitored participating sites for compliance with AdSense policies". TAC ¶ 51. In addition, Plaintiffs do not allege that FRC served ads on 100, 000 domains and they argue that Google cannot negate FRC's allegations with assertions of its own. Opp. at 4, ECF 103. Finally, Plaintiffs contend that this is not the proper time for factual determinations. Id. The Court agrees with Plaintiffs. Defendant's arguments are based on purported facts not before the Court and thus fail to override Plaintiffs' allegations.

b. CIS

With regard to CIS, Defendant argues that screenshots of its website, which the Court previously judicially noticed, see First Dismissal Order at n.1, contradict its allegations of performance because CIS' ad placements were identical to examples of "unacceptable implementations" included in a Google page that set forth the AdSense policies in more detail. Mot. at 9 (citing Exhs.25 and 26 to Wong Decl., ECF 95-13, 95-14 ; Exh.2 to Gray Decl.).

Plaintiffs argue that this position is misleading for two reasons. First, they note that the screenshots of CIS' website were taken in 2014, seeWong Decl.¶¶ 14-15, ECF 95, nearly two years after Google terminated CIS, see TAC ¶ 70, and therefore cannot demonstrate how CIS placed ads when it was an AdSense publisher. In addition, Google admits that the Program Policies did not link to the detailed article when CIS was a Publisher, see Gray Decl.¶ 5, ECF 94-1, and so, Plaintiffs argue, Google has not established that the article was in effect then. Opp. at 4.

The Court agrees with Plaintiffs. While the Court need not accept as true allegations that are contradicted by judicially-noticed documents, Defendant fails to establish such contradiction here.

c. Taylor Chose

The parties' arguments with regard to Ms. Chose are similar to those regarding CIS. Defendant argues that Ms. Chose's allegations regarding compliance, see, e. g., TAC ¶ 74, are contradicted by a cached screenshot of her now inactive website, which Defendant contends is largely composed of scraped content. Mot. at 9, see also Wong Decl. Exh.27, ECF 95-15. Plaintiffs respond, again, that Defendant's assertions are misleading—this time because Defendant compares a November 2013 screenshot, see Wong Decl.¶ 16, with a help page that was not only published in October 2014, see Gray Decl.¶ 9, but was also too many clicks away from the Program Policies to be deemed part of the contract. The Court again agrees with Plaintiffs ; the screenshot does not suffice to contradict Ms. Chose's allegations of performance.

d. Matthew Simpson

*6 Finally, Defendant argues that Mr. Simpson's allegations of performance are insufficient because he alleges only that he neither conducted nor is aware of any invalid activity on his websites—not that it did not occur. Mot. at 9 (citing TAC ¶ 91). Plaintiffs argue that this reads the TAC too narrowly, focusing on one paragraph when numerous paragraphs allege performance. Opp. at 5. The Court agrees with Plaintiffs. See, e. g., TAC ¶ 88 (Mr. Simpson "complied with all terms set forth in Google's AdSense terms and conditions…"). Thus, the Court finds that each Plaintiff has sufficiently alleged performance.[2]

e. Excuse by Force Majeure

Defendant additionally challenges Plaintiffs' allegations that any invalid activity on their sites must be excused as a force majeure because it was outside of their control. Mot. at 10 ; see also TAC ¶¶ 55, n.16, n.18, 92. The Court has reviewed Plaintiffs' theory and finds that, while creative, it is not sound.

Under California law, unless a contract explicitly identifies an event as a force majeure, the event must be unforeseeable at the time of contracting to qualify as such. See *Watson Laboratories Inc. v. Rhone-Poulenc Rorer, Inc., 178 F. Supp.2d 1099, 1111 (C. D. Cal.2001).*[3] Applying that rule here, the Court finds that invalid activity cannot be excused as a force majeure because, while the Terms foresaw the risk, they explicitly placed the burden on Plaintiffs and did not identify invalid activity as a qualifying force majeure. See Exhs. A, C ¶¶ 5, 14. Accordingly, the Court GRANTS Defendant's Motion to Dismiss this theory of excuse.

2. Termination for "No Reason"

Defendant also challenges Plaintiffs' allegations that Google breached by terminating them for "no reason". Mot. at 17-18. The Court agrees that each Plaintiff's termination notice identified a reason. See TAC ¶¶ 58, 70, 79, 91. However, because Plaintiffs' breach of contract claim is based on other alleged misconduct, the Court cannot dismiss the claim on this basis.

3. Unconscionability

Defendant next argues that Plaintiffs have failed to sufficiently allege the third element of breach of contract—defendant's breach—because Google acted in accordance with the Terms when it terminated Plaintiffs and withheld their payments. Mot. at 10-17. Google first argues that the Challenged Terms are not unenforceable as unconscionable. Id. at 10-13.

"[U]nconscionability has both a procedural and a substantive element…" *Armendariz v. Found. Health Psychcare Servs., Inc., 24 Cal.4th 83, 114 (2000)* (internal citations omitted). "The prevailing view is that procedural and substantive unconscionability must both be present in order for a court to exercise its discretion to refuse to enforce a contract or clause under the doctrine of unconscionability." Id. (internal citations omitted). "But they need not be present in the same degree… the more substantively oppressive the contract term, the less evidence of procedural unconscionability is required to come to the conclusion that the term is unenforceable, and vice versa." Id. (internal citations omitted). Defendant argues that neither element is present here, and the Court considers each in turn.

a. Procedural

*7 Procedural unconscionability exists where a contract imposes "oppression or surprise due to unequal bargaining power". Id. Here, Plaintiffs allege that the Challenged Terms are oppressive because they are non-negotiable, see TAC ¶¶ 62, 65, 75, 87, 140 ; see also Opp. at 7. Defendant responds that this, by itself, is insufficient because Plaintiffs had other options for website monetization and because monetization is not essential. Mot at 11-12.

Defendant offers two cases that reach this result. First, *Belton v. Comcast Cable Holdings, LLC, 151 Cal. App.4th 1224, 1246 (2007)* found an adhesive contract for cable services not oppressive because customers could obtain the desired service, which was "a nonessential recreational activity", from alternative sources. Similarly, *Morris v. Redwood Empire Bancor*, *128 Cal. App.4th 1305*, *1320 (2005)* found a contract of adhesion not oppressive where "the complaining party has a meaningful choice of reasonably available alternative sources of supply from which to obtain the desired goods and services free of the terms claimed to be unconscionable". Defendant argues that the same result is proper here because Plaintiffs had other choices for the non-essential service of website monetization.

Plaintiffs respond with several cases from this district and the Ninth Circuit that find allegations of an adhesive contract sufficient to establish procedural unconscionability because "California law treats contracts of adhesion, or at least terms over which a party of lesser bargaining power had no opportunity to negotiate, as procedurally unconscionable to at least some degree". *Bridge Fund Capital Corp. v. Fastbucks Franchise Corp.*, *622 F.3d 996*, *1004 (9th Cir.2010)*, (citing *Armendariz*, *24 Cal.4th at 114*). For example, Plaintiffs offer *Newton v. Am. Debt Servs., Inc.*, *854 F. Supp.2d 712*, *723 (N. D. Cal.2012)*, aff'd, *549 Fed. Appx.692 (9th Cir.2013)*, which considered an adhesive debt-settlement contract. Newton expressly rejected the arguments Defendant makes here, finding that the "other choices" argument "ignores California case law finding that 'use of a contract of adhesion establishes a minimal degree of procedural unconscionability notwithstanding the availability of market alternatives'". Id. at 723 (emphasis in original) (quoting *Sanchez v. Valencia Holding Co., LLC*, *201 Cal. App.4th 74*, *91 (2011)*). The court similarly found the defendants' argument that unconscionability is not present where the good at issue is non-essential to contradict a string of California cases. Id. at 723.

In addition to offering cases that challenge Defendant's reading of California law, Plaintiffs argue that, under California Civil Code § 1670.5, it is too early to dismiss the unconscionability claims. Opp. at 7. Section 1670.5 provides, "When it is claimed…that the contract or any clause thereof may be unconscionable the parties shall be afforded a reasonable opportunity to present evidence as to its commercial setting, purpose, and effect to aid the court in making the determination". Plaintiffs contend that they have not had such an opportunity here.

Defendant responds that § 1670.5 is satisfied because Defendant has provided exhibits showing that CIS and Mr. Simpson display ads from other networks on their sites and therefore have other alternatives. Mot. at 12 (citing Wong Decl.

Exhs.25, 26, 28-30, ECF 95-13, 95-14, 95-16 to 18). Plaintiffs argue that this is insufficient to overcome their allegation that "Google touts AdSense as sui generis" with "the largest global advertiser pool on the web". TAC ¶ 20.

*8 Given the early stage of this case, the Court agrees with Plaintiffs. The parties have not had a "reasonable opportunity to present evidence as to [the contract's] commercial setting, purpose, and effect". See Cal. Civ. Code § 1670.5. Thus, the Court finds that Plaintiffs have sufficiently alleged at least a degree of procedural unconscionability. See *Bridge Fund*, *622 F.3d at 1004*.

b. Substantive

" [e] ven if the evidence of procedural unconscionability is slight, strong evidence of substantive unconscionability will tip the scale and render the provision unconscionable." Nagrampa v. MailCoups, Inc., 469 F.3d 1257, 1281 (9th Cir.2006) (citing Armendariz, 24 Cal.4th at 113). Substantive unconscionability exists where a term is "so one-sided as to shock the conscience, or impose harsh or oppressive terms". *Walnut Producers*, *187 Cal. App.4th at 648*.

Defendant argues that, far from being shocking, oppressive, or overly harsh, the Challenged Terms are justified by Google's need to improve AdSense's integrity, which in turn helps publishers because they benefit from the success of the platform. Mot. at 12-13. Defendant explains that Google's discretion in termination is justified by the need to prevent fraudulent clicks and undesirable content and to compensate advertisers, and that Google's ability to withhold earnings is limited to a short, finite period that is proportional to the harm invalid activity causes to AdSense's integrity. Id. at 13. In support of its position, Defendant offers two cases it distinguishes as considering far harsher terms, Hahn and Pardee, and two cases that uphold terms that Defendant contends are similar to those at issue here, Am. Software and Schuman.

In Hahn, the plaintiff challenged a term in a massage-services membership agreement that forfeited any pre-purchased massages upon cancellation of the membership. *Hahn v. Massage Envy Franchising, LLC, No.12-CV-153 DMS BGS, 2014 WL 5100220 (S. D. Cal. Sept.25, 2014)*. The court found the term substantively unconscionable, in part because no legitimate business reason supported the term, which was " [a] t bottom...a deceptive way for a business to extract relatively small monthly sums from thousands of consumers (generating large sums over time) in exchange for an illusory service". Id. at 9, 11.

Defendant asserts that the Challenged Terms do not resemble the clause in Hahn, but offers no explanation. Mot. at 13. On the other hand Plaintiffs, who also rely on Hahn, contend that, just as the forfeiture clause in Hahn "negate [d] the reasonable expectation" that consumers will receive pre-purchased services, 2014 WL 5100220, at 9, the Challenged Terms negate the reasonable expectation that a party will be paid for services it rendered. Opp. at 9.

Defendant next offers Pardee as a distinguishing case. Mot. at 13. In Pardee, the court found terms waiving the parties' rights to punitive damages and a jury trial in a real estate contract "so one-sided as to be substantively unconscionable". *Pardee Constr. Co. v. Superior Court, 100 Cal. App.4th 1081, 1092 (2002)*. The court explained that the waiver of punitive damages was "in practical reality, only for Pardee's benefit" and that nothing in the record showed that waiver of a jury trial "would in fact result in any significant saving of time or costs" or any other gain for the buyers. Id. at 1091-92. Defendant argues that these terms constituted hidden and complex waivers, unlike the terms at issue here. Mot. at 13.

*9 In contrast, Defendant contends that the Challenged Terms are similar to the terms considered in Am. Software and Schuman. In Am. Software, the court found a term in a software salesperson's employment contract that terminated her right to receive commissions on payments received 30 days after her severance enforceable. *Am. Software, Inc. v. Ali, 46 Cal. App.4th 1386 (1996)*. The court found that the term was not substantively unconscionable because the contract "was the result of an arm's-length negotiation between two sophisticated and experienced parties of comparable bargaining power and is fairly reflective of prevailing practices in employing commissioned sales representatives". Id. at 1394-95. The court recognized the company's need to compensate the individual who services the account after the seller leaves. Id. at 1393. In addition, the court noted that the relevant terms "involved certain risks to both parties". Id. at 1393.

Schuman similarly found a term deferring commissions until payment is received or reasonably certain to be enforceable. *Schuman v. Ikon, 232 Fed. Appx.659, 663 (9th Cir.2007)*. In this unpublished opinion, the Ninth Circuit was persuaded by the fact that the commissions were paid to the plaintiff's successor, rather than the employer, and noted that the plaintiff had not actually forfeited any commissions as he had not executed any sales pursuant to the contract. Id.

Defendant contends that the Challenged Terms similarly authorize withholding payments during a short, finite period. Mot. at 13. Plaintiffs argue that the Terms are not similar because the contracts in both Am. Software and Schuman provided for other compensation—a base salary in Am. Software and 30 percent commissions for six months in Schuman—and withheld payments to compensate the plaintiff's successor, not employer. Opp. at 9. In addition, Plaintiffs note that the parties shared risks regarding compensation in Am. Software and argue that the Schuman plaintiff was not terminated arbitrarily. Id.

Having reviewed the cases offered by the parties, [4] most of which considered unconscionability at summary judgment, the Court finds that Plaintiffs have sufficiently alleged substantive unconscionability. Taking the allegations are true, the Challenged Terms are one-sided because they let Google withhold funds for up to two months regardless of the severity of the purported breach and even if the funds are earned through valid activity, notwithstanding Google's supposed ability to distinguish between valid and invalid ad serves. TAC ¶ 32. In addition, Plaintiffs allege that Google, unlike the defendants in Am. Software and Schuman, withholds payments not to compensate other publishers or even advertisers, but solely for its own profit. Id.¶ 46. While a more developed record may reveal that Google is justified in withholding the entirety of unpaid earnings, Plaintiffs offer sufficient allegations to survive the pleading stage on this issue.

4. Liquidated Damages

Defendant next challenges Plaintiffs' allegations that the Terms contain an unenforceable liquidated damages provision. Mot. at 14-15, 25. The parties agree that this concerns the Termination Term and Plaintiffs allege that the Payment Term is also implicated to the extent that Google uses it to withhold 100 percent of a publisher's reported earnings upon termination for supposed breach. Opp. at 9 (citing TAC ¶ 36). Having found that Plaintiffs sufficiently allege that the terms are unenforceable as unconscionable, the Court nevertheless considers this argument because it determines whether or not Plaintiffs' § 1671 (b) claim survives.

*10 The Court most recently considered Plaintiffs' liquidated damages theory in the Order Granting Plaintiffs' Motion for Reconsideration. ECF 91 ("Recon. Order"). The Court explained that, under California law, liquidated damages are defined as "an amount of compensation to be paid in the event of a breach of contract, the sum of which is fixed and certain by agreement..." *Chodos v. W.*

Publ'g Co., *292 F.3d 992*, *1002 (9th Cir.2002)* (quoting *Kelly v. McDonald*, *98 Cal. App.121*, *125 (1929)*). "Thus, to constitute liquidated damages, the contractual provision must : (1) arise from a breach, and (2) provide a fixed and certain sum". *Ruwe v. Cellco P'ship*, *613 F. Supp.2d 1191*, *1196 (N. D. Cal.2009)*.

In the Reconsideration Order, the Court dismissed the allegations that Defendant withheld earnings from FRC and Mr. Simpson pursuant to a liquidated damages provision because Plaintiffs had alleged that Google terminated them due to invalid activity rather than breach based on Plaintiffs' own actions. Recon. Order at 5. The Court granted leave to amend and Plaintiffs have cured the defect by alleging that invalid activity is a form of breach, see TAC ¶ 38, and therefore any damages due as a result of invalid activity "arise from a breach". See *Ruwe*, *613 F. Supp.2d at 1196*. Defendant does not contest Plaintiffs' allegation that invalid activity constitutes breach of the Terms.

The parties' current disagreement focuses on the second requirement—that the provision identify a fixed and certain sum. The Court previously found Plaintiffs' allegations sufficient to survive a motion to dismiss on this issue. Recon. Order at 6-8. The Court explained that "unpaid amounts" could refer to the entirety of a terminated publisher's unpaid but earned balance—a fixed, ascertainable sum to which Plaintiffs were entitled. Defendant challenges this finding.

Defendant first contends that, rather than require Plaintiffs to forfeit a deposit or pay a fee, as is common in liquidated damages provisions, Google simply exercised its right to not pay for work done in violation of the Terms. Id. at 14-15. Plaintiffs respond that Google's own word choice, which refers to money generated by terminated publishers as "earnings", reveals that Google is withholding money Plaintiffs have already earned. Opp. at 11-12 ; see also TAC ¶¶ 32, 40-44, 83, 96. Plaintiffs also allege that Google tallies and reports each publisher's earnings for serving ads in the publisher's account. Id.¶ 44, 53, 57. As before, the Court finds Plaintiffs argument more persuasive. SeeRecon. Order at 7 (Because the Termination Term "also states ' [a] ny earned balance below the applicable threshold will remain unpaid'", unpaid amounts could refer to an earned balance).

Defendant next argues that the withheld sum is insufficiently certain for the Challenged Terms to constitute a liquidated damages provision. Defendant bases this argument in large part on Bayol, which found that Zipcar's late fees constitute liquidated damages because the subscriber agreement provides a high degree of certainty regarding the fee amount for a late return. *Bayol v. Zipcar, Inc.*, *78 F. Supp.3d 1252, 1258 (N. D. Cal.2015)*. Defendant highlights two portions of the decision : that "courts will find fees that are not a single, fixed number to be liquidated damages provisions where they can easily be determined from the contract at the time of breach" and that " [t] o be sufficiently fixed and certain to qualify as liquidated damages, a provision must either set the exact amount (i. e., a single number) , or provide some formula by which the amount is certain or readily ascertainable". Mot. at 15 (quoting *Bayol, 78 F. Supp.3d at 1256*) (internal citations omitted) (emphasis in Motion). Defendant argues that the Terms fail to satisfy either requirement, as they identify neither an amount nor a formula. Instead, Defendant argues, the Terms explicitly build in discretion for the amount and they result in amounts that vary widely in terms of both absolute number and percentage of a publisher's previous earnings. Mot. at 15.

*11 Plaintiffs respond that the Terms specify a formula : 1.00 × unpaid earnings at termination. Opp. at 13. In addition, as noted above, Plaintiffs allege that Google reports each publisher's earnings to the publisher. TAC ¶¶ 44, 53, 57.

As before, the Court finds that the amount is "readily ascertainable". While Defendant may be correct that the Terms do not specify a formula or set amount, the Court finds Plaintiffs' allegations that, in practice, Google always withholds the entire sum sufficient to establish that the parties "possess some degree of certainty regarding their liability in the event of a breach". *Ruwe, 613 F. Supp.2d at 1198* (amount was sufficiently certain because same amount was charged to each customer in practice).

Defendant next argues that, even if the Challenged Terms constitute a liquidated damages provision, it is not unreasonable and is therefore enforceable under § 1671 (b) , which presumes enforceability "unless the party seeking to invalidate the provision establishes that the provision was unreasonable under the circumstances existing at the time the contract was made". Cal. Civ. Code § 1671 (b). The statute "casts the burden on the opposing party to prove unreasonableness and requires only that the liquidated damages bear a reasonable relationship to the range of harm that might reasonably be anticipated". *Weber, Lipshie & Co. v. Christian, 52 Cal. App.4th 645, 656 (1997)*.

Defendant argues that Plaintiffs fail to meet this burden because the amount Google withholds relates to the anticipated harm to AdSense's integrity in two ways. Mot. at 16. First, the amount is a reasonable estimate of damages at the time of contracting and, second, the penalty is greater for sites with higher traffic, which cause greater harm than do less popular sites. Id.

Plaintiffs respond that they have adequately pled a lack of reasonable relationship by alleging that Google withholds all earned but unpaid funds, regardless of the magnitude of the breach and despite Google's purported ability to separate valid from invalid activity. Opp. at 14-15 ; see also TAC ¶¶ 6, 32, 132. In addition, Plaintiffs contend that Google does not refund the money to advertisers and that it often terminates accounts without any prompting by an advertiser, thus cutting any link to harm. Opp. at 14 (citing TAC ¶ 48). Finally, Plaintiffs argue that the reasonableness of a liquidated damages provision is too fact-intensive to be determined at this stage. Id.

The Court agrees with Plaintiffs. " [T] he validity of a liquidated damages provision is a fact-based inquiry not appropriately determined on a motion to dismiss." *Bayol v. Zipcar, Inc.*, *78 F. Supp.3d 1252, 1255 (N. D. Cal.2015)*. Defendant argues that Bayol is different because factual questions suggested a mismatch between the liquidated damages amount and the damage Zipcar actually suffers, see Reply at 9 n.6, but the Court finds that the same is true here. As Defendant admits, the harm caused by publishers' invalid activity or other breaches is difficult to measure, see Mot. at 16, and Plaintiffs have raised factual questions regarding the link to harm by alleging that Google does not refund the withheld money to advertisers. Accordingly, the Court DENIES Defendant's Motion to Dismiss Plaintiffs' breach of contract and § 1671 (b) claims.

5. Waiver

*12 Defendant separately challenges Ms. Chose and Mr. Simpson's breach of contract claims on the basis that they waived any payment-related claim, including breach of contract, by failing to timely dispute the withholding of their payments pursuant to the Terms. Mot. at 18-19.

The Payment Term provides, "If you dispute any payment made or withheld relating to the Services, you must notify Google in writing within 30 days of any such payment. If you do not, any claim relating to the disputed payment is waived". TOS ¶ 5. Plaintiffs do not argue that Ms. Chose and Mr. Simpson timely challenged their payments, see TAC ¶¶ 82, 95, but they argue that this should not translate into waiver for several reasons. The Court begins with the first four arguments, which it finds entirely unpersuasive.

First, Plaintiffs argue that Google failed to inform Ms. Chose and Mr. Simpson of the dispute requirement. Plaintiffs argue that, because the language about dispute appears in the Payment Term and not the Termination Term, it applies to active rather than terminated publishers. Opp. at 15. The Court finds this argument unavailing because, as Defendant points out, the term opens by explaining that payments are made " [s] ubject to this Section 5 [Payments] and Section 10 [Termination] ". Reply at 9 (citing TOS ¶ 5).[5] Second, the Court agrees with Defendant that the Terms gave Ms. Chose and Mr. Simpson sufficient instruction on how to dispute a payment, specifying that publishers should "notify Google in writing". TOS ¶ 5. Third, the Court agrees with Defendant that Plaintiffs' allegations that Google's support pages tell publishers that they cannot appeal withholding are irrelevant because Plaintiffs do not allege that Ms. Chose or Mr. Simpson read or relied on those pages. See Reply at 10 ; see also Opp. at 15-16 ; TAC ¶¶ 83, 96. Fourth, the Court also agrees with Defendants that, even if the condition is a forfeiture clause that must be "strictly interpreted against the party for whose benefit it is created", see Opp. at 16 (quoting Cal. Civ. Code § 1442) , the result is the same : a publisher waives any payment-related claim by failing to dispute the payment or withholding within 30 days. See Reply at 10, n.7.

Finally, Plaintiffs contend that the requirement is a private statute of limitations and that it is unenforceable because thirty days is not enough time for former publishers to consult with an attorney or even identify the precise cause for their termination. Opp. at 17-18. Plaintiffs rely on two cases employment cases, Ellis and Assaad, and one far more applicable case from the Eastern District of Pennsylvania, which considers Google's contract for its AdWords program.

The plaintiffs in both Ellis v. U. S. Security Associates and Assaad v. Am. Nat. Ins. Co. sought to sue their former employers after signing employment agreements that barred them from bringing employment claims after a certain time—more than six months after any incident in *Ellis*, *224 Cal. App.4th 1213*, *1217 (2010)* , and if the employee failed to timely request arbitration within 30 days of termination in *Assaad*, *No. C 10-03712*, *2010 WL 5416841*, *at 7 (N. D. Cal. Dec.23*, *2010)*. Both plaintiffs filed their claims within the statutory time but outside of the contractual terms. Id. at 7 ; *Ellis*, *224 Cal. App.4th at 1222*. Both courts held that the provisions functioned as a private statute of limitations. *Id. at 1222-23* ; *Assaad*, *2010 WL 5416841*, *at 7*. The Ellis court explained that a private period of limitation is enforceable if it is reasonable, and that it is reasonable "if the plaintiff has a sufficient opportunity to investigate and file an action, the time is not so short as to work a practical abrogation of the right of action, and the action is not barred before the loss or damage can be ascertained". *Ellis*, *224 Cal. App.4th at 1223*.

*13 Applying that standard, Ellis found six months insufficient to bring an employment claim, noting that "most reported decisions upholding shortened periods involve straightforward commercial contracts plus the unambiguous breaches or accrual of rights under those contracts". Id. (quoting *Moreno*, *106 Cal. App.4th at p.1430*, *131 Cal. Rptr.2d 684*). Assaad found 30 days to be an unreasonable, "vastly shortened statute of limitations". *Assaad*, *2010 WL 5416841*, *at 7-8*.

Much more applicable to the case at hand, Plaintiffs also offer Feldman, which considered the following provision in Google's AdWords terms : "You waive all claims relating to charges unless claimed within 60 days after the charge..." *Feldman v. Google*, *Inc.*, *513 F. Supp.2d 229*, *243 n.7 (E. D. Pa.2007)*. The court found that the provision constituted a contractual limitations period, but determined that it was enforceable because it was reasonable. Id. at 243. "Contractual limitations periods are valid and can be shorter than limitations periods prescribed by statute so long as the period for bringing claims is reasonable." Id. (citing Han v. Mobil Oil Corp., 73 F.3d 872, 877 (9th Cir.1995)). The Feldman court enforced the provision because 60 days provided the plaintiff, an attorney, "sufficient time to identify, investigate, and report billing errors". Id. at 243.

Defendant responds that those cases do not apply, as each required a party to file suit within a shortened period of time, but that here the notice is simply a condition precedent to filing suit. In support of its position, Defendant offers Brosnan, which found that " [f] ailure to mediate a dispute pursuant to a contract that makes mediation a condition precedent to filing a lawsuit warrants dismissal". *Brosnan v. Dry Cleaning Station Inc.*, *No. C-08-02028 EDL*, *2008 WL 2388392*, *at 1 (N. D. Cal. June 6, 2008)*. However, the contract placed no time limit on when such mediation could be initiated and therefore did not bar later suit.

Defendant also points to a decision finding that a purchase agreement barring attorney fees for a party who commences litigation without first attempting to mediate the dispute "means what it says : plaintiff's failure to seek mediation precludes an award of attorney fees". *Lange v. Schilling, 163 Cal. App.4th 1412, 1414.* Finally, Defendant offers a case that finds a term barring a plaintiff from compelling arbitration after a contractually-set time to be an enforceable condition precedent to arbitration. *Platt Pacific, Inc. v. Anderson 6 Cal.4th 307, 313 (1993).*

Having reviewed these cases, the Court finds that the Payment Dispute Term constitutes a private statute of limitations. As in the cases offered by Plaintiffs, failure to comply with the term bars claims in their entirety, rather than only alternative dispute resolution or recovery of attorneys' fees. Thus, as in those cases, the Court next considers whether the 30-day period is reasonable. See Han, 73 F.3d at 877 ("California permits contracting parties to agree upon a shorter limitations period for bringing an action than that prescribed by statute, so long as the time allowed is reasonable.").

Though Plaintiffs argue in their Opposition that 30 days was an insufficient amount of time in which to raise a payment-related dispute, they do not allege the same. To the contrary, they plead that both CIS and FRC succeeded in disputing their payments within that time, TAC ¶¶ 59, 71, and explain that Ms. Chose and Mr. Simpson failed to do the same based on the four reasons the Court rejected above, id.¶ 82, 95. Accordingly, the Court GRANTS Defendant's Motion to Dismiss to the extent that it seeks to dismiss all payment-related claims by Ms. Chose and Mr. Simpson.

*14 In addition, the Court finds that amendment would be futile because 30 days is a reasonable amount of time in which to notify Google of a dispute. The Court finds a comparison to Feldman instructive. There, the court found 60 days sufficient for the plaintiff to make any charge-related "claim". Here, publishers have less time (30 days) , but they need only "dispute" a payment or withholding, not file a full claim. Moreover, the adequacy of the time period is demonstrated by FRC and CIS' admitted compliance. The Court finds 30 days sufficient for this task, particularly as publishers regularly receive payments and earnings estimates from Google and, as discussed above, the Terms identify how to communicate the dispute. Thus, the Court does not grant Ms. Chose and Mr. Simpson leave to amend their payment-related claims.

B. Implied Covenant of Good Faith and Fair Dealing

Defendant next challenges Plaintiffs' breach of covenant claim. Mot. at 20-21. "Under California law, a claim for breach of the covenant of good faith and fair dealing requires that a contract exists between the parties, that the plaintiff performed his contractual duties or was excused from nonperformance, that the defendant deprived the plaintiff of a benefit conferred by the contract in violation of the parties' expectations at the time of contracting, and that the plaintiff's damages resulted from the defendant's actions." *Avila v. Countrywide Home Loans*, *No.10-CV-05485-LHK*, *2010 WL 5071714*, *at 5 (N. D. Cal. Dec.7, 2010)*.

Defendant's first two challenges to the breach of covenant claim are identical to arguments the Court considered and rejected above : that Plaintiffs failed to plead performance or excuse and that Defendant cannot be held liable for acting in accordance with an express contractual provision. As above, the Court rejects these arguments.

Defendant next argues that Plaintiffs' breach of covenant claim should be dismissed as duplicative of their breach of contract claim. Mot. at 20. Defendant relies on *Careau & Co. v. Sec. Pac. Bus. Credit, Inc.*, *222 Cal. App.3d 1371 (1990)*, as modified on denial of reh'g (Oct.31, 2001) , which dismissed as duplicative a breach of covenant claim brought against a defendant that had refused to provide a $13 million loan after the plaintiff had allegedly completed the conditions precedent to disbursement. The court explained that " [i] f the allegations do not go beyond the statement of a mere contract breach and, relying on the same alleged acts, simply seek the same damages or other relief already claimed in a companion contract cause of action, they may be disregarded as superfluous". Id. at 1395. To plead a separate breach of covenant claim, the plaintiff must offer allegations "demonstrat [ing] a failure or refusal to discharge contractual responsibilities, prompted not by an honest mistake, bad judgment or negligence but rather by a conscious and deliberate act, which unfairly frustrates the agreed common purposes and disappoints the reasonable expectations of the other party". Id. at 1395. Applying that rule to the facts before it, the court upheld the trial court's summary adjudication of the breach of covenant claim because it "alleged nothing more than a duplicative claim for contract damages". Id. at 1401.

Defendant also offers *Bionghi v. Metro. Water Dist. of S. Cal.*, *70 Cal.*

App.4th 1358, *(1999)* , which reached the same result. In Bionghi, the owner of a temporary employment agency sued the defendant for breach of contract and breach of covenant for allegedly terminating the agency due to office politics and racial prejudice. Id. at 1361-63. Relying on Careau, the appellate court upheld the trial court's summary adjudication of the breach of covenant claim because it "relies on the same acts, and seeks the same damages, as its claim for breach of contract". Id. at 1370.

*15 Defendant argues that the Court should reach the same result because Plaintiffs' breach of contract and covenant claims rest on the same allegations : that Plaintiffs entered into and performed under a contract yet were denied payment by Google. Mot. at 20. Plaintiffs respond that they have additionally alleged bad faith on Google's part. Plaintiffs allege that Google showed its bad faith when it terminated Ms. Chose and CIS while leaving other publishers with the same types of displays active, and by withholding all unpaid earnings notwithstanding the agreement's language that Google "may" withhold unpaid amounts. TAC ¶¶ 70, 79, 137.

Plaintiffs rely on *Celador Int'l Ltd. v. Walt Disney Co.*, *347 F. Supp.2d 846 (C. D. Cal.2004)* , which denied dismissal of a breach of covenant claim as duplicative. Celador considered breach of contract and covenant claims brought by the creators of a television show against the parent company of their production and distribution partners for allegedly causing those partners not to seek competitive deals and failing to renegotiate a higher licensing fee when custom and practice dictated that it should. Id. at 850-851. The court explained that, because breach of contract and covenant claims "will always be based on the same facts [since] a certain set of circumstance gives rise to a lawsuit" and "will always seek the same remedy [since] the same remedies are available for both claims…the challenge brought by Careau and its progeny is to distinguish two claims based on the same facts". Reviewing the allegations before it, the court found that the plaintiff had pled two claims—they "allege that Defendants' actions breached the contract. If not, the actions, allegedly taken in bad faith, frustrated the actual benefits of the contract". Id. at 853.

Plaintiffs contend that the same is true here : they allege that Google breached the Terms by terminating Publishers arbitrarily and withholding all unpaid earnings. If not, they allege that those actions, taken in bad faith, removed any consideration for Plaintiffs serving ads. TAC ¶ 154.

In support of their argument that the withholding breached the covenant, Plaintiffs offer *Storek & Storek, Inc. v. Citicorp Real Estate, Inc., 100 Cal. App.4th 44 (2002)*, which considered whether a bank breached the covenant by refusing to disburse a loan after determining, allegedly in bad faith, that the plaintiff failed to complete a condition precedent—specifically, to satisfy the bank that the loan amount would cover the costs of the project. The court explained that, when a party's satisfaction is a condition precedent, that party must either make a purely subjective decision in good faith or an objectively reasonable decision. The choice depends on the parties' intent as expressed in the contract or defaults to the reasonableness standard. Id. at 59. The court found that, because the loan contract was for a commercial transaction and the decision to be made by the bank was a matter entirely of financial concern, with no implication for aesthetics or personal taste, the bank was required to make an objectively reasonable decision. Id. at 60, 64.

Plaintiffs argue that, here, Google's satisfaction with their websites and ad serves was a condition precedent to payment and that they have pled that Google neither exercised its discretion in an objectively reasonable manner nor in good faith. Opp. at 20-21. The Court first reviews the Terms to determine whether they include a condition precedent and finds that Plaintiffs are correct. Under the Payment Term, Publishers "will receive a payment related to the number of…valid events performed in connection with the display of Ads on [their] Properties, in each case as determined by Google". TOS ¶ 5 ; see also T&C ¶ 11 (emphasis added). Thus, Google's determination of valid activity is a condition precedent to it paying publishers.

*16 Under Storek, only one test can apply to any given contract. In this one regard, the Court finds that the express language of the TOS and T&C differ in a material way. The TOS provide, "Payments to you may be withheld to reflect… any amounts arising from invalid activity, as determined by Google in its sole discretion", while the T&C stated, "Google reserves the right to withhold payment…due to [invalid activity or breach] by You, pending Google's reasonable investigation". TOS ¶ 5 ; T&C ¶ 11 (emphasis added). Thus, the Court finds that the TOS require Google to make a purely subjective determination in good faith, see TOS ¶ 5, while the T&C require Google to make an objectively reasonable determination without an accompanying good faith requirement, see

T&C ¶ 11. As a result, Plaintiffs' claims regarding withholding under the T&C are subsumed by their breach of contract claim, [6] while their claims that Google withheld payments under the TOS without exercising discretion in good faith suffice to go forward.

With regard to Plaintiffs' allegations that Defendant exercised bad faith when terminating Ms. Chose and CIS by allowing similar websites to remain active, Defendant argues that the websites are not similar and that, even if they were, Google's failure to terminate other violators is not enough to establish bad faith. The Court agrees that allegations of selective enforcement are not enough to plead bad faith.

Thus, the Court GRANTS Defendant's Motion to Dismiss Plaintiffs' breach of the implied covenant claim to the extent that it relies on allegations of termination and payments withheld under the T&C and DENIES the motion to the extent that the claim relies on allegations of payments withheld under the TOS.

C. Unjust Enrichment

In the First Dismissal Order, the Court dismissed Plaintiffs' unjust enrichment claim for failing to comply with Klein v. Chevron, which held that a plaintiff could plead claims based both on the existence and the absence of an agreement if the plaintiff "was uncertain as to whether the parties had entered into an enforceable agreement". *Klein v. Chevron U. S. A. Inc.*, *202 Cal. App.4th 1342*, *1388.* "A plaintiff may not, however, pursue or recover on a quasi-contract claim if the parties have an enforceable agreement regarding a particular subject matter." Id. at 1388. The Court granted leave to amend to allege uncertainty regarding the existence of a contract here.

Plaintiffs now allege that " [f] or purposes of this cause of action, plaintiffs deny the enforceability of the terms at issue, and, as needed to enable the recovery of the earnings due them for serving AdSense program ads, the enforceability of the entire AdSense contracts with Google". TAC ¶ 159. Defendant argues that this conclusory allegation fails to cure the deficiency because the parties do not dispute that the Terms exist and are, as a whole, enforceable. Mot. at 21-22.

Plaintiffs respond that they satisfy Klein by alleging that the Challenged Terms are unenforceable. Opp. at 21-22. Plaintiffs rely on *Bear, LLC v. Marine Grp. Boat Works, LLC, No.3 : 14-CV-02960-BTM, 2015 WL 4255061 (S.*

D. Cal. July 14, 2015) to argue that contesting only some of a contract›s terms suffices. However, in Bear, the defendant conceded that the complaint "contests the validity of...the amendments pursuant to which [the defendant] performed its work, labor and services..." Id. at 5. In other words, in Bear, the heart of the contract was in dispute. In contrast, here, Plaintiffs allege that "[s]ave for certain terms alleged to be invalid and unenforceable, the [Terms] are valid". TAC ¶ 130.

Thus, the Court agrees with Defendant. Because the parties agree that there is an enforceable contract here, Plaintiffs cannot bring a claim for unjust enrichment. Accordingly, the Court GRANTS Defendant's Motion to Dismiss Plaintiffs' unjust enrichment claim.

D. UCL Claim

*17 Defendant next challenges the UCL Claim, arguing that Plaintiffs lack standing to bring it and that they fail to state that Defendant engaged in "any unlawful, unfair or fraudulent business act or practice". Mot. at 22-25 ; see also Cal. Bus. & Prof. Code § 17200.

1. Standing

Defendant contends that Plaintiffs lack standing under § 17200 because they are businesses, not the consumers or competitors the law was written to protect. Mot. at 22-23. Defendant relies on Linear Tech Corp, which upheld dismissal of a UCL claim brought by "sophisticated corporate customers who have entered or will enter their own contracts with respondents" because "where a UCL action is based on contracts not involving either the public in general or individual consumers who are parties to the contract, a corporate plaintiff may not rely on the UCL". *Linear Tech Corp. v. Applied Materials, Inc., 152 Cal. App.4th 115, 135 (2007)*. See also *Dollar Tree Stores Inc. v. Toyama Partners LLC, 875 F. Supp.2d 1058, 1083 (N. D. Cal.2012)* (dismissing corporation's UCL claim because the "claim is based on a breach of a contract that does not implicate the public in general or individual consumers.").

Defendant misreads Linear Tech to suggest that a business can never bring a UCL claim. Linear Tech instead states that a business cannot bring such a claim when the contract does not involve "the public in general or individual consumers..." See also *In re Webkinz Antitrust Litig., 695 F. Supp.2d 987, 999*

(*N. D. Cal.2010*) (finding that the "UCL grants standing to companies of varying size" as long as they "state a connection to the protection of the general public" or "to individual consumer's interest"). Thus, the Court considers whether Plaintiffs have stated a connection to the interests of the public or individual consumers.

Plaintiffs argue that their allegations implicate the public and individual consumers because of AdSense's size and consumers' interactions with Plaintiffs' pages. Plaintiffs argue that this case is like Ewert, which allowed corporate and individual sellers to bring a UCL claim against eBay for preventing them from listing their products for the full contractual period. *Ewert v. eBay, Inc., No. C-07-02198 RMW, 2010 WL 4269259, at 1, 8-9* (N. D. Cal. Oct.25, 2010). Applying Linear Tech, the court found that this group of sellers could bring a UCL claim because it dealt "exclusively with form contracts...and involve [d] individual consumers". Id. at 9.

Plaintiffs argue that the same is true here : the Terms are form contracts and consumers who click on AdSense ads are involved. Mot. at 23. Defendant argues that users who click on ads are different than users who buy products. The Court agrees with Plaintiffs. Plaintiffs allege that publishers use their content "as the driving force for attracting legitimate ad consumers to their sites". TAC ¶ 32. Thus, as in Ewert, the interests of individual consumers are implicated because consumers may be harmed if a Publisher who caters to their interests is terminated. Thus, the Court finds that Plaintiffs have sufficiently alleged their standing under the UCL.

2. Fraudulent Prong

Defendant next argues that Plaintiffs fail to allege that Google engaged in a fraudulent act or practice, to plead reliance on any alleged omission, and to satisfy the pleading standards for fraud. Mot. at 23-24 ; see also Fed. R. Civ. P.9 (b) (plaintiff must "state with particularity the circumstances constituting fraud"). Plaintiffs respond that Google's policy of withholding all of a publisher's unpaid earnings at termination while stating only that it "may" withhold unpaid amounts constitutes a material misrepresentation. Opp. at 24 (citing TAC ¶ 171). In addition, they contend that they have pled reliance by alleging that they would not have expended time, energy, and money in serving AdSense ads had they known that Google would withhold all of their unpaid earnings upon termination. Opp. at 24 (citing TAC ¶ 171).

*18 "Generally, to be actionable under the UCL, a concealed fact must be material in the sense that it is likely to deceive a reasonable consumer." *Clemens v. DaimlerChrysler Corp.*, *534 F.3d 1017, 1025-26 (9th Cir.2008)* (citing *Aron v. U-Haul Co. of Cal.*, *143 Cal. App.4th 796, 806 (2006)*). "［T］he plaintiff must produce evidence showing 'a likelihood of confounding an appreciable number of reasonably prudent purchasers exercising ordinary care'". Id. (quoting *Brockey v. Moore*, *107 Cal. App.4th 86, 99 (2003)*). In addition, "a class representative proceeding on a claim of misrepresentation as the basis of his or her UCL action must demonstrate actual reliance on the allegedly deceptive or misleading statements". *In re Tobacco II Cases*, *46 Cal.4th 298, 306 (2009)*. "Reliance is proved by showing that the defendant's misrepresentation or nondisclosure was an immediate cause of the plaintiff's injury-producing conduct. A plaintiff may establish that the defendant's misrepresentation is an immediate cause of the plaintiff's conduct by showing that in its absence the plaintiff in all reasonable probability would not have engaged in the injury-producing conduct." Id. at 326 (internal citations omitted).

The Court agrees with Defendant that Plaintiffs have failed to plausibly allege reliance. Instead, CIS and FRC allege that they received AdSense payments for more than seven and nearly two years, respectively, before their final payments were withheld. In addition, CIS alleges that "a substantial portion of the family income" of its owner came from AdSense. TAC ¶ 66. Based on these allegations, the Court finds it entirely implausible that Plaintiffs would not have invested in their work as publishers if they knew Google would withhold earnings from up to two pay periods upon termination.[7] In addition, Plaintiffs have not met Rule 9 (b) because they failed to plead Google's intent to withhold and its knowledge of withholding the entirety of every publisher's unpaid earnings at termination. Thus, the Court GRANTS Defendant's Motion to Dismiss Plaintiffs' fraudulent UCL claim without leave to amend.

3. Unlawful Prong

Defendant argues that Plaintiffs have failed to allege any unlawful activity because the Terms are not unconscionable and contain no liquidated damages provision. See Mot. at 24-25. As above, the Court finds that Plaintiffs have sufficiently alleged unlawful conduct. Thus, the Court DENIES Defendant's Motion to Dismiss Plaintiffs' unlawful UCL claim.

4. Unfair Prong

Defendant's challenge to Plaintiffs' claim under the UCL's unfair prong fares no better. Again, Defendant argues that Plaintiffs do not explain how Google's alleged conduct violates a legislative public policy that is "tethered to specific constitutional, statutory, or regulatory provisions". Mot. at 25 (quoting *Drum v. San Fernando Valley Bar Ass'n, 182 Cal. App.4th 247, 257 (2010)*).[8] As discussed above, the Court finds that Plaintiffs' sufficiently allege a claim under § 1671 (b). Thus, the Court DENIES Defendant's Motion to Dismiss Plaintiffs' unfair UCL claim.

E. Declaratory Relief - Counts Six and Seven

Defendant finally seeks to dismiss Plaintiffs' declaratory relief claims, which ask for a declaration that certain terms are unconscionable and improper liquidated damages. Mot. at 25. Defendant argues that the declaratory relief claims fail because the underlying claims fail. As discussed above, the Court disagrees with Defendant about the underlying claims. Accordingly, the Court DENIES Defendant's Motion to Dismiss Plaintiffs' claims for declaratory relief.

IV. ORDER

*19 For the foregoing reasons, IT IS HEREBY ORDERED that Defendant's Motion to Dismiss is GRANTED IN PART and DENIED IN PART as follows. The Motion is GRANTED without leave to amend with regard to :

1. Plaintiffs' force majeure theory of excuse ;

2. any payment-related claims by Ms. Chose and Mr. Simpson ;

3. Plaintiffs' claim of breach of the implied covenant of good faith and fair dealing to the extent that it relies on allegations of termination or payments withheld under the T&C ;

4. Plaintiffs' unjust enrichment claim ; and

5. Plaintiffs' fraudulent UCL claim.

The Motion is DENIED with regard to :

1. Plaintiffs' § 1671 (b) claim ;

2. Plaintiffs' breach of contract claim, except as outlined above regarding payment-related claims by Ms. Chose and Mr. Simpson and Plaintiffs' force

majeure theory ;

　　3. Plaintiffs' breach of the implied covenant of good faith and fair dealing claim to the extent that it relies on allegations of payments withheld under the TOS ;

　　4. Plaintiffs' unlawful and unfair UCL claims ; and

　　5. Plaintiffs' claims for declaratory relief.

　　IT IS SO ORDERED.

　　All Citations

　　Not Reported in F. Supp.3d, 2016 WL 2902332.

Footnotes

　　1. Plaintiffs seek to represent a worldwide class for the first time in their Third Amended Complaint. Because Defendant does not challenge this class definition, the Court does not reach the issue, but notes that the amendment exceeds the leave granted in the First Dismissal Order.

　　2. In addition, having determined that Plaintiffs have sufficiently alleged performance, the Court does not reach Plaintiffs' two alternative arguments— that, even if Google can establish that Plaintiffs breached, it may only withhold payment for invalid activity because the Terms are a divisible contract, see Opp. at 6, and that, even if the Court finds the allegations of performance insufficient, Plaintiffs have sufficiently pled a "common count" of breach of contract, id at 2.

　　3. Plaintiffs argue that Watson misstates California law and offer Eastern Air Lines, Inc. for the proper statement. However, Eastern Airlines' statement of the law is identical to that set forth in Watson : a foreseeable event can qualify as a force majeure if the contract explicitly identifies it as such. See *Eastern Airlines v. McDonnell Douglas Corp.*, *532 F.2d 957, 991 (5th Cir.1976)*.

　　4. Plaintiffs also rely on *Dean Witter Reynolds, Inc. v. Superior Court, 211 Cal. App.3d 758 (1989)* , see Opp. at 9, but the defendant in that case conceded that "some measure of substantive unconscionability might be present" and the parties disputed only procedural unconscionability.

　　5. Plaintiffs additionally argue that the termination notices failed to offer sufficient notice because, while they inform terminated publishers that the termination can be appealed, they do not state that the withholding of earnings

can be disputed. Id. at 16 ; see also Exh.12 to Gray Decl, ECF 94-13. Defendant responds that Google was not under any obligation to remind publishers of the dispute requirement as it is clearly set forth in the Terms. The Court has previously considered this argument and, as before, agrees with Defendant.

6. As the court in Storekexplained, a challenge to a party's reasonableness under a contract is a claim of nonperformance of the express terms of the contract, not a claim for breach of the implied covenant. *Storek, 100 Cal. App.4th at 62.*

7. The only Plaintiff for whom reliance may have been plausible is Ms. Chose, who alleges that she was a publisher for only 2 months and lost $25,000 in unpaid earnings. TAC ¶¶ 74, 80-81. However, her payment-related claims were dismissed above.

8. The Court notes that the precise test for the UCL's unfair prong has not been definitively established. Other formulations include whether the conduct was "immoral, unethical, oppressive, unscrupulous or substantially injurious to consumers", *Drum, 182 Cal. App.4th at 257* ; see also *In re Google, Inc. Privacy Policy Litig., 58 F. Supp.3d 968, 984 (N. D. Cal.2014)* (citation omitted). As noted above, while a more-developed record may prove otherwise, the Court finds that Plaintiffs have sufficiently alleged harm to consumers to satisfy this test as well.

美国加利福尼亚州北部联邦地区法院，圣何塞分院。

5　Free Range Content 公司等诉谷歌公司

案件编号：14-cv-02329-BLF

签署时间：2016 年 5 月 13 日

部分批准、部分驳回了驳回起诉动议的命令

［答复：电子案例第 94 号档案］

贝丝·兰博逊·弗里曼，地区法院法官

*1 作为原 AdSense 广告发布商，原告提出本案集体诉讼，指控谷歌公司无故封停其账户，并非法扣留其最近一到两个月作为发布商的累积收入。法院此前驳回了原告的起诉，并允许其进行修正。（见电子案例第 66 号档案，第一份驳回令）被告现请求法院撤销之前不公平的驳回裁定。（见电子案例第 94 号档案）基于下述理由，法院部分批准、部分驳回了被告驳回起诉的动议，并不允许修改。

一、背景

通过 AdSense for Content 计划（以下简称"AdSense"），谷歌公司与在其网站上发布广告的网站运营商签约，约定网站运营商可以从广告主支付的广告费用中提取一定比例的费用。［第三版修正起诉状（以下简称"TAC"）第 23 段；电子案例第 92 号档案］原告是原 AdSense 广告发布商，其称谷歌公司无故封停其账户，并且扣留了他们应计但在账户封停时尚未收到的全部收入。（同上，第 14-17、第 50、第 63、第 73、第 85、第 134 段）原告试图代表 40 个国家 / 地区的原发布商起诉，这些发布商在账户封停时都被谷歌公司扣留了全部的应得余额。（同上，第 115 段）[1]

A. AdSense 条款

AdSense 条款（以下简称"条款"）构成了谷歌公司与美国发布商之间的合同。（同上，第 27 段）原告声称，在其作为出版商的数年中，合同条款采用了多种形式（同上，第 27 段）：截至 2013 年年中，采用的是共 10 页的"条款和条件"（以下简称"T&C"）（电子案例第 92-2 号档案），之后用 5 页的"服务条款"（以下简称"TOS"）取代了 T&C（电子案例第 92-1、92-3 号档案）。这两项条款均为不可议价的条款，并与不可议价的"计划政策"和"品牌指南"相关。（TAC 第 27 段）原告声称，作为诉讼核心的支付和终止条款（"受质疑的条款"）在两份合同中基本相似。（同上第 23—25 段、第 29—31 段）法院对每一条款的相关部分作出如下认定：

1. 支付条款

支付条款中规定："您将收到与在您的媒体资源上显示的广告的有效点击次数、有效展示次数或相关的有效事件等因素相关的款项，具体情况以谷歌公司判定为准。"（TOS 第 5 段；另见 T&C 第 11 段）原告声称这构成谷歌公司向发布商支付与其发布的广告互动的费用的允诺。（TAC 第 23 段）

同时，原告声称"支付条款"允许谷歌公司自行决定是否扣留发布商因无效活动获得的收入。（同上，第 25 段）TOS 规定："付款的唯一标准在于谷歌公司的会计核算，可能对您的付款予以扣留，以作出反映或调整，从而避免……因无效活动产生的金额。具体情况以谷歌公司行使自由裁量权判定为准"。（TOS 第 5 段）T&C 规定："对于'无效活动'所产生的金额，谷歌公司概不负责"，并且"如果您有任何'无效活动或违约行为'，谷歌公司保留扣留付款的权利……并交由谷歌公司合理调查……"（T&C 第 11 段）

*2 根据支付条款的定义，"无效活动"包括：（①）垃圾邮件或"由个人、机器人、自动程序或类似设备操作的点击"；（②）因付款、虚假陈述或要求而造成的点击；（③）向 JavaScript 被禁用的用户投放的广告；（四）"由谷歌公司决定的由无效活动产生的任何款项"的点击。（TOS 第 5 段）原告声称，任何非由其导致的无效行为应根据本条款的不可抗力条款免责（见 TAC 第 55 段第 16、第 18、第 92 段），其中规定："任何一方对于因超出该方合理控制的条件（如自然灾害、战争或恐怖主义行为、暴动、劳动条件、政府行为和网络干扰）所致的合同不充分履行不承担责任。"（TOS 第 14 段；另见 T&C 第 10 段）

支付条款还规定："如果您对支付服务或扣留的任何款项有异议，您必须在该款项发生后 30 天内以书面形式通知谷歌公司。如果您未提交书面通知，

则视为您放弃与争议款项有关的任何权利主张。"（TOS 第 5 段；另见 T&C 第 11 段）

2. 终止条款

终止条款规定："谷歌公司可以随时无条件终止本协议，或者以任何理由中止或终止所有涉财产服务。"（TOS 第 10 段；T&C 第 6 段）TOS 还规定："如果我方由于您的违约或无效活动而终止协议，我方可以扣留您的未付款项……"（TOS 第 10 段）

原告声称，本条款赋予谷歌公司在扣留无效活动的款项时行使自由裁量权，但谷歌公司实施一揽子政策，即因无效活动封停账户时扣留发布商的所有未付收入。（TAC 第 31—32 段）原告辩称，无论发布商合法提供多少广告，也无论谷歌公司是否有能力区分有效和无效活动，都会发生一揽子扣留。（同上，第 32—33 段）原告还声称，扣留款项并不能转化为向广告客户的退款。（同上，第 8、第 46、第 48 段）

此外，原告声称，前述受质疑的条款无法执行，因为它们构成不合理的违约赔偿金条款。（同上，第 139—142 段）关于不合理，原告声称发布商通常是无代表的个人或小型企业，他们没有能力也不能就任何条款进行谈判。（同上，第 28 段）原告声称尽管如此，他们仍然签订了合同，因为他们"坚信在网络媒体资源上发布广告方面，AdSense 还没有对手"，AdSense 有能力定位广告，利用谷歌公司的搜索技术，快速设置账户和轻松地访问全球最大的网络广告客户群。（同上，第 20 段）

B. 原告

原告以自己的经历、据称是原发布商的网上评论、自称是谷歌公司前雇员的匿名报告以及其他诉讼中的诉状来说明谷歌公司的行为。（同上，第 50—113 段）法院在下文中分别总结了每位原告所述经历。

1. Free Range Content 公司

Free Range Content 公司（以下简称"FRC"）位于加利福尼亚州，大约在 2012 年 7 月至 2014 年 3 月期间担任发布商。（同上，第 14、第 51 段）FRC 在各个网站上发布了广告，谷歌公司对其进行监视以确保其遵守条款。（同上，第 51 段）2014 年 2 月，根据谷歌公司估计，FRC 的收入开始以前所未有的速度增长；到 2 月底，收益已超过 40 000 美元。（同上，第 53、第 57 段）。FRC 向谷歌公司报告了这一增长，要求谷歌公司提供帮助，以确定增长来源并纠正问题。（同上，第 54 段）FRC 公司预计于 2014 年 3 月 6 日与谷歌公司代表举行会议，但谷歌公司于 3 月 4 日以"无效活动"为由冻结了 FRC 的账户，并扣留了 FRC 的全部未付收益。（同上，第 58 段）终止通知明确了内部申诉程序，FRC 及时使用该程序，要求恢复其账户并追回谷歌公司扣留的收益。（同上，第 59 段）3 月 6 日，FRC 进行了预定的听证；3 月 7 日，FRC 公司的申诉被驳回。（同上，第 60 段）

　　*3 FRC 认为，即使其站点上存在"无效活动"，也不是 FRC 方造成的。（同上，第 55 段）而且任何"无效活动"都可以因不可抗力而免责。（同上，第 55 段）FRC 进一步声称，谷歌公司至少应支付其在最后付款期内有效活动的收益，是 8 000 美元至 11 000 美元，但谷歌公司扣留了其 2014 年 2 月的全部收入，而没有试图将扣留范围限制在无效活动上。（同上，第 57、第 61 段）。

　　2. 椰岛软件

　　椰岛软件位于夏威夷，在 2005 年 3 月至 2012 年 11 月期间担任发布商。（同上，第 15、第 64 段）与 FRC 一样，椰岛软件声称它在符合合同条款的网站上成功投放了数千个广告。（同上，第 66 段、第 68 段）椰岛软件声称，其所有者为了加入 AdSense，在编程、网络连接和设备上花费了数千美元，并且 AdSense 的收入占其所有者家庭收入的很大一部分。（同上，第 66 段、第 69 段）

　　尽管椰岛软件称其遵守规定，但谷歌公司仍于 2012 年 11 月 16 日终止了与椰岛软件的合同，理由是谷歌公司"发现椰岛软件不符合谷歌公司政策"，包括网站管理指南和 AdSense 条款的"实质内容"。（同上，第 70 段）同日，椰岛软件使用和 FRC 相同的程序提起申诉，三天后被驳回。（同上，第 71 段）椰岛软件声称，账户禁用时，谷歌公司欠其前一个半个月的收益，总共约为 2 400 美元。（同上，第 71、第 72 段）

　　3. 泰勒·肖兹

　　肖兹女士居住于明尼苏达州，大约在 2013 年 9 月至 2013 年 11 月期间担任发布商。（同上，第 16、第 74 段）肖兹女士声称她遵守了前述条款。（同上，第 76—77 段）和椰岛软件一样，肖兹女士为了加入 AdSense 支付了托管费用并获取域名。（同上，第 78 段）2013 年 11 月 27 日，谷歌公司禁用了肖兹女士的账户，声称："对于显示 AdSense 广告的网站来说，重要的是通过提供独特的相关内容为用户提供重要价值，而不是在自动生成的页面或几乎没有内容的页面上投放广告。"（同上，第 79 段）肖兹女士表示她的网站由原创内容构成，并非有意违反谷歌公司的任何政策。（同上，第 79 段）肖兹女士估算，账户禁用时，谷歌公司尚欠其 25 000 美元，而谷歌公司全额扣留了这笔款项。（同上，第 80—81 段）肖兹女士声称，她未对账户禁用提起申诉是因为她不知道可以提起申诉。（同上，第 82 段）与送达给 FRC 与椰岛软件的终止通知不同，谷歌公司发送给肖兹女士的通知没有提及申诉程序。（同上，第 82 段，引用谷歌公司第一项驳回起诉的动议，电子案例第 39–11 号档案）

4. 马修·辛普森

辛普森先生居住于加拿大，从 2012 年 2 月至 2013 年 6 月中旬担任发布商。（同上，第 17、第 86 段）辛普森先生声称，他遵守前述条款成功投放了数千个广告。（同上，第 88—89 段、第 91 段）然而，2013 年 6 月，谷歌公司以无效活动为由禁用了辛普森的账户。（同上，第 91 段）当时，他的未付收益约为 147 美元，全部被谷歌公司扣留。（同上，第 93—94 段）和 FRC 一样，辛普森先生认为，他在网站上的任何无效活动都应因不可抗力而予以免责，因为这不是他造成的。（同上，第 92 段）辛普森先生还声称，他为了加入 AdSense 支付了托管和域名注册的费用，以及他在自己的网站上浏览过的产品的费用。（同上，第 90 段）辛普森先生没有对他的账户禁用提起申诉，也没有就扣留他的未付收入提出异议。（同上，第 95 段）

*4 基于这些指控，原告试图代表来自 40 个国家 / 地区的一批前发布商（不受任何时间范围限制）提出以下指控（同上，第 115 段）：（1）谷歌公司违反《加利福尼亚州民法典》第 1671 节第 2 分节；（2）谷歌公司违反合同；（3）谷歌公司违反诚信和公平交易的默示契约；（4）构成不当得利；（5）谷歌公司违反《反不正当竞争法》（以下简称 "UCL"）、《加州商业职业守则》第 17200 节等；以及两项确认赔偿请求，一项是根据《加利福尼亚州确认判决法》、《加利福尼亚州民法典》第 1060 节，另一项是根据《联邦确认判决法》、《美国法典》第 28 卷第 2201 节第 1 分节，声明受质疑的条款作为不合情、不合理的违约赔偿金条款，不可强制执行。

二、法律标准

欲使根据《联邦民事诉讼规则》第 12 节 b 条第 6 款规定提出的驳回起诉的动议生效，"起诉状必须包含充分且真实的事实材料，以'陈述形式上合理的救济请求'"。参见 "阿什克罗夫特诉伊克巴尔案"，《联邦最高法院判例》第 556 卷第 662—678 页（2009 年）［引用 "贝尔大西洋公司诉托姆布雷案"，《联邦最高法院判例》第 550 卷第 544—570 页（2007 年）］。考虑驳回起诉的动议时，法院 "将起诉状中的事实主张视为真实予以接受，并从最有利于被告的角度对诉状进行解释"。参见 "曼扎莱克诉 St. Paul Fire & Marine 保险公司案"，《美国联邦法院判例集》第三辑第 519 卷第 1025—1031 页

（第九巡回法院，2008 年）。然而，法院认为："不需要将那些与适当的司法认知或证据事项相矛盾的指控认可为真实予以接受。"参见"斯普雷维尔诉金州勇士队案"，《美国联邦法院判例集》第三辑第 266 卷第 979—988 页（第九巡回法院，2001 年）。

三、讨论

A. 违约

被告辩称，原告关于违约的主张不成立，因为在他们的第一次诉状中没有充分主张履行或免除。（动议第 7—10 点）被告还对原告关于质疑条款不可执行的主张提出质疑。（同上，第 10—17 点，最后，被告试图驳回肖兹女士和辛普森先生的控诉，辩称他们未能及时与谷歌公司就扣留款项提出异议，因此视为放弃了提出任何与付款相关的诉求权利。（同上，第 18—19 点）法院依次考虑每个论点。

1. 履约或免责

"在加利福尼亚州，为了证明其违约主张成立，原告必须出示以下证据：（1）合同的存在；（2）原告的履约或不履约的免责事由；（3）被告违约；（4）原告因此遭受的损失。"参见"谷歌公司诉杰克曼案"，案件编号 5：10-CV-04264 EJD，2011 WL 3267907，at 4（加利福尼亚州北区法院，2011 年 7 月 28 日）[引用 "Careau 公司诉 Sec. Pac. Bus. Credit 公司案"，《加利福尼亚州上诉判例汇编》第三辑第 222 卷第 1371—1388 页（1990 年）]。法院此前驳回了原告因未能充分主张履行或免责事由而提出的违约主张。（第一份驳回令第 1 页）但法院允许原告进行修改，原告如今声称其遵守了合同条款。（TAC 第 51—52 段、第 67—68 段、第 76—77 段、第 79 段、第 88—89 段、第 91 段、第 132 段；第 11 款、第 15 款、第 20 款、第 22 款）。被告辩称这些补充不充分，并分别对每一位原告提出质疑。（动议第 7—10 点）

a. FRC

首先，被告辩称 FRC 在最初的起诉状中承认违约，声称其"是由于［其估计的 40000 美元收入］的很大一部分……可能在 8 000 美元到 11 000 美元范围内，是因为最后一段时间内，尽职尽责地投放 AdSense 广告……"（动议，第 8 点；引用起诉状第 22 段，电子案例 第 1 号档案）被告认为这代表 FRC 承认在其最后付款期间 75%—80% 的广告点击无效。（同上）

TAC 中，原告预料到被告的反驳，并声称 FRC 没有承认这一点，而是"善

意地提到在谷歌公司禁用其账户之前在谷歌咨询主页上看到的内容"。(TAC第57段)

*5 法院同意原告的意见。FRC 不承认违规,相反,FRC 声称并坚持其网站上的活动激增,但无法确定原因。(起诉状第20段)因为 FRC 不知道导致激增的原因,所以它不能承认存在无效活动。因此,法院不能判定 FRC 未履约。

被告进一步辩称,FRC 的合规指控不能成立,因为 FRC 的商业模式是"在数千个第三方网站上投放广告",包括"100 000 多个域名"。(动议,第8点)前述条款允许发布商在第三方网站上显示广告,前提是这些网站"符合 AdSense 计划政策"。(见"格雷声明",第12点附件2,电子案例第94-3号档案)被告指出 FRC 肯定构成违约,因为它不可能持续审查展示广告的每个网站,TAC 也没有声称它做到了这点。(动议第8点)

原告回应说,他们认为"FRC 监测参与网站是为了顺应 AdSense 政策"。(TAC 第51段)此外,原告声称 FRC 没有在10多万个域名上提供广告,他们认为谷歌公司不能用他们自己的主张来否定 FRC 的指控。(异议答辩状第4点,电子案例第103号档案)最后,原告辩称现在不是事实认定的适当时机。(同上)法院同意原告的观点。被告的论点是基于法院尚未审理的所谓事实,因此不能推翻原告的指控。

b. 椰岛软件

关于椰岛软件,被告辩称,法院先前通过司法程序认证的其网站截图(第一份驳回令第1款),与椰岛软件声称履约行为相悖,因为椰岛软件的广告投放与谷歌公司详细列出 AdSense 政策的网页中所包含的"不可接受的行为"实例完全相同。(动议第9点;引用"Wong 声明"附件第25—26段,电子案例第95-13号、第95-14号档案;"格雷声明"附件2)。

原告认为,这一立场具有误导性,原因有二:首先,他们指出,椰岛软件网站的截图是在2014年拍摄的(见"Wong 声明"第14—15段、电子案例第95号档案),即谷歌公司禁用椰岛软件账户近两年后(TAC 第70段),因此不能证明椰岛软件在作为 AdSense 发布商时是如何投放广告的。此外,谷歌公司承认,椰岛软件作为发布商时,AdSense 计划政策并未链接到具体的条款(见"格雷声明"第5段、电子案例第94-1号档案),因此,原告认为谷歌公司无法证明该条款当时就已生效。(异议答辩状第4点)

法院同意原告的观点。虽然法院无须将与司法程序认定的文件相矛盾的指控视为真实,但被告在此未能证明这一矛盾成立。

c. 泰勒·肖兹

双方关于肖兹女士的争论与关于椰岛软件的争论相似。被告质疑肖兹女士关于合规性的说法（TAC 第 74 段），与其现已停用的网站的缓存截图相矛盾，被告认为该网站的内容由抓取的内容组成。（见动议第 9 点，另见 Wong 声明，电子案例 第 95–15 号档案）原告再次回应说，被告的主张具有误导性，因为被告将 2013 年 11 月的截图（见"Wong 声明"第 16 段）与 2014 年 10 月发布的帮助页面比较（见"格雷声明"第 9 段），但是该网页与 AdSense 计划政策所要求的点击量相去甚远，不能被视为合同的组成部分。法院再次同意原告的观点，该截图不足以反驳肖兹女士关于履约的指控。

d. 马修·辛普森

*6 最后，被告认为辛普森先生对履行协议的指控是不充分的，因为他只声称他既没有作出也不知道网站上有任何无效活动，而不是说没有发生无效活动。（动议第 9 点，引用 TAC 第 91 段）原告认为，在许多段落都写明履约行为的情况下，只关注其中一个段落对 TAC 的解读过于狭隘。（异议答辩状第 5 点）法院同意原告的观点。（见 TAC 第 88 段，辛普森先生"遵守了谷歌 AdSense 中规定的所有条款……"）因此，法院认为每个原告都充分地证明了履约行为。[2]

e. 因不可抗力免责

被告还质疑原告的指控，即他们在网站上的任何无效活动都可以因不可抗力而予以免责，因为这不在他们的控制范围之内。（动议第 10 点；另见 TAC 第 55 段第 16、第 18 和第 92 款）法院复查了原告的意见，发现它虽然有创意，但并不合理。

根据加利福尼亚州的法律，除非合同明确规定某一事件为不可抗力，否则该事件必须是在订约时不可预见的，才能被认定为不可抗力。参见"沃森实验室公司诉罗讷 – 普伦茨罗雷公司案"，《美国联邦法院判例集》副刊第二辑第 178 卷第 1099—1111 页（加利福尼亚州中区联邦地区法院，2001 年）。[3] 在此适用该规则时，无效的活动不能因不可抗力而被免责。因为该条款虽然预见了风险，但也明确地将举证责任分配在了原告身上，且并未将无效活动认定为不可抗力。（附件 A、附件 C，第 5、第 14 段）因此，法院同意被告的动议，驳回这一免责理论。

2. 无故终止

被告还质疑原告关于谷歌公司"无故"终止他们的账户违反了合同的指控。（动议第 17—18 点）法院认可被告在每一份封停原告账户的通知中都明确了原因。（见 TAC 第 58、第 70、第 79、第 91 段）但是，由于原告提出的违反合同的主张是基于其他所谓的不当行为，因此法院不能以此为由驳回该主张。

3. 显失公平

被告接着辩称，原告未能充分指控违反合同的第三项内容——被告违约，因为谷歌公司在终止原告的账户并扣留其款项时遵循了前述条款规定。（动议第 10—17 点）谷歌公司主张，受质疑的条款不存在因为显失公平而无法执行的情况。（同上，见第 10—13 点）

"显失公平既具有程序性又具有实质性因素……"参见"阿门达李兹诉健康心理保健服务基金会案"，《加利福尼亚州判例汇编》第四辑第 24 卷第 83—114 页（2000 年）（内部引证略去）。"主流观点是，程序性和实质性的不公平必须同时存在，法院才能行使自由裁量权，依据显失公平原则拒绝执行合同或条款。"（同上，省略内部引用）"但它们不需要以相同的程度存在……合同条款在实质上越具有压迫性，则得出该条款不可执行的结论所需要的证明程序不公平的证据越少，反之亦然。"（同上，省略内部引用）被告辩称，本案中这两个要素都不存在，法院需依次考虑。

a. 程序性

*7 如果合同"由于不平等的谈判力量而施加压迫或突袭"，就存在程序不公平的情况。（同上）本案中，原告声称受质疑的条款具有压迫性，因为这些条款无法协商。（见 TAC 第 62 段、第 65 段、第 75 段、第 87 段、第 140 段，另见异议答辩状第 7 点）被告回应称，仅凭这一点是不够的，因为原告有其他选择来获得网站盈利，并且盈利并不是必要的。（动议第 11—12 点）

被告提供了两个支持这一结论的案例。首先，贝尔顿诉康卡斯特电缆控股有限责任公司案，《加利福尼亚州上诉判例汇编》第四辑第 151 卷，第 1224—1246 页（2007 年），该案认为有线电视服务的附合性合同不具有压迫性，因为客户可以从其他来源获得所需的服务，这是"非必要的娱乐活动"。同样，莫里斯诉红杉帝国银行案，《加利福尼亚州上诉判例汇编》第四辑第 128 卷第 1305—1320 页（2005 年），该案认为在"起诉方可以选择可合理获得的其他供应来源，以获得所需的商品和服务，从而不受不公平条款约束"的情况下，附合性合同并不具有压迫性。被告认为，同样的结论应用在本案中也是正确的，因为原告对于非必要的网站营利服务还有其他的选择。

原告援引本地区和第九巡回法院的几个案例进行回应，认为附合性合同的指控足以证明程序上的不公平，因为"加利福尼亚州法律认为附合性合同，或者至少是那些谈判力量较弱的一方没有机会谈判的条款，在某种程度上是有失程序公平的"。"桥基金资本公司诉快步车特许经营公司案"，《联邦判例补编》第三辑第 622 卷第 996—1004 页（第九巡回法庭，2010 年，引用阿门达利兹市案，《加利福尼亚州判例汇编》第四辑第 24 卷第 114 页）。例如，原告方援引了"牛顿诉美国债务服务公司案",《联邦判例补编》第二辑第 854 卷第 712—723 页（加利福尼亚州北区法院一审判决，2012 年），《美国联邦法院判例集》附录第 549 卷第 692 页（第九巡回法庭，2013 年）。这一案件涉及对附和性债务清偿合同的认定。"牛顿案"明确反驳了被告在本案中提出的论点，认为"其他选择"的论点"无视加利福尼亚州判例法的裁定，即'尽管存在市场替代方案，但使用附和性合同仍会造成最小限度的程序不公平'"。（同上，第 723 页）；引用"桑切斯诉瓦伦西亚控股有限责任公司案"，《加利福尼亚州上诉判例汇编》第四辑第 201 卷第 74—91 页（2011 年）] 被告认为，如果存在争议的货物无关紧要，那么就不存在不合理性，而法院认为这一说法与一系列加利福尼亚州案例判决结果相悖。（同上，第 723 页）

　　除了援引案例来推翻被告对加利福尼亚州法律的解读，原告还认为，根据《加利福尼亚州民法典》第 1670.5 节规定，驳回不合情理的指控还为时过早。（异议答辩状第 7 点）第 1670.5 节规定："若要主张合同或合同的某条款可能不合情理，应为各方当事人提供合理的机会就其商业背景、合同目的和合同效力提供证据，以协助法院作出裁决。"原告争辩说他们在本案中没有这样的机会。

　　被告回应称其符合第 1670.5 节的规定，因为被告提供的证据显示椰岛软件和辛普森先生在其网站上展示了来自其他网络的广告，因此他们有其他选择。（动议第 12 点，引用"Wong 声明"第 25 段、第 26 段、第 28-30 段，电子案例第 95-13 号、第 95-14 号、第 95-16 号至 18 号档案）原告认为，这一说法不足以推翻他们提出的"谷歌公司将 AdSense 吹嘘为其特有"和"拥有全球最大的网络广告客户群"的指控。（TAC 第 20 段）

　　*8 鉴于此案还处于早期阶段，法院认同了原告的观点。双方当事人没有"合理的机会就合同的商业背景、合同目的和合同效力提供证据"。（参见《加利福尼亚州民法典》第 1670.5 节）因此，法院认为原告已至少针对程序不合理进行了充分指控。参见"桥基金案"，《美国联邦法院判例集》第三辑第 622 卷第 1004 页。

　　b. 实质性

　　"即使证明程序性不公平的证据很少，但实质性不公平的有力证据将足够证明合同条款不公平。"参见"纳格拉帕诉梅尔科斯案"，《美国联邦法院判例集》第三辑第 469 卷第 1257—1281 页（第九巡回法院，2006 年）（引用"阿门达利兹市案"，《加利福尼亚州判例汇编》第四辑第 24 卷第 113 页）。"条款过于片面到令人震惊的程度，或施加苛刻的或压迫性的条款"，则构成实质不公平。参见"核桃生产商案"，《加利福尼亚州上诉判例汇编》第四辑

第 187 卷第 648 页。

被告辩称，那些受质疑的条款并非是令人震惊、具有压迫性或过于苛刻的，理由是谷歌公司需要提高 AdSense 的诚信度，这反过来又对广告发布商有所帮助，因为发布商能够从平台的成功中获利。（动议第 12—13 点）被告解释说，谷歌公司有权选择终止合同以防止欺诈性点击和不良内容并对广告客户作出补偿。而且，谷歌公司扣留收入的权利仅限于一段较短而有限的期间，该期间与无效活动对 AdSense 诚信度造成的损害成正比。（动议第 13 点）被告援引了哈恩案和帕迪案来支持其立场，认为这两个案件中的合同条款要严苛得多。此外，还援引了 Am 软件公司案和舒曼案。被告声称，上述两案所裁定的条款与本案中争点条款相似。

哈恩案中，原告质疑按摩服务会员协议中的一项条款，该条款规定会员资格取消后一切预先购买的按摩服务也会取消。参见"哈恩诉特许经营按摩店案"，案件编号 12–CV–153 DMS BGS，2014 WL 5100220（加利福尼亚州南区法院，2014 年 9 月 25 日）。法院认为该条款实质上是不公平的，其中部分原因是没有合法的经营性理由来支持该条款，即该条款实质经营者提供虚幻服务，每月从众多消费者那里提取少量金额（随时间推移，金额增加）的欺骗性方式"。（动议第 9 点、第 11 点，第 9 页、第 11 页）

被告宣称，本案中受质疑的条款与哈恩案中的条款并不相似，但未提供任何解释。（动议第 13 点）而同样援引哈恩案的原告辩称，正如哈恩案的没收条款"否定了消费者将获得预购服务的合理期待"一样（2014 WL 5100220，at 9），本案中受质疑的条款否定了发布商因其提供服务而获得报酬的合理期待。（异议答辩状第 9 点）

被告随后提出了帕迪案这一特殊案例。（动议第 13 点）帕迪案中，法院裁定，放弃房地产合同中当事方获得惩罚性赔偿金和陪审团审判权利的条款"过于片面，造成了实质性不公平"。参见"帕迪建筑公司诉高等法院"，《加利福尼亚州上诉判例汇编》第四辑第 100 卷第 1081—1092 页（2002 年）。法院解释说，放弃惩罚性赔偿金是"实际上，仅对帕迪公司有利"，并且记录中没有任何证据表明放弃陪审团审判"实际上会为买方节省大量时间或费用成本"或带来任何其他收益。（同上，第 1091—1092 页）被告辩称，这些条款构成隐秘且复杂的弃权，与本案中讨论的条款不同。（动议第 13 点）

*9 相反，被告辩称受质疑的条款与 Am 软件公司案和舒曼公司案中所涉及的条款相似。Am 软件公司案中，在软件销售员的雇佣合同中有一项条款终止了其在离职 30 天后从所获报酬中收取佣金的权利，法院认为该条款是可执行的。参见"Am 软件公司诉阿里案"，《加利福尼亚州上诉判例汇编》第

四辑第 46 卷第 1386 页（1996 年）。法院认为，该条款不属于实质性不公平，因为该合同"是两个具有相当议价能力且经验丰富的当事方之间公平谈判的结果，并充分体现了雇佣委托销售代表的通行惯例"。（同上，第 1394—1395 页）法院承认，公司需要在销售员离职后向提供该账户服务的个人支付报酬。（同上，第 1393 页）此外，法院指出相关条款"给双方都造成了特定的风险"。（同上，第 1393 页）

舒曼案同样认为，将佣金推迟到收到付款或合理确定时再予以支付的条款是可执行的。"舒曼公司诉伊康案"，《美国联邦法院判例集》附录第 232 卷第 659—663 页（第九巡回法院，2007 年）。在这个未公开的判决书中，第九巡回法院认定佣金是支付给原告的继任人而不是雇主，并指出，由于其并未根据合同完成任何销售，因此原告并未实际丧失任何佣金。（同上）

被告辩称，受质疑的条款也同样允许在较短的、有限的期限扣留款项。（动议第 13 点）原告辩称，本案中的条款与上述两个案例中的条款均不相同，因为 Am 软件公司案和舒曼公司案的合同均提供了其他补偿（Am 软件公司提供了基本工资，而舒曼公司提供了 6 个月内 30% 的佣金），并且扣留了款项以补偿原告的继任人，而不是雇主。（参见异议答辩状第 9 点）此外，原告指出，在 Am 软件公司案的赔偿责任中，双方当事人分担了风险，并认为舒曼案中，原告与公司的合作并不是任意终止的。（同上）

在审查各当事方提出的案例后，[4] 法院认为，其中大多数案件在简易判决中都不尽合理，原告充分地指控了条款的实质性不公平之处。假设指控属实，受质疑的条款就是片面的，因为这些条款允许谷歌公司罔顾所谓的违约严重程度，以及分辨有效和无效广告服务的义务，而扣留资金长达 2 个月之久，即使这些资金都是通过有效活动赚取的。（TAC 第 32 段）此外，原告对谷歌公司的指控与 Am 软件公司案和舒曼公司案不同，谷歌公司扣留款项的目的不是补偿其他发布商或广告商，而仅仅是为了自己的利益。（同上，第 46 段）虽然更详细的记录可能表明谷歌公司有理由扣留全部未支付的收入，但原告提出了充分的指控，可以在这个问题的辩诉阶段中暂时获胜。

4. 违约赔偿金

被告接下来反驳了原告指控的另一个观点，即原告认为条款包含不可执行的违约赔偿金条款。（动议第 14—15 点、第 25 点）。当事方一致认为这一条款与终止条款有关，原告认为支付条款关系范围十分广泛，根据这一条款，一旦协议因所谓的违约而终止，谷歌公司即可扣留发布商 100% 的广告收益。参见异议答辩状第 9 点，引用 TAC 第 36 段在原告已经充分指控这些条款因不公平而不可行后，法院仍然考虑这一论点，因为这决定了原告根据《美国法典》第 1671 节第 2 分节提出的主张是否成立。

　　*10 法院在最近一次准予原告复议动议的复议令中,考虑了原告主张的违约赔偿金论点,即电子案例第 91 号档案"复议令"。法院解释说,根据加利福尼亚州法律,违约赔偿金的定义为:"因违约而支付由协议确定的的赔偿金额……"参见"肖多斯诉 Publ'g 公司案",《美国联邦法院判例集》第三辑第 292 卷第 992—1002 页(第九巡回法院,2002 年)。[引用"凯莉诉麦当劳案",《加利福尼亚州上诉判例汇编》第 98 卷第 121—125 页(1929 年)]"因此,要构成违约赔偿金,合同条款必须规定以下要件:(1)由违约引起,以及(2)规定了一个确定的金额。"参见"如威诉 Cellco P'ship 案",《联邦判例补编》第二辑第 613 卷第 1191—1196 页(加利福尼亚州北区法院,2009 年)。

　　复议令中,法院驳回了被告依据违约赔偿金条款从 FRC 与辛普森先生处扣取收益的主张,因为原告指控谷歌公司终止他们的账户是基于无效活动,而不是因为原告自身行为违约。(复议令第 5 点)法院批准了原告的修正请求,原告改称无效活动是一种违约形式(见 TAC 第 38 段),且因此由无效活动引发的所有损害赔偿金均"由违约产生",已经弥补了这一缺陷。参见"如威案",《联邦判例补编》第二辑第 613 卷第 1196 页。被告并未对原告关于无效活动构成违约的指控提出异议。

　　当事方现在的争议焦点是第二个要求——条款需确定一个固定的金额。法院之前认为原告的指控足够在这个问题的驳回起诉动议中成立。(复议令第 6—8 点)法院解释称,"未付金额"可以指终止账户的发布商未被支付但实际赚取的总余额数、即原告有权获得的一个固定的、可确定的金额。被告对这一裁决提出异议。

　　被告首先辩称,谷歌公司只是行使了其对违反条款的工作拒绝付款的权利,而不是要求原告支付费用或者没收原告押金,这在违约赔偿条款中很常见。(复议令第 14—15 页)原告回应称,谷歌公司将终止账户的发布商产生的金钱称为"收入",即表示谷歌公司扣留了原告已经赚取的金钱。(异议答辩状第 11—12 点;另见 TAC 第 32 段、第 40—44 段、第 83 段、第 96 段)原告还指控,谷歌公司记录并报告了每一个发布商在其账户中投放广告服务的收入。(异议答辩状第 44 段、第 53 段、第 57 段)与之前一样,法院认为原告的论证更具有说服力。(复议令第 7 点,因为"终止条款"还规定低于适用阈值的任何收益余额将保持未付状态,未付金额可以指收益余额)

　　被告接着辩称,扣留的金额不足以使被质疑的条款构成违约赔偿条款。被告的观点在很大程度上基于贝约尔案,该案中贝约尔认为热布卡公司的滞纳金构成违约赔偿金,因为用户协议中延迟返还的费用金额具有高度的确定性。参见"贝约尔诉热布卡公司案",《联邦判例补编》第三辑第78卷第1252—1258页(加利福尼亚州北区法院,2015年)。被告强调了该判决中的两个部分:"如果费用不是一个单一、固定的数字,且该费用无法在违约时从合同中轻易确定,则法院会认定该费用不属于违约金条款",以及"为了充分固定和确定是否符合违约金的条件,该条款必须设定确切的金额(即一个单一的数字),或者提供一个确定的或易于确定的公式"。[动议第15点;引用"贝约尔案,《联邦判例补编》第三辑第78卷第1256页(内部引用省略)(动议中强调)]被告辩称,这些条款无法满足其中任何一项要求,因为这些条款既未标识金额,也未标识公式。而且,被告还辩称,这些条款明确规定了其可自行决定违约金额,因此得出的金额与发布商之前收入的绝对数量和百分比方面差异很大。(动议第15点)

*11 原告回应说,这些条款明确提出了一个公式:1.00 × 合同终止时的未付收益。(异议答辩状第13点)此外,如上所述,原告声称谷歌公司会向发布商报告每个发布商的收入。(TAC第44段、第53段、第57段)

如前所述,法院认为金额"易于确定"。虽然被告可能纠正说条款没有详细规定公式或设定金额,但法院认为原告关于谷歌公司总是扣留全部金额的指控事实上足以证明双方"在违约时的责任具有一定程度的确定性"。参见"如威案",《联邦判例补编》第二辑第613卷第1198页(由于在实际操作中向每个客户收取的金额是相同的,所以金额是完全能够确定的)。

被告接着辩称,即使受质疑的条款构成违约赔偿金条款,也是合理的,因此可以强制执行,因为根据《加利福尼亚州民法典》第1671节第2分节强制实施受质疑的条款,该条款可以推定具有可执行性,"除非寻求使条款无效的一方当事人能够证明该条款在订立合同时存在不合理的情况"。该法规"将证明不合理的责任分配给对方当事人,只要求违约赔偿金与可合理预期的损害范围有合理的关系"。参见"Weber, Lipshie公司诉克里斯蒂安案",《加利福尼亚州上诉判例汇编》第四辑第52卷第645—656页(1997年)。

被告辩称,原告未能尽到这一证明责任,因为谷歌公司扣留的金额在两个方面涉及对AdSense诚信度的预期损害。(动议第16点)首先,这一数额是在签约时对损害的合理估计;其次,之所以对流量较大的网站处以更多罚款,是由于流量较大的网站给AdSense带来的损害要比流量较少的网站更大。(同上)

原告回应道,尽管谷歌公司声称有能力区分有效活动和无效活动,但谷歌公司仍然在罔顾违约程度的情况下扣留了所有已赚但未付的收益,这充分证明了违约赔偿金和损害范围之间缺乏合理关系。(异议答辩状第14—15点;

另见 TAC 第 6 段、第 32 段、第 132 段）此外，原告还声称，谷歌公司不仅不退款给广告商，而且经常在没有预警的情况下终止广告商账户，从而切断了任何可能造成损害的联系。（异议答辩状第 14 点；引用 TAC 第 48 段）最后，原告辩称，违约赔偿金条款的合理性涉及的事实太多，因而现阶段无法确定下来。（同上）

法院同意原告的观点。"违约赔偿金条款的有效性需要基于事实调查，不适合在驳回起诉的动议中确定下来。"参见"贝约尔诉热布卡公司案"，《联邦判例补编》第三辑第 78 卷第 1252—1255 页（加利福尼亚州北区法院，2015 年）。被告辩称贝约尔案的情况与本案不同，因为事实问题表明违约赔偿金金额与热布卡公司实际遭受的损失不匹配。（见答辩状第 9 条第 6 款）但法院认为本案与其相同。正如被告所承认的那样，发布商的无效活动或其他违约行为所造成的损害难以衡量。（动议第 16 点）而原告通过指控谷歌公司没有将扣留款项退还给广告商，从而提出了与损害有关的事实问题。因此，法院驳回了被告因原告违约和第 1671 节第 2 分节下的指控而提出的驳回原告起诉的动议。

5. 弃权

*12 被告分别对肖兹女士和辛普森先生的违约指控提出质疑，理由是他们放弃了所有与付款有关的指控，包括违约指控，因为他们没有及时根据条款对扣留他们的付款提出申诉。（动议第 18—19 点）

支付条款规定："如果您对与服务相关的任何付款或扣款有异议，您必须在该种付款发生后 30 天内，以书面形式通知谷歌公司。如果您没有这样做，则视为您放弃与争议付款有关的任何主张"。（见 TOS 第 5 段）原告并没有辩称肖兹女士和辛普森先生及时对他们的付款提出了质疑（见 TAC 第 82 段、第 95 段），但他们认为基于一些原因，未能及时提出质疑不应被视为放弃。法院从前四个论点入手，发现这些论点完全没有说服力。

首先，原告辩称，谷歌公司没有将申诉权利告知肖兹女士和辛普森先生。原告认为，由于有关申诉的描述出现在支付条款而非终止条款中，因此支付条款适用于现行的发布商，而不适用于已终止合同的发布商。（异议答辩状第 15 点）法院认为这一论点不成立。首先，正如被告所指出的那样，支付条款开篇就规定，付款是在"遵守第 5 条［支付条款］和第 10 条［终止条款］的情况下进行的"。[5]（答辩状第 9 点；引用 TOS 第 5 段）其次，法院同意被告的观点，即条款给予了肖兹女士和辛普森先生足够的提示，告诉他们如何对付款提出申诉，并且明确了发布商应"以书面形式通知谷歌公司"。（TOS 第 5 段）再次，法院同意被告的观点，即原告关于谷歌公司在支持页面告诉发布商不能对扣留款项提出申诉的指控与本案无关，因为原告并未声称肖兹女士或辛普森先生阅读或参考过这些页面。（见答辩状第 10 点；另见异议答辩状第 15—16 点；TAC 第 83 段、第 96 段）最后，法院也认同被告的观点，即使该条件是一个必须"严格解释为不利于其利益的一方"的没收条款（异议答辩状第 16 点，引用《加利福尼亚州民法典》第 1442 节），结果也是一样的：发布商在 30 天内没有对付款或扣款提出申诉，就视为放弃了与付款有关的权利主张。（见答辩状第 10 点第 7 款）

其次，原告认为，该要求是一种私人时效法规，无法执行，因为 30 天的时间不足以让前发布商咨询律师，甚至无法确定其账户终止的确切原因。（异议答辩状第 17—18 点）原告依据的是埃利斯案和阿萨德案的雇佣案例，还有一个来自宾夕法尼亚州东区法院的案例，这一案例更为符合，因为该案例涉及的是谷歌公司旗下的"关键字广告"项目合同。

埃利斯诉美国安全协会案和阿萨德诉美国国家保险公司案中的原告在签署了禁止他们在一定时间后提出雇佣诉讼的雇佣协议之后，试图起诉其前雇主。在埃利斯案中，时间期限为任何事件发生后超过 6 个月。《加利福尼亚州上诉判例汇编》第四辑第 224 卷第 1213—1217 页（2010 年）。而阿萨德案中的雇佣协议规定，如果雇员未能在解雇后 30 天内及时请求仲裁，则不得提出仲裁。参见"阿萨德案"，案件编号 C 10–03712，2010 WL 5416841，at 7（加利福尼亚州北区法院，2010 年 12 月 23 日）。两个案件中的原告都在法定时间内提起了诉讼，但超过了合同条款规定的时间。（同上，第 7 点："埃利斯案"，《加利福尼亚州上诉判例汇编》第四辑第 224 卷第 1222 页）两个案件中的法院都认为，这些条款形同私人时效法规。（同上，第 1222—1223 页；"阿萨德案"，2010 WL 5416841，at 7）埃利斯案中的法院解释说，私人时效期间如果合理，则具有可强制执行性，"如果原告有足够的机会调查和提起诉讼，时间并未短到导致原告实际上丧失诉权，且在其能够确定损失或损害之前未被禁止提起诉讼"，则该条款是合理的。参见"埃利斯案"，《加利福尼亚州上诉判例汇编》第四辑第 224 卷第 1223 页。

*13 根据该项标准，埃利斯案中法院认为 6 个月不足以提出劳动争议主张，并指出："大多数报道的支持缩短期限的裁决都涉及简单的商业合同，以及该等合同明确规定的违约行为或产生的权利。"（参见"埃利斯案"；引用"莫雷诺案"，《加利福尼亚州上诉判例汇编》第四辑第 106 卷第 1430 页；《加利福尼亚判例汇编》第二辑第 131 卷第 684 页）阿萨德案中法院认为 30 天的期限不合理，"大大缩短了诉讼时效"。"阿萨德案"，2010 WL 5416841，at 7–8。

原告还提供了费尔德曼案，它更适用于本案，该案涉及谷歌公司旗下"关键字广告"条款中的以下规定："您放弃与收费有关的所有权利主张，除非在收费后 60 天内提出……"参见"费尔德曼诉谷歌公司案"，《联邦判例补编》第二辑第 513 卷第 229—243 页（宾夕法尼亚州东区法院，2007 年）。法院认为尽管该条款构成合同时效限制期，但由于具备合理性从而认定该条款具有可执行性。（同上，第 243 页）"合同时效期是有效的，并且可以短于法规规定的时效期限，只要提出权利主张的期限是合理的即可。"［《联邦判例补编》第二辑第 513 卷第 243 页，引用"韩诉美孚石油公司案"，《美国联邦法院判例集》第三辑第 73 卷第 872—877 页（第九巡回法院，1995 年）］费尔德曼案中，法院之所以执行这一规定，是因为 60 天为原告律师提供了"足够的时间来进行识别、调查和报告账单错误"。（同上，第 243 页）

被告回应称，这些案件不适用于本案，因为每个案件都要求当事方在较短的时间内提起诉讼，但本案通知仅是提起诉讼的先决条件。为了支持其立场，被告援引了布罗斯南案，该案中认为"如果不能根据合同调解纠纷，而该合同将调解作为提起诉讼的先决条件，那么就需要驳回诉讼"。参见"布罗斯南诉干洗站公司案"，案件编号 C-08-02028 EDL，2008 WL 2388392, at 1（加利福尼亚州北区法院，2008 年 6 月 6 日）。但是，合同没有对何时开始进行调解设置时间限制，因此并不妨碍日后提起诉讼。

被告还指出，一项裁决认定，购买协议禁止提起诉讼的一方在未先行寻求争议调解的情况下追偿律师费，"也就是说，原告若未能先行寻求调解，则不能获得律师费支持"。参见"兰格诉希林案"，《加利福尼亚州上诉判例汇编》第四辑第 163 卷第 1412—1414 页。最后，被告还援引了一个案例，该案例认为，该案例裁决，合同中一项条款规定，若原告未在合同规定时间后强制进行仲裁，则仲裁得以执行。参见"普拉特太平洋公司诉安德森案"，《加利福尼亚州判例汇编》第四辑第 6 卷第 307—313 页（1993 年）。

审查了这些案件之后，法院认为付款争议期限构成私人时效法规。与原告援引的案例一样，不遵守这些条款将妨碍其全部的诉讼请求，而不仅仅是禁止替代性的争议解决或律师费追偿。因此，正如这些案件一样，法院接下来将考虑 30 天的期限是否合理。参见"韩案"，《美国联邦法院判例集》第三辑第 73 卷第 877 页（"加利福尼亚州允许缔约各方就诉讼时效期限达成协议，只要所允许的时间合理，诉讼时效期限可以短于法令规定的期限"）。

尽管原告在异议答辩状中辩称，30 天不足以提出与付款相关的申诉，但他们并没有提出相同的主张。相反，他们辩称椰岛软件和 FRC 在这段时间内都成功地就其付款提出了申诉（TAC 第 59 段、第 71 段），并解释说，基于法院驳回的四个理由，肖兹女士和辛普森先生未能提出同样的申诉（同上，第 82 段、第 95 段）。因此，法院批准了被告要求驳回肖兹女士和辛普森先生所有与付款有关的诉求的驳回起诉动议。

*14 此外，法院认为修正条款是徒劳的，因为 30 天是将申诉通知给谷歌公司的合理时间。法院认为此案与布罗斯南案的比较十分有意义。布罗斯南案中，法院裁定原告有 60 天的时间足够提出与收费有关的任何"诉求"。而本案中，发布商的时间更少（30 天），但是他们只需要对付款或预扣款项提出"申诉"，而无须提出全部诉求。此外，FRC 和椰岛软件承认的合规情况也证明了该期限是足够的。法院认为 30 天足以完成这项任务，特别是因为发布商会定期从谷歌公司收到付款和收益估算值，并且如上所述，条款确定了如何协商纠纷。因此，法院不予批准肖兹女士和辛普森先生修改其与付款有关的诉求。

B. 诚实信用和公平交易的默示契约

被告接下来对原告提出的违反契约主张提出质疑。（动议第 20—21 点）"根据加利福尼亚州法律，对违反诚实信用和公平交易契约的主张要求双方之间存在合同关系，原告履行了合同义务或免除了不履行责任，被告违反了双方在订立合同时的期望，剥夺了原告应得的合同利益，并且原告的损失是由被告的行为造成的。"参见"阿维拉诉全国住房贷款公司案"，案件编号 10-CV-05485-LHK，2010 WL 5071714，at 5（加利福尼亚州北区法院，2010 年 12 月 7 日）。

被告对违反契约主张的前两个异议与法院在上文中考虑并驳回的观点相同：原告未能就履行或免除义务提出抗辩，且被告不承担根据明确合同规定行事的责任。如上所述，法院驳回了这些论点。

被告接着辩称，原告违反契约的主张与违反合同的主张重复，应予以驳回。（动议第 20 点）被告援引"Careau 公司诉 Sec. Pac. Bus. Credit 公司案"，《加利福尼亚州上诉判例汇编》第三辑第 222 卷第 1371 页（1990 年），经拒绝修改（2001 年 10 月 31 日），法院以主张重复为由驳回了对被告提出的违约主张，即被告在原告据称完成了支付贷款的先决条件后拒绝提供 1 300 万美元的贷款。法院解释说："如果这些主张没有超出合同约定的违约范围，基于相同被指控的行为，仅仅是为了寻求相同的损害赔偿或其他已经在相关合同案由中主张的救济，则这些主张可以被视为是多余的。"（同上，第 1395 页）为了提出另一项违约的主张，原告必须提出指控，"证明（被告）没有履行或拒绝履行合同义务，不是由于无心的错误、错误的判断或疏忽，而是基于故意，这种行为不公平地违背了合同约定的共同目的，并使另一方的合理期望落空"。（同上，第 1395 页）将这一规则应用于本案中的事实，法院维持了初审法院对违反契约主张的简易判决，因为其"只不过是对合同损害赔偿提出了重复的主张"。（同上，第 1401 页）

被告还提出"Bionghi 诉加利福尼亚州南部地区供水及污水处理协会案"，《加利福尼亚州上诉判例汇编》第四辑第 70 卷 1358 页（1999 年），该案也作出了相同的判决。Bionghi 案中，一家临时就业中介机构起诉被告违反合同和默示契约，声称被告因办公室斗争和种族歧视与该机构解约。（同上，第 1361—1363 页）上诉法院以 Careau 案为依据，支持了初审法院对违反契约主张作出的简易判决，因为该主张"与违约诉求一样，二者属于依据相同的法令，要求相同的损害赔偿"。（同上，第 1370 页）

*15 被告辩称，法院应当作出相同的判决，因为原告的违反合同和默示契约主张都基于相同的指控，即原告签订并履行了合同，但是谷歌公司拒绝支付。（动议第 20 点）原告回应，他们还指控了谷歌公司的不诚信行为。原告声称尽管协议约定了谷歌公司"可以"扣留未支付的收益，但是谷歌公司在终止肖兹女士和椰岛软件账户的同时，未对其他发布同类广告的发布商作出处置，并扣留了前者所有的未支付收益，该等行为显示了谷歌公司的不诚信。（见 TAC 第 70 段、第 79 段、第 137 段）

原告提出了"塞拉多公司诉华特迪士尼公司案"，《联邦判例补编》第二辑第 347 卷第 846 页（加利福尼亚州中部法院，2004 年），此案以重复为由驳回了原告的违反契约主张。"塞拉多案"中，一档电视节目的创作者对该节目制作和发行合作伙伴的母公司提出了违反合同和默示契约的主张，该主张声称其合作伙伴未寻求竞争性交易，并且在惯例要求应该重新协商更高的许可费时未进行重新协商。（同上，第 850—851 页）法院解释说，因为违反合同和契约的主张"总是基于相同的事实（因为某些特定的情况会引发诉讼）"，并且"总是寻求相同的救济（因为相同的救济对两种诉讼都适用）……Careau 和其子公司需要在相同事实的基础上区分两种主张。"审查之前的指控后，法院裁决原告提出了两项主张，即"声称被告的行为违反了合同。即使被告没有违反合同，这些不诚信的行为也会使原告的实际合同利益受损"。（同上，第 853 页）

原告认为本案也是如此，原告主张谷歌公司任意终止发布商账户并扣留未支付收益的行为违反了条款，即使没有违反条款，谷歌公司的这些不诚信行为，也使原告提供广告所应得的对价受损。（见 TAC 第 154 段）

为了支持谷歌公司扣留未支付收益系违反契约这一主张，原告提供了"Storek & Storek 公司诉花旗房地产公司案"（《加利福尼亚州上诉判例汇编》

第四辑第 100 卷第 44 页，2002 年）。该案审议了银行在确定原告没有完成先决条件——让银行相信贷款金额足以覆盖项目的成本——之后拒绝发放贷款这一不诚信行为是否违反了合同。法院解释说，一方当事人的意愿为前提条件时，他必须要么基于诚信原则作出纯粹出于善意的主观决定，要么作出客观理性的决定。这个选择取决于双方当事人在合同中表达的意向或者默认的合理性标准。（同上，第 59 页）法院认为，由于贷款合同用于商业交易，而且银行作出的决定也是出于对金融问题的考虑，与审美或个人品位无关，所以银行必须作出客观合理的决定。（同上，第 60 页、第 64 页）

原告声称，本案中谷歌公司对原告网站和广告服务的满意度是付款的先决条件，并且他们提出证据表明谷歌公司既没有以客观合理的方式，也没有善意地行使自由裁量权。（异议答辩状第 20—21 点）法院首先审查条款是否包括先决条件，并裁定原告的说法是正确的。根据支付条款，发布商"将收到的款项取决于有效活动的数量，即广告在网络媒体资源上得以展示的数量，一切解释权归谷歌公司"。[TOS 第 5 段；另见 T&C 第 11 段（添加强调）]因此，谷歌公司对于有效活动的确定是其向发布商付款的前提条件。

*16 根据"Storek 案"，只有一项测试适用于全部的特定合同。在这一点上，法院认为 TOS 和 T&C 的明确描述存在重大差别。TOS 规定："若存在无效行为，则谷歌公司可能会扣留由此产生的金额，一切解释权归谷歌公司。"而 T&C 表明："谷歌公司保留因您的'无效行为或违约行为'而扣留付款的权利，并有待谷歌的合理调查。"[TOS 第 5 段；T&C 第 11 段（添加强调）]因此，法院认为，TOS 要求谷歌公司出于诚信原则基于善意作出主观判断（见 TOS 第 5 段），而 T&C 要求谷歌公司作出客观合理的决定，但不附带任何善意要求（见 T&C 第 11 段）。因此，原告根据 T&C 提出的扣留付款主张被其违约主张所覆盖，[6] 而原告关于谷歌公司在没有依照诚信原则行使自由裁量权的情况下根据 TOS 扣留付款的主张可以继续进行。

关于原告的指控，即被告在终止肖兹女士和椰岛软件的账户时没有遵循诚信原则而允许类似的网站继续活跃，被告辩称，这些网站并不相似，即使它们相似，谷歌公司未能终止其他违规账户并不足以构成不诚信行为。法院认为，选择性执行的指控不足以作为不诚信的抗辩理由。

因此，关于被告要求驳回原告对被告违反诚实守信和公平交易的默示契约主张的动议，若该主张是根据 T&C 提出的终止账号和扣留付款的指控，则法院对被告的动议予以批准；若该主张是根据 TOS 提出的扣留付款的指控，则法院对被告的动议予以驳回。

C. 不当得利

在第一份驳回令中，法院驳回了原告有关不当得利的主张，因为该指控与"克莱因诉谢弗龙案"的情况不一致。该案中，法院认为如果原告"不确定双方是否达成了可执行的协议"，可以协议本身存在与否提出权利主张。参见"克莱因诉美国谢弗龙公司案"，《加利福尼亚州上诉判例汇编》第四辑第202 卷第 1342—1388 页。"然而，如果双方就某一标的物达成了可执行协议，那么原告不能以准合同主张权利进行起诉或追偿。"（同上，第 1388 页）法院批准原告修改请求，以指控本案合同存在不确定性。

原告声称："出于诉讼目的，原告否认争议条款具有可执行性，并且根据需要，为了能够收回原告因提供 AdSense 项目广告而应得的收益，否认与谷歌公司签订的整个 AdSense 合同的可执行性。"（TAC 第 159 段）被告辩称，该结论性指控未能解决其内在缺陷，因为双方并未对条款的存在以及整体上的可执行性提出异议。（动议第 21—22 点）

原告回应称，其认为受质疑的条款是不可执行的，这一点与"克莱因案"情况相同。（异议答辩状第 21—22 点）原告根据"贝尔有限责任公司诉船用玻璃钢公司案"（案件编号 3 : 14-CV-02960-BTM，2015 WL 4255061），加利福尼亚州南区法院，2015 年 7 月 14 日），认为只对合同的部分条款提出异议即可。然而，在"贝尔案"中，被告承认起诉状中"质疑被告工作、劳动及服务所依据的修正案的有效性"。（同上，第 5 页）换句话说，"贝尔案"中合同的核心存在争议。相比之下，本案中原告声称"除了某些条款被认为无效和不可执行，其余的条款均为有效"。（TAC 第 130 段）

因此，法院同意被告的观点。因为双方都同意本案中的合同具有可执行性，原告不得主张不当得利。由此，法院同意被告关于驳回原告不当得利主张的动议。

D. UCL 诉讼

*17 被告接下来对 UCL 诉讼提出质疑，认为原告没有诉权（起诉资格）提起该主张，且原告没有说明被告参与了"任何非法、不公或欺诈的商业行为"。（动议第 22—25 点；另见《加州商业职业守则》第 17200 节）

1. 起诉资格

被告声称，根据《加州商业职业守则》第 17200 节规定，原告没有起诉资格，因为其是企业，而不是法律规定要保护的消费者或竞争者。（动议第 22—23 点）被告援引了"凌力尔特公司案"，该公司提出驳回由"已经或将要与被告签订合同的成熟企业客户"提出的 UCL 诉讼，因为"如果 UCL 诉讼是基于既不涉及一般公众也不涉及作为合同一方的个人消费者的合同，则作为公司的原告不应依赖 UCL"。参见"凌力尔特公司诉应用材料公司案"，《加利福尼亚州上诉判例汇编》第四辑第 152 卷第 115—135 页（2007 年）。另见"美元树商店股份有限公司诉富山公司案"，《联邦判例补编》第二辑第 875 卷第 1058—1083 页（加利福尼亚州北区法院，2012 年）（因为"诉讼是基于合同违约，不涉及一般公众或个人消费者"，所以驳回公司的 UCL 主张）。

被告误解了"凌力尔特公司案"，认为企业不是提起 UCL 诉讼的适格主体。相反，"凌力尔特公司案"指出，如果合同不涉及"一般公众或个人消费者……"，则企业不能提起该主张。另见 Webkinz 反托拉斯诉讼案，《联邦判例补编》第二辑第 695 卷第 987—999 页（加利福尼亚州北区法院，2010 年）（该案中，"UCL 对不同规模的公司赋予起诉资格"，只要这些企业"声明与保护公共利益有关"或"与个人消费者利益有关"）。因此，法院要考虑原告是否声明了与公众或个人消费者利益的联系。

原告辩称，由于 AdSense 的规模以及消费者与原告网页的互动，他们的主张牵涉公众和个人消费者。原告认为，本案类似"埃韦特案"，该案中允许公司和个人卖家就易趣网在整个合同期内禁止他们将产品上架的行为提起 UCL 诉讼。参见"埃韦特诉易趣网案"，案件编号 C-07-02198 RMW，2010 WL 4269259，at 1, 8-9（加利福尼亚州北区法院，2010 年 10 月 25 日）。在参考"凌力尔特公司案"后，法院认为这群卖家可以提起 UCL 诉讼，因为该案"只涉及格式合同……并涉及个人消费者"。（同上，第 9 页）

原告认为本案情况相同：条款也是格式合同，点击 AdSense 广告的消费者也被牵涉其中。（动议第 23 点）被告认为，点击广告的用户与购买产品的用户不同。法院同意原告的观点。原告声称，发布商将他们的内容"用作吸引合法广告消费者访问其网站的驱动力"。（TAC 第 32 段）因此，同"埃韦特案"一样，本案牵涉个人消费者的利益，因为如果迎合消费者利益的发布商被封停账户，则消费者利益可能会受到损害。因此，法院认为原告有充分的起诉资格提起 UCL 诉讼。

2. 欺诈性原则

被告接着辩称，原告没有指控谷歌公司作出欺诈行为，原告没有对任何声称的被告不作为建立信赖，也没有达到欺诈的诉求标准。（动议第 23—24 条；另见《联邦民事诉讼规则》第 9 节第 2 分节，原告必须"特别说明构成欺诈的具体情况")原告回应称，谷歌公司关于在合同终止时扣留发布商所有未付收益的规定仅声明谷歌公司"可能"扣留未付金额，这构成重大虚假陈述。（异议答辩状第 24 点；引用 TAC 第 171 段）此外，原告声称，如果他们知道谷歌公司在合同终止时会扣留他们所有的未付收益，他们就不会花费时间、精力和金钱来提供 AdSense 广告，从而证明了信赖已经得以建立。（异议答辩状第 24 点；引用 TAC 第 171 段）

*18 "一般来说，要提起 UCL 诉讼，隐藏的事实必须是实质性的，即其可能会欺骗理性的消费者。"参见"克莱门斯诉戴姆勒克莱斯勒公司案"，《美国联邦法院判例集》第三辑第 534 卷第 1017 页、第 1025—1026 页（第九巡回法院，2008 年）（引用"阿隆诉 U-Haul 加利福尼亚公司案"，《加利福尼亚州上诉判例汇编》第四辑第 143 卷第 796—806 页，2006 年）。"原告必须出示证据，证明'给相当数量的尽正常注意义务的、合理谨慎的购买者造成混淆的可能性'"。[同上，引用"布洛克基诉摩尔案"，《加利福尼亚州上诉判例汇编》第四辑第 107 卷第 86—99 页（2003 年）]此外，"在集体代表人以虚假陈述主张作为其 UCL 诉讼依据所提起的诉讼中，其必须证明其对所指控的欺骗性或误导性陈述的实际依赖性"。参见"烟草 II 案"，《加利福尼亚州判例汇编》第四辑第 46 卷第 298—306 页（2009 年）。"通过证明被告的虚假陈述或拒绝披露是导致原告受损害事实的直接原因可以证明信赖得以建立。原告可以通过证明如果被告不存在虚假陈述，原告在所有合理的可能性下均不会从事产生损害后果的行为，来证明被告的虚假陈述是其行为的直接原因。"[同上，第 326 页（内部引用省略]

法院同意被告的观点，即原告未能充分主张其存在信赖。相反，椰岛软件和 FRC 声称，在最后一笔付款扣留之前，他们从 AdSense 那里收到付款的时间已经分别为 7 年以上和接近 2 年了。此外，椰岛软件称，其所有者的"大部分家庭收入"来自 AdSense。（TAC 第 66 段）

基于这些指控，法院认为，如果原告知道谷歌公司在合同终止时将扣留至多两个付款期的收益，他们就不会投资于他们作为发布商的工作这一说法完全不可信。[7]此外，原告不符合《联邦民事诉讼规则》第 9 节第 2 分节规定，因为他们未能就谷歌公司扣留付款的意图以及在合同终止时扣留每位发布商的全部未付收益提出抗辩。因此，法院批准被告要求驳回原告提起 UCL 欺诈性诉讼的动议，且不允许修改。

3. 非法原则

被告辩称，原告未能指控被告存在任何非法活动，因为这些条款并非不合情理,且不包含违约赔偿金条款。(动议第 24—25 点)如上所述,法院认为原告充分主张了非法行为。因此,法院驳回被告要求驳回原告 UCL 非法诉讼的动议。

4. 不公平原则

被告依然无法质疑原告根据不公平原则提出的 UCL 诉讼。被告辩称,原告并没有解释谷歌公司被指控的行为如何违反了"受具体宪法、法规或监管规定约束"的法律公共政策。[动议第 25 点;引用"德拉姆诉圣费尔南多山谷律师协会案",《加利福尼亚州上诉判例汇编》第四辑第 182 卷第 247—257 页(2010 年)][8]。如上所述,法院认为原告根据《加利福尼亚州民法典》第 1671 节第 2 分节充分提出了主张。因此,法院驳回了被告要求驳回原告 UCL 不公平诉讼的动议。

E. 确认性救济——第六和第七条诉因

最后,被告寻求驳回原告的确认性救济请求,原告的该等请求主张宣布某些条款为不合理和不适当的违约赔偿金条款。(动议第 25 点)被告辩称,确认性救济请求不成立是因为基础主张不成立。如上所述,法院不同意被告关于原告基础主张的观点。因此,法院驳回被告关于驳回原告确认性救济请求的动议。

四、判决

*19 基于上述原因,兹裁决针对被告驳回起诉的动议部分批准、部分驳回,动议下列部分得到批准,无须修改:

1. 原告的不可抗力免责请求;

2. 肖兹女士和辛普森先生提出的任何与付款相关的诉讼请求;

3. 原告关于被告违反诚实信用和公平交易的默示之约的诉讼请求,只要该请求是根据 T&C 终止合同或扣留付款提出的指控;

4. 原告的不当得利主张;

5. 原告 UCL 欺诈性诉讼请求。

动议下列部分被驳回:

1. 原告依据《加利福尼亚州民法典》第 1671 节第 2 分节提出的诉讼请求;

2. 原告的合同违约主张,除了上述关于肖兹女士和辛普森先生提出的与付款相关的主张以及原告的不可抗力主张;

3. 原告关于被告违反诚实信用和公平交易的默示之约的诉讼请求,只要该请求是根据 TOS 扣留付款提出的指控;

4.原告不合法和不公平的 UCL 诉讼请求；

5.原告的确认性救济请求。

作出如上判决。

所有引文

在《联邦判例补编》第三辑，2016 年 WL 2902332 中未见报道。

脚注

1.原告在第三版修正起诉状中试图首次代表来自世界各地的（本案受害者）群体。由于被告没有质疑这一群体的定义，因此法院没有讨论该问题，但指出修正超出了第一份驳回令所授权的许可范围。

2.此外，法院在确认原告进行了充分指控后，没有涉及原告的两个可替代性论点：即使谷歌公司能够证明原告违约，但由于该条款是可以分割的合同条款，因此只能扣留无效活动的付款（异议答辩状第 6 点）；即便法院认为关于履行的指控不充分，原告也充分地提出了能够证明被告违反合同的基本诉因（同上，第 2 点）。

3.原告认为，"沃森案"误述了加利福尼亚州法律，还提供了"美国东部航空公司案"中的正确陈述。然而，美国东部航空公司关于法律的声明与沃森所提出的是一样的：如果合同明确将可预见的事件认定为不可抗力，则可以将其视为不可抗力。参见"美国东部航空公司诉麦克唐奈道格拉斯公司案"，《美国联邦法院判例集》第二辑第 532 卷第 957—991 页（第五巡回法院，1976 年）。

4.原告依据了"迪恩威特公司诉最高法院案"，《加利福尼亚州上诉判例汇编》第三辑第 211 卷第 758 页（1989 年）（异议答辩状第 9 点），但该案中的被告承认"可能存在某种程度的实质性不公平"，而当事人仅对程序性不公平提出异议。

5.原告还辩称终止未能提供充分的通知，因为这些通知虽然告知了终止的发布商有权对终止提出申诉，但是没有表明发布商可以对被扣留的收益提出申诉。（异议答辩状第 16 点；另见"格雷声明"附件 12，电子案例第 94-13 号档案）被告回应称，谷歌公司没有任何义务提醒发布商注意申诉的要求，因为该要求在本条款中有明确规定。法院已经考虑过这个论点，并同意被告的观点。

6.正如"Storek 案"中法院的解释，根据合同对某一方当事人合理性的质疑是对合同明示条款不履行的主张，而不是对违反默示条款的主张。参见

"Storek 案",《加利福尼亚州上诉判例汇编》第四辑第 100 卷第 62 页。

　　7. 唯一可能合理的依赖来自原告肖兹女士,她声称担任了两个月的发布商,损失了 25 000 美元的未付收益。(TAC 第 74 段、第 80 段—81 段)然而,她对付款相关的主张已在上文中被驳回。

　　8. 法院指出,UCL 尚缺乏确切的不公平原则标准。其他表述包括行为是否"不道德、无伦理、具有压迫性、具有侮辱性,或对消费者造成巨大伤害"。参见"德拉姆案",《加利福尼亚州上诉判例汇编》第四辑第 182 卷第 257 页。另见"谷歌公司隐私政策诉讼案",《联邦判例补编》第三辑第 58 卷第 968—984 页(加利福尼亚州北区法院,2014 年)(引用省略)。如上文所述,虽然更完善的证据有助于达到证明目的,但是法院认为原告已经充分指控了本案对消费者造成的伤害,已满足了该标准。

United States District Court, N. D. California, San Francisco Division.

VI Jeffrey WILENS, Plaintiff, v. AUTOMATTIC INC., et al., Defendants.

No. C 14-02419 LB
Signed February 5, 2015

Attorneys and Law Firms

Jeffrey Neil Wilens, Yorba Linda, CA, for Plaintiff.

ORDER (1) GRANTING PLAINTIFF'S MOTION FOR LEAVE TO SERVE DOE 1 BY EMAIL

[Re : ECF No.45]

LAUREL BEELER, United States Magistrate Judge

INTRODUCTION

*1 On May 25, 2014, Plaintiff Jeffrey Wilens filed a complaint against Defendants Automattic, Inc., TLDS LLC, Google, Inc., and Does 1-100 for trademark infringement in violation of the Lanham Act, 15 U. S. C.§ 1125 (a) (1), and for violation of the Anticybersquatting Consumer Protection Act, 15 U. S. C.§ 1125 (d). (Original Complaint, ECF No.1.[1]) Automattic, TLDS, and Google have been dismissed from this action, and now Mr. Wilens is attempting to identify and serve Doe 1. Mr. Wilens now moves for leave to serve Doe 1 by email or, alternatively, by publication. (Motion, ECF No.45.) Pursuant to Civil Local Rule 7-1 (b), the court finds this matter suitable for determination without oral argument and vacates the February 5, 2015 hearing date. Upon consideration of

Mr. Wilens's motion, the declarations and evidence he filed in support of it, and the applicable authority, the court grants his motion and allows him to serve Doe 1 by email.[2]

STATEMENT

A. MR. WILENS'S ALLEGATIONS

Plaintiff Jeffrey Wilens is an attorney specializing in consumer and employment law. (First Amended Complaint ("FAC"), ECF No.23 ¶¶ 1, 8, 11.) The name of his law firm is Lakeshore Law Center. (Id.¶¶ 10-11.) He is the only attorney in the United States with his and his law firm's name. (Id.¶ 11.) He maintains websites at www. lakeshorelaw. org and www. creditrepairdebt. org. (Id.¶ 10.) He holds trademark rights in the marks JEFFREY WILENS and LAKESHORE LAW CENTER and has spent tens of thousands of dollars advertising and promoting his personal and business name. (Id.¶¶ 9, 13.)

Mr. Wilens alleges that Doe 1 created, at Defendants' allowance, seven websites that violate his rights in the JEFFREY WILENS and LAKESHORE LAW CENTER marks and tarnish and disparage him and his law practice. (See id.¶¶ 14-20.) TLDS is the domain name registrar for one of those websites : www. jeffreywilens. com. (Id.¶¶ 16, 20.) Google hosts another one : jeffreywilens. blogspot. com. (Id.¶¶ 15, 19.) The other five websites—lakeshorelawcenter. wordpress. com ; attorneyjeffreywilens. wordpress. com ; jeffreywilenslawyer. wordpress. com ; unitedvictimsofjeffreywilens. wordpress. com ; and jeffreywilenslakeshorelaw. wordpress. com—are hosted by Automattic. (Id.¶¶ 14, 18.) Those websites criticize Mr. Wilens and his firm. (See id.¶¶ 33 (Doe 1 "stated that 'Jeffrey Wilens is engaging in the same activity that many lawyers, disbarred and/or jailed were engaging in' ".), 36 (Doe 1 "stated [that] 'JEFFREY WILENS IS USING SAME TACTICS [sic] AS ATTORNEY'S [sic] WHO HAVE BEEN JAILED AND DISBARRED. Many lawyers using the same unethical tactics as Jeffrey Wilens and [sic] have been disbarred and jailed. Jeffrey Wilens [sic] unethical moves will catch up to him and he will be next to be disbarred' ".), 38 (Doe 1 "stated [that] 'Jeffrey Wilens gets the millions while his clients the "victims" get nothing' ".), 39 (Doe 1 "stated [that] 'Jeffrey

Wilens makes up victims for his baseless class action suit' ".), 40 (Doe 1 "created and published a false review from supposedly an actual client" of Mr. Wilens, and the review stated that Mr. Wilens "contacted me and asked me to be a victim in one of his frivolous litigation against a major corporation").The websites also link to articles about "lawyers who have committed various crimes" or have been disbarred. (Id.¶¶ 34, 36.) Mr. Wilens alleges that all of Doe 1's statements are false and defamatory and that Doe 1's websites have "no legitimate purpose for using[Mr. Wilens's] personal or business name in" their domain names. (See id.¶¶ 21, 32, 35, 37-40.)

*2 Mr. Wilens alleges that Doe 1 "admitted [that] his goal was to cause [Mr. Wilens] to suffer 'agony'", and the statements were made intentionally and maliciously with the intent to cause pain and suffering and to "destroy [Mr. Wilens's] professional reputation and to cause him to lose clients". (Id.¶ 42.) Mr. Wilens also alleges that Doe 1 created the websites "for the purposes of diverting search engine traffic by clients and potential clients of [Mr. Wilens] from [Mr. Wilens's] websites controlled by" Doe 1, and that Doe 1 "did this for purposes of commercial gain and with intent to tarnish and disparage [Mr. Wilens's] marks by creating likelihood of confusion". (Id.¶ 17.) Mr. Wilens also alleges that Defendants were aware that their actions were and are contributing to Doe 1's trademark infringement because on March 3, 2014 he provided to them written notice with specific information describing the infringement and their role in perpetrating it. (Id.¶ 22.) Each Defendant responded in writing that it would not take any action absent an order from a court of competent jurisdiction. (Id.) Mr. Wilens also alleges that if Defendants had not allowed Doe 1 to use JEFFREY WILENS or LAKESHORE LAW CENTER in the domain names of the websites, search engines would have placed them so prominently upon a search of those terms. (Id.¶ 24.)

B. PROCEDURAL HISTORY

On May 25, 2014, Mr. Wilens filed his original complaint against Automattic, Google, and TLDS LLC for trademark infringement and cybersquatting. (See Original Complaint, ECF No.1.) In response to TLDS's motion to dismiss, and pursuant to Federal Rule of Civil Procedure 15 (a) (1) (B), on July 1, 2014, Mr. Wilens filed a First Amended Complaint that dropped TLDS as a defendant to the action, realleged his claims for trademark infringement and cybersquatting against Automattic, Google, and Doe 1, and added a claim for defamation against Doe 1. (See FAC, ECF No.23 ; see also Schwarzer, Tashima & Wagstaffe, CALIFORNIA PRACTICE GUIDE : FEDERAL CIVIL PROCEDURE BEFORE TRIAL §§ 8 : 1386 (amendment under Rule 15 may be used to drop a party) , 8 : 1551 (amended complaint that voluntarily drops a defendant named in the original complaint effectively dismisses that defendant from the action).) In light of the First Amended Complaint, the court denied as moot TLDS LLC's motion to dismiss. (See Order, ECF No.26.)

Then, on July 10, 2014, Automattic and Google jointly filed a motion to dismiss the First Amended Complaint. (See Motion, ECF No.28.) Mr. Wilens filed an opposition on July 24, 2014. (See Opposition, ECF No.30.) On July 31, 2014, Mr. Wilens and Google filed a stipulation dismissing with prejudice Mr. Wilens's claims against Google, and Automattic filed a reply. (See Stipulation of Dismissal, ECF No.31 ; Reply, ECF No.32.) On September 10, 2014, Mr. Wilens's voluntarily dismissing without prejudice his claims against Automattic. (Voluntary Dismissal, ECF No.35.) The court then dismissed the pending motion to dismiss as moot. (9/12/2014 Order, ECF No.37.) Thus, only Doe 1 remains as a defendant to this action.

Since that time, Mr. Wilens has been diligently attempting to identify and locate Doe 1 so that he may serve him or her. In support of his motion for leave to serve Doe 1 by email or, alternatively, by publication, Mr. Wilens states (and provides evidence to show) that he has taken the following steps :

• Mr. Wilens served a subpoena on TLDS, the registrar listed for jeffreywilens. com. According to documents provided by TLDS, the website was registered on December 9, 2013, and the person listed as the registrant is Konstantin Petrov at address "Montazhnikov 24, Sankt-Peterburg, 190000, Russia". The registrant's listed email address isjeffypetrov@mail. ru. Mr. Wilens has never represented a client or sued a person or company with an officer or director named "Konstantin Petrov" or "Jeffy Petrov". Mr. Wilens determined that the address Montazhnikov 24 appears in a number of Russian cities but does not appear in Saint Petersburg, that the "postal code" 19000 is for Kaniv in the Ukraine, and is not in Saint Petersburg. (12/26/2014 Wilens Decl., ECF No.45 at 24 ¶¶ 14-16 ; 2/3/2015 Wilens Decl., Ex.1, ECF No.52 at 6-9.)

• Mr. Wilens determined that the IP address hosting jeffreywilens. com is

217.112.35.87. An Internet search at w3bin. com, a tool that analyzes where websites are hosted, shows that the website is hosted in a server located in Russia and owned by Utransit International Carrier Limited. (12/26/2014 Wilens Decl., ECF No.45 at 25 ¶ 17.)

　　*3 • Mr. Wilens did, however, successfully correspond with someone at the email addressjeffypetrov@mail. ru. In June 2014, Mr. Wilens sent an email to that address complaining about the trademark violations. On July 16, 2014, a person responded to the email using thejeffypetrov@mail. ru email address. Mr. Wilens and that person then had a series of email communications, in which Mr. Wilens told the person that the websites and blogs were violating his trademarks and were defamatory, and the person defended the accuracy of contents of the websites and blogs and repeated many of the allegedly defamatory statements. The instant lawsuit was specifically discussed. The person stated on August 13, 2014 : "Your lawsuit is baseless so go ahead and make our day and continue to fight it. We are only posting the truth." At one point, the person stated that he or she wanted Mr. Wilens to dismiss one or more pending class actions that Mr. Wilens is prosecuting. In exchange, the person said that he or she would stop posting information about Mr. Wilens and would transfer the website's domain name to him. These discussions never went anywhere because the person would not specifically identify which class action or actions he or she wanted dismissed. In total, the person used thejeffypetrov@mail. ru email address to send Mr. Wilens at least 20 emails between July 16, 2014 and December 20, 2014. (12/26/2014 Wilens Decl., ECF No.45 at 23-24 ¶¶ 10, 13 ; 2/3/2015 Wilens Decl., Ex.2, ECF No.52 at 10-31.)

　　• According to the TLDS records, Doe 1 switched the registrar for jeffreywilens. com from TLDS to Enom. com on August 3, 2014. The listed registrant is not "Konstantin Petrov" but instead is "Anonymous Speech, 1-3-3 Sakura House, Tokyo, JP 169-0072". According to the website www. anonymousspeech. com, Anonymous Speech is a company that helps website owners and email senders conceal their identity. Anonymous Speech's website states that it will not disclose the identity of its members who use it to send anonymous emails or to have domains and websites hosted and that it will not respond to inquiries or subpoenas. Enom's listed email address to report abuse isabuse@enom. com. Mr. Wilens submitted a complaint to that email address but Enom responded that it could not do anything to help him. (12/26/2014 Wilens

Decl., ECF No.45 at 25 ¶ 18 ; 2/3/2015 Wilens Decl., Ex.1, ECF No.52 at 6-9.)

• The www. lakeshorelawcenter. com website is similarly protected. According to www. networksolutions. com, the listed registrar is "Reg. RU LLC", a Russian domain registration company. Mr. Wilens emailed an abuse report to that company but it took no action. The registrant's identity is hidden by PrivacyProtect. org, a company in Australia similar to the Anonymous Speech company described above. Mr. Wilens emailed an abuse report to that company but it would not reveal the identity of the registrant. (12/26/2014 Wilens Decl., ECF No.45 at 25-26 ¶ 19.)

• Mr. Wilens determined that the IP address hosting www. lakeshorelawcenter. com is 217.112.35.87, which is the same IP address that hosts jeffreywilens. com. (12/26/2014 Wilens Decl., ECF No.45 at 25-26 ¶ 20.)

• Mr. Wilens served a subpoena on Google regarding jeffreywilens. blogspot. com. According to the information produced in response, the blog was created on December 17, 2013, and the listed name of the owner is "Johnny Troll". The email address associated with the blog isjohnytroll2@gmail. com. (12/26/2014 Wilens Decl., ECF No.45 at 26 ¶ 22 ; 2/3/2015 Wilens Decl., Ex.3, ECF No.52 at 32-38.)

• Mr. Wilens served a subpoena on Automattic regarding lakeshorelawcenter. wordpress. com, attorneyjeffreywilens. wordpress. com jeffreywilenslawyer. wordpress. com, unitedvictimsofjeffreywilens. wordpress. com, and jeffreywilenslakeshorelaw. wordpress. com. According to the information produced in response, the blogs were created in December 2013 and January 2014. The names of the blog owners are not listed, but the email address associated with the blogs isjohnytroll2@mail. ru. (12/26/2014 Wilens Decl., ECF No.45 at 26 ¶ 23 ; 2/3/2015 Wilens Decl., Ex.4, ECF No.52 at 39.)

• The IP address 66.240.210.100 was used to createjeffreywilens. blogspot. com and three of the five Wordpress blogs. However, 22 different IP addresses were used to create the other blogs or to make posts on the blogs. Based on Mr. Wilens's search on who. is, the vast majority of the IP addresses used to post blog entries are owned by Nobis Technology Group, LLC. and Cari. net. (12/26/2014 Wilens Decl., ECF No.45 at 26-27 ¶¶ 25-26.)

*4 • Mr. Wilens served subpoenas on Nobis Technology and Cari. net. Both companies produced documents showing that the IP addresses were associated with a subscriber named "Brent Hather". One set of documents listed Brent Hather's address as 16192 Coastal Highway, Lewes, Delaware 19958, his phone number as 866-343-6722, and his email address asbhather@gmail. com. The other set of documents listed his address as 7770 Regents Road, San Diego, California 92122, his phone number as 866-343-6722, and his email address astech@myprivacytools. com. This contact information is associated with a Delaware corporation named My Privacy Tools, Inc., which is located in San Diego, California. According to its website, My Privacy Tools, Inc. sells Windows software that includes an IP proxy program that allows its customers to engage in "anonymous web surfing" and "send anonymous emails". (12/26/2014 Wilens Decl., ECF No.45 at 27-28 ¶¶ 27, 28, 31 ; 2/3/2015 Wilens Decl., Ex.5, ECF No.52 at 40-49.)

• According to his LinkedIn profile, Brent Hather is a Vice President at My Privacy Tools, Inc. Mr. Wilens emailed Mr. Hather at the listed email addresses. Mr. Hather responded, confirmed My Privacy Tools is his company, and said it would comply with a subpoena, and stated he did not use the IP addresses but they would have been used by the company's customers. (12/26/2014 Wilens Decl., ECF No.45 at 27 ¶¶ 29-30 ; 2/3/2015 Wilens Decl., Ex.6, ECF No.52 at 50-51.)

• Mr. Wilens served a subpoena on My Privacy Tools asking it to produce any contact information for the person who used the exact IP addresses on the particular dates and times (going up to August 2014) that correspond to the creation of the blogs and the postings on them. The company stated that it did not have that information. Mr. Wilens then communicated with Mr. Hather, who confirmed that his company leased the IP addresses in question on the specified dates and times and that they were used by one of its customers, but he also informed Mr. Wilens that it did not maintain (except for perhaps a short time) a log tracking which customers using particular IP addresses on particular dates in the past. Thus, the company had no information about the IP addresses used. Mr. Hather also indicated that customers could use the service for free or without providing a valid name and address. (12/26/2014 Wilens Decl., ECF No.45 at 28 ¶¶ 32-34 ; 2/3/2015 Wilens Decl., Ex.6, ECF No.52 at 50-51.)

In light of his fruitless efforts to determine the identify of Doe 1, Mr. Wilens now asks the court to allow him to serve Doe 1 by email or, alternatively, by publication. (Motion, ECF No.45.) As for service by email, Mr. Wilens proposes to serve Doe 1 by emailing the complaint and summons tojeffypetrov@mail. ru, johnnytroll2@mail. ru, andjohnnytroll2@gmail. com, andabuse@enom. com. (Id. at 17.) He also proposes to post a comment that links to a copy of the complaint and summons on www. jeffreywilens. com, jeffreywilens. blogspot. com, lakeshorelawcenter. wordpress. com, attorneyjeffreywilens. wordpress. com, jeffreywilenslawyer. wordpress. com, unitedvictimsofjeffreywilens. wordpress. com, and jeffreywilenslakeshorelaw. wordpress. com. (Id.)

ANALYSIS

In his motion, Mr. Wilens asks the court to permit him to serve Doe 1, who appears to be located in Russia, by e-mail. Federal Rule of Civil Procedure 4 (f) authorizes service of process on an individual in a foreign country in the following ways :

(1) by any internationally agreed means of service that is reasonably calculated to give notice, such as those authorized by the Hague Convention on the Service Abroad of Judicial and Extrajudicial Documents ;

(2) if there is no internationally agreed means, or if an international agreement allows but does not specify other means, by a method that is reasonably calculated to give notice :

(A) as prescribed by the foreign country's law for service in that country in an action in its courts of general jurisdiction ;

(B) as the foreign authority directs in response to a letter rogatory or letter of request ; or

*5 (C) unless prohibited by the foreign country's law, by :

(i) delivering a copy of the summons and of the complaint to the individual personally ; or

(ii) using any form of mail that the clerk addresses and sends to the individual and that requires a signed receipt ; or

(3) by other means not prohibited by international agreement, as the court orders.

"As obvious from its plain language, service under Rule 4 (f) (3) must be (1) directed by the court ; and (2) not prohibited by international agreement. No other limitations are evident from the text." *Rio Props. , Inc. v. Rio Intern. Interlink, 284 F.3d 1007, 1014 (9th Cir.2002)* (affirming propriety of service of process by e-mail). While Rule 4 (f) (3) gives the court discretion to "craft alternate means of service", such means still must comport with constitutional notions of due process. Id. at 1016. "To meet this requirement, the method of service crafted by the district court must be 'reasonably calculated under all the circumstances, to apprise interested parties of the pendency of the action and afford them an opportunity to present their objections'". Id. at 1016-17 (quoting *Mullane v. Cent. Hanover Bank & Trust Co., 339 U. S.306, 314 (1950)* (Jackson, J.)).

Here, Mr. Wilens has made substantial efforts to locate and identify Doe 1, to no avail. He has served six subpoenas and submitted three abuse-related complaints on companies related to the registration of the allegedly offending websites and blogs, and although he has received some information in response, it has not been sufficient to pin-point Doe 1's location or identify him or her. Mr. Wilens also has taken more informal steps to correspond with those identified with the allegedly offending websites and blogs, and while he has communicated with someone at the email addressjeffypetrov@mail. ru who may be Doe 1, that person has not provided Mr. Wilens with his or her location or true identity, either.

In addition, assuming that Doe 1 is located in Russia (which appears to be most likely location, based on the evidence submitted) , neither Mr. Wilens nor the court is not aware of any international agreement that would prohibit Mr. Wilens from serving Doe 1 via email. (SeeMotion, ECF No.45 at 15.) And in light of the correspondence that Mr. Wilens has had with the person at jeffypetrov@ mail. ru, the court finds that service by email is reasonably calculated under all the circumstances to apprise interested parties of the pendency of the action and afford them an opportunity to present their objections. Given this ruling, the court does not address Mr. Wilens's argument in support of service by publication.

CONCLUSION

For the foregoing reasons, the court grants Mr. Wilens's motion. By February 20, 2015[3], he must serve Doe 1 by emailing the complaint and summons to jeffypetrov@mail. ru, johnnytroll2@mail. ru, andjohnytroll2@gmail. com, andabuse@enom. com. By that same date he also must post a comment that links to a copy of the complaint and summons on www. jeffreywilens. com, jeffreywilens. blogspot. com, lakeshorelawcenter. wordpress. com, attorneyjeffreywilens. wordpress. com, jeffreywilenslawyer. wordpress. com, unitedvictimsofjeffreywilens. wordpress. com, and jeffreywilenslakeshorelaw. wordpress. com. Mr. Wilens must file either proof of service or a status update explaining why service has not been made by February 20, 2015 as well.

　　*6 IT IS SO ORDERED.

All Citations

Not Reported in Fed. Supp., 2015 WL 498745.

Footnotes

　　1 Record citations are to documents in the Electronic Case File ("ECF"); pinpoint citations are to the ECF-generated page numbers at the top of the documents.

　　2 Along with his motion for leave to serve Doe 1 by email, Mr. Wilens also filed a motion to shorten the time for hearing his motion for leave. Motion to Shorten Time, ECF No.46. Because the court in this order finds that a hearing is not necessary and grants Mr. Wilens's motion for leave to serve Doe 1 by email, the court denies as moot Mr. Wilens's motion to shorten time.

　　3 The current deadline for Mr. Wilens to serve Doe 1 is February 5, 2015. (11/10/2014 Order, ECF No.44.) In light of this order, the court hereby extends that deadline to February 20, 2015.

美国加利福尼亚州北部联邦地区法院，旧金山分院。

6　杰弗里·威伦斯诉 Automattic 公司等

案件编号：C 14-02419 LB
签署时间：2015 年 2 月 5 日

律师和律师事务所

原告代理律师：加利福尼亚州约巴林达的杰弗里·威伦斯
裁决（1）批准原告请求以电子邮件的方式向 DOE 1 送达（起诉状和传票）
的动议
［答复：电子案例 第 45 号档案］
劳尔·贝勒，美国地方法官

简介

*1 2014 年 5 月 25 日，原告杰弗里·威伦斯针对被告 Automattic 公司、
TLDS 公司、谷歌公司和 Does 1-100 提交起诉状，指控被告构成商标侵权，
违反了《美国法典》第 15 卷第 1125 节第 1 分节第 1 款的《拉纳姆法》和《美
国法典》第 15 卷第 1125 节第 4 分节的《反域名抢注消费者保护法》。（原
起诉状，电子案例 第 1 号档案[1]）原告已经在该诉讼中撤回了对 Automattic
公司、TLDS 公司和谷歌公司的指控，现在威伦斯先生正试图查明 Doe 1 的
信息并向其送达起诉状和传票。威伦斯先生现在请求通过电子邮件或公告送
达的方式向 Doe 1 送达起诉状和传票。（动议，电子案例 第 45 号档案）根据
《地方民事规则》第 7 节第 1 分节第 2 款，法院认为该诉讼适用无须口头辩
论即可裁决的程序，并取消了 2015 年 2 月 5 日的听证会。考虑了威伦斯先
生的动议，并审查了为支持该动议而提交的声明和证据，以及可适用的授

权后，法院批准了他的动议，并允许他通过电子邮件向 Doe 1 送达起诉状和传票。[2]

陈述

A. 威伦斯先生的指控

原告杰弗里·威伦斯是一名消费法和就业法领域的专业律师。[第一版修正起诉状（"FAC"），电子案例 第 23 号档案第 1 段、第 8 段、第 11 段]他的律师事务所名为湖滨法律中心。（同上，第 10—11 段）他是美国唯一一位拥有自己姓名商标权和自己的律师事务所商标权的律师。（同上，第 11 段）其维护 www. lakeshorelaw. org 和 www. creditrepairdebt. org 等两个网站（同上，第 10 段），拥有"杰弗里·威伦斯"和"湖滨法律中心"的商标权，并花费了数万美元为其个人和律师事务所的名称做广告和宣传（同上，第 9 段、第 13 段）。

威伦斯先生声称，Doe 1 在被告的允许下创建了 7 个网站，侵犯了他对"杰弗里·威伦斯"和"湖滨法律中心"这两个商标的权利，玷污和诋毁了他本人及其法律业务（同上，第 14—20 段）TLDS 是其中一个网站（www. jeffreywilens. com）的域名注册商（同上，第 16 段、第 20 段），谷歌公司则是另一个网站（jeffreywilens. blogspot. com）的域名注册商（同上，第 15 段、第 19 段）。其他 5 个网站（lakeshorelawcenter. wordpress. com；attorneyjeffreywilens. wordpress. com；jeffreywilenslawyer. wordpress. com；unitedvictimsofjeffreywilens. wordpress. com；jeffreywilenslakeshorelaw. wordpress. com）均在 Automattic 上注册。（同上，第 14 段、第 18 段）这些网站批评威伦斯先生及其公司。[（同上，第 33 段（Doe 1 称"杰弗里·威伦斯正在从事许多与被吊销律师资格和 / 或入狱的律师相同的活动"），第 36 段（Doe 1 称"杰弗里·威伦斯使用的伎俩与被吊销律师资格并入狱的律师相同。许多使用与杰弗里·威伦斯同样的不道德手段的律师已被吊销律师资格并入狱。杰弗瑞·威伦斯作出这些不道德行为，最终将自食其果，成为下一个被吊销律师资格的人"），第 38 段（Doe 1 声明"杰弗里·威伦斯赚取了数百万美元，而他的'受害者'客户什么也得不到"），第 39 段（Doe 1 写道"杰弗里·威伦斯为他虚假的集体诉讼编造受害者"），第 40 段（Doe 1 以一位威伦斯先生的真实客户的口吻，编造并发布了一个虚假评论，该评论称威伦斯先生"联系我假扮他对一家大型公司提起无谓诉讼的受害者"）。这些网站提供有关"犯下各种罪行的律师"或被吊销律师资格的律师的文章链接。（同上，第 34 段、第 36 段）威伦斯称，Doe 1 的所有陈述都是虚假和诽谤性的，Doe 1 的网站在其域名上使用威伦斯先生的个人或公司名称不具有正当目的。（同上，第 21 段、第 32 段、第 35 段、第 37~40 段）

　　*2 威伦斯先生声称，Doe 1 "承认他的目的是使威伦斯先生遭受'痛苦'"，Doe 1 作出这些陈述的主观心态带有恶意，目的就是让威伦斯先生感到痛苦、遭受折磨，并 "破坏威伦斯先生的职业声誉，使他失去客户"。（同上，第 42 段）威伦斯先生还声称，Doe 1 创建这些网站试图 "将［威伦斯先生］的既有客户、潜在客户和搜索引擎的流量从 Doe 1 控制的［威伦斯先生的］网站转移出来"，目的是 "为了商业利益，并意图通过可能让公众感到混淆的方式来玷污和诋毁［威伦斯先生的］商誉"。（同上，第 17 段）威伦斯先生还声称，被告自始至终都知晓其行为正在导致 Doe 1 的商标侵权行为，因为威伦斯先生已于 2014 年 3 月 3 日书面通知各被告，通知中包含了各被告侵权行为及其在实施侵权行为中所扮演的角色等具体信息。（同上，第 22 段）每名被告均以书面形式答复称，如果没有具备管辖权的法院发布的命令，他们不会采取任何行动。（同上，第 17 段）威伦斯先生还声称，如果被告不允许 Doe 1 在网站域名中使用 "杰弗里·威伦斯" 或 "湖滨法律中心" 的名字，搜索引擎就会在用户搜索这些名字时，将其显示在非常突出的位置。（同上，第 24 段）

B. 历审程序

　　2014 年 5 月 25 日，威伦斯先生提交起诉状，最初对 Automattic 公司、谷歌公司和 TLDS 公司提起了商标侵权和域名抢注的诉讼。（见原始起诉状，电子案例第 1 号档案）根据《联邦民事诉讼规则》第 15（a）（1）（B）条，针对 TLDS 公司驳回起诉的动议，威伦斯先生于 2014 年 7 月 1 日提交了第一版修正起诉状，放弃将 TLDS 公司作为该诉讼的被告，调整了其针对 Automattic 公司、谷歌公司和 Doe 1 侵犯商标权和域名抢注的诉讼请求，并对 Doe 1 提起（商业）诽谤的诉讼请求。［见 FAC，电子案例 第 23 号档案；另见施瓦泽、田岛 & 瓦格斯塔夫，《加州实践指南：联邦民事审前程序》第 8：1386 节（根据《联邦民事诉讼规则》第 15 条所作的修正案可用于撤销对一方的起诉），第 8：1551 节（在修改后的起诉状中自愿放弃原始起诉中的被告可有效地将被告从诉讼中排除出去）］根据第一版修正起诉状，法院驳回了 TLDS 公司的驳回起诉动议，因为这份动议已经不具实际意义。（见命令，电子案例第 26 号档案）

　　随后，2014 年 7 月 10 日，Automattic 公司和谷歌公司联合提交了要求驳回第一版修正起诉状的动议。（见动议，电子案例第 28 号档案）威伦斯先生于 2014 年 7 月 24 日提交了反对书。（见反对书，电子案例第 30 号档案）2014 年 7 月 31 日，威伦斯先生和谷歌公司提交了一份协议，撤回威伦斯先生针对谷歌公司的所有权利主张，Automattic 公司提交了答辩状。（见驳回诉讼请求的规定，电子案例第 31 号档案；答辩状，电子案例第 32 号档案）2014 年 9 月 10 日，威伦斯先生自愿不再对 Automattic 公司提起诉讼。（见自愿撤诉申请书，电子案例第 35 号档案）法院随后驳回了未决的驳回起诉动议，因为这份动议已无实际意义。（2014 年 9 月 12 日命令，电子案例第 37 号档案）因此，只有 Doe 1 仍是该诉讼的被告。

自此开始，威伦斯先生就一直在努力试图查明并定位 Doe 1，以便向其送达起诉状和传票。为了支持威伦斯先生提出的允许通过电子邮件或公告送达的方式向 Doe 1 送达起诉状和传票的动议，威伦斯先生声明（并提供证据证明）他已经采取了以下措施：

• 威伦斯先生对 jeffreywilens. com 的注册商 TLDS 公司送达了起诉状和传票。根据 TLDS 公司提供的文件，该网站注册于 2013 年 12 月 9 日，记录的注册人是康斯坦丁·彼得罗夫，地址为"俄罗斯圣彼得堡蒙塔泽尼科夫 24 号，邮编 190000"。注册人列出的电子邮件地址是 jeffypetrov@mail. ru。无论是威伦斯先生代表过的客户，还是起诉过的个人或公司的管理人员或董事，都没有叫"康斯坦丁·彼得罗夫"或"杰菲·彼得罗夫"的人。威伦斯先生确定在俄罗斯某些城市确有蒙塔泽尼科夫 24 号这个地方，但圣彼得堡没有这个地方，"邮政编码"19000 是乌克兰卡尼夫的，而非圣彼得堡的。（2014 年 12 月 26 日，"威伦斯声明"，电子案例第 45 号档案第 24 点第 14—16 段；2015 年 2 月 3 号，"威伦斯声明"附件 1，电子案例 第 52 号档案第 6—9 点）。

• 威伦斯先生确定托管 jeffreywilens. com 的 IP 地址是 217.112.35.87。他在分析网站托管地位置的工具 w3bin. com 上进行了搜索，结果显示该网站托管在俄罗斯的一个服务器上，该服务器的所有者是 Utransit 国际保险人有限公司。（2014 年 12 月 26 日，"威伦斯声明"，电子案例第 45 号档案第 25 点第 17 段）。

• *3 然而，威伦斯先生确实通过电子邮件地址 jeffypetrov@mail. ru 成功地与某人通信。2014 年 6 月，威伦斯先生向该地址发送了一封电子邮件，起诉商标侵权一事。2014 年 7 月 16 日，有人使用 jeffypetrov@mail. ru 电子邮件地址回复了威伦斯先生发出的电子邮件。随后，威伦斯先生与该人进行了一系列电子邮件通信，威伦斯先生在这些电子邮件中告诉此人，相关网站和博客侵犯了他的商标权，相关内容构成诽谤，该人为相关网站和博客内容的准确性进行辩护，并重复了许多据称是诽谤的言论。法院具体讨论了这一即时诉讼。该人于 2014 年 8 月 13 日表示："你的诉讼毫无根据，所以继续吧，我们也会继续下去。我们只是在公布真相。"该人曾表示，希望威伦斯先生撤回其正在起诉的一项或多项未决集体诉讼。作为交换，此人表示他或她将停止发布有关威伦斯先生的信息，并将该网站的域名转让给他。由于该人没有具体指明希望威伦斯先生撤回哪项集体诉讼，上述讨论并未取得任何进展。2014 年 7 月 16 日至 2014 年 12 月 20 日期间，该人使用 jeffypetrov@mail. ru 电子邮件地址向威伦斯先生发送了至少 20 封电子邮件。（2014 年 12 月 26 日，"威伦斯声明"，电子案例第 45 号档案第 23—24 点第 10、13 段；2015 年 2 月 3 日，"威伦斯声明"附件 2，电子案例 第 52 号档案第 10—31 点）

• 根据 TLDS 公司记录，Doe 1 于 2014 年 8 月 3 日将 jeffreywilens. com 网站的注册商从 TLDS 公司切换到 Enom. com。记录的注册人不是"康斯坦丁·彼得罗夫"，而是"匿名言论，日本东京樱花之家 1-3-3 号，邮编 JP 169-0072"。根据 www. anonymousspeech. com 网站介绍，匿名言论公司是一家帮助网站所有者和电子邮件发件人隐藏身份的公司。匿名言论公司声明它不会披露使用该网站发送匿名电子邮件或利用该网站托管域名和网站的成员身份，也不会回应查询或传票。Enom 列出了报告滥用行为的电子邮件地址是 abuse@enom. com。威伦斯先生就该电子邮件地址提交了起诉状，但 Enom 回应说对此无能为力。（2014 年 12 月 26 日，"威伦斯声明"，电子案例 第 45 号档案第 25 点第 18 段；2015 年 2 月 3 日，"威伦斯声明"附件 1，电子案例第 52 号档案第 6—9 点。）

• www. lakeshorelawcenter. com 网站也受到了类似的保护。根据 www. networksolutions. com 网站，被记录的注册商是一个俄罗斯域名的注册公司"Reg. Ru 公司"。威伦斯先生用电子邮件发送了一份滥用报告给该公司，但是该公司并没有任何回应。该公司注册人身份被一家名为 PrivacyProtect. org 的类似于上述匿名言论公司的澳大利亚公司隐藏。此外，威伦斯先生向 PrivacyProtect. org 公司发送了一份滥用报告的电子邮件，但其并未回复注册人的身份。（2014 年 12 月 26 日，"威伦斯声明"，电子案例第 45 号档案第 25—26 点第 19 段）

• 威 伦 斯 先 生 发 现 托 管 www. lakeshorelawcenter. com 的 IP 地 址 为 217.112.35.87,这与托管 jeffreyWilens. com 的 IP 地址一样。（2014 年 12 月 26 日，"威伦斯声明"，电子案例第 45 号档案第 25—26 点第 20 段）

• 威伦斯先生向谷歌公司发出了一份关于 jeffreywilens. blogspot. com 的传票。根据回应提供的信息，该博客创建于 2013 年 12 月 17 日，记录的所有者姓名为"约翰尼·特罗"。与博客关联的电子邮件地址是 johnytroll2@

gmail. com。（2014 年 12 月 26 日，"威伦斯声明"，电子案例第 45 号档案第 26 点第 22 段；2015 年 2 月 3 日，"威伦斯声明"附件 3，电子案例第 52 号档案第 32—38 点）

• 威伦斯先生就 lakeshorelawcenter. wordpress. com, attorneyjeffreywilens. wordpress. com, jeffreywilenslawyer. wordpress. com, unitedvictimsofjeffreywilens. wordpress. com 和 jeffreywilenslakeshorelaw. wordpress. com 等网站向 Automattic 公司发出传票。根据回应提供的信息，这些博客是在 2013 年 12 月和 2014 年 1 月创建的。虽然没有记录博客所有者的姓名，但与博客相关的电子邮件地址是 johnnytroll2@mail. ru。（2014 年 12 月 26 日，"威伦斯声明"，电子案例第 45 号档案第 26 点第 23 段；2015 年 2 月 3 日，"威伦斯声明"附件 4，电子案例第 52 号档案第 39 点）

• 创建 jeffreywilens. blogspot. com 和其中三个 Wordpress 博客的 IP 地址为 66.240.210.100。但是，共有 22 个不同的 IP 地址用于创建其他博客或在博客上发布帖子。根据威伦斯先生在 who. is 上的搜索，绝大多数用于发布博客条目的 IP 地址都归诺比斯科技集团有限公司和卡里网（Cari. net）所有。（2014 年 12 月 26 日，"威伦斯声明"，电子案例第 45 号档案第 26—27 点第 25—26 段）

• *4 威伦斯先生向诺比斯科技集团有限公司和卡里网送达了传票。这两家公司出示的文件显示，这些 IP 地址与一个名叫"布伦特·海瑟"的用户有关。一组文件列出了布伦特·海瑟的地址为美国特拉华州刘易斯市滨海公路 16192 号，邮编 19958，电话号码为 866-343-6722，电子邮件地址为 bhather@gmail. com。另一组文件列出其地址为美国加利福尼亚州圣地亚哥摄政道 7770 号，邮编 92122，电话号码为 866-343-6722，电子邮件地址为 astech@myprivacytools. com。此联系信息与位于加利福尼亚州圣地亚哥的名为"我的隐私工具"的特拉华州公司相关联。根据其网站，"我的隐私工具"公司销售的 Windows 软件包括一个 IP 代理程序，该程序允许客户参与"匿名上网"和"发送匿名电子邮件"。（2014 年 12 月 26 日，"威伦斯声明"，电子案例 第 45 号档案第 27—28 点第 27 段、第 28 段、第 31 段；2015 年 2 月 3 日，"威伦斯声明"附件 5，电子案例 第 52 号档案第 40—49 点）

• 他的"领英"个人资料显示，布伦特·海瑟是"我的隐私工具"公司的副总裁。威伦斯先生通过记录的电子邮件地址向海瑟先生发送了电子邮件。海瑟先生回应，确认"我的隐私工具"是他的公司，公司会遵守传票，并表示他没有使用这些 IP 地址，但公司客户会使用这些 IP 地址。（2014 年 12 月 26 日，"威伦斯声明"，电子案例第 45 号档案第 27 点第 29—30 段；2015 年 2 月 3 日，"威伦斯声明"附件 6，电子案例第 52 号档案第 50-51 点）

· 威伦斯先生向"我的隐私工具"公司送达了传票，要求该公司提供与创建博客和在博客上发布内容相对应的特定日期和时间（截至 2014 年 8 月）的确切 IP 地址使用人的联系信息。该公司表示没有这方面的信息。威伦斯先生随后与海瑟先生进行了沟通，海瑟先生证实其公司在指定的日期和时间内租用了有关 IP 地址，一个客户使用了这些地址，但他也告诉威伦斯先生，该公司没有对客户在过去特定日期内使用特定 IP 地址保持（也许只有很短的时间）追踪。因此，该公司没有使用 IP 地址的信息。海瑟先生还表示，客户可以不提供有效的姓名和地址而免费使用这项服务。（2014 年 12 月 26 日，"威伦斯声明"，电子案例第 45 号档案第 28 点第 32—34 段；2015 年 2 月 3 日，"威伦斯声明"附件 6，电子案例第 52 号档案第 50—51 点）

鉴于威伦斯先生曾试图确定 Doe 1 身份但无果而终，他现在请求法院允许他通过电子邮件或公告送达的方式向 Doe 1 送达起诉状和传票。（动议，电子案例 第 45 号档案）至于如何通过电子邮件送达，威伦斯先生建议将起诉状和传票通过以下电子邮件送达至 Doe 1：jeffypetrov@mail. ru, johnnytroll2@mail. ru, johnytroll2@gmail. com, 以及 abuse@enom. com。（同上，第 17 页）他还提议在 www. jeffreywilens. com, jeffreywilens. blogspot. com, lakeshorelawcenter. wordpress. com, attorneyjeffreywilens. wordpress. com, jeffreywilenslawyer. wordpress. com, unitedvictimsofjeffreywilens. wordpress. com 和 jeffreywilenslakeshorelaw. wordpress. com. 等网址上发表评论，链接到起诉状和传票的副本。（同上）

分析

威伦斯先生在动议中请求法院允许他通过电子邮件向 Doe 1 送达起诉状和传票。Doe 1 目前似乎在俄罗斯。《联邦民事诉讼规则》第 4 节第 6 分节授权以下列方式向外国个人送达诉讼文件：

（1）通过经国际条约确定的、能够合理发出通知的送达方式，如《关于向国外送达司法和司法外文件的海牙公约》授权的送达方式；

（2）如果没有国际条约确定的方式，或者国际条约允许但未指定其他方法的，则采用能够合理发出通知的如下送达方式：

（A）在具有一般管辖权的法院的诉讼中，按照外国法律所规定的在该国进行送达的方式送达；

（B）外国当局在回应调查委托书或请求函时所指示的送达方式；

*5（C）除非外国法律禁止，否则可通过以下途径：

（i）将传票及起诉状的副本亲自交付该人；

（ⅱ）使用书记员指定地址邮寄给该人且要求带有签名回执的邮件；

（ⅲ）按照法院要求，通过国际条约不禁止的其他方式。

"显而易见，根据《联邦民事诉讼规则》第 4（f）（3）条的规定，送达必须（1）由法院指示；（2）不受国际条约禁止。文本中没有其他明显的限制。"参见"里约热内卢房地产公司诉里约国际互联公司案"，《美国联邦法院判例集》第三辑第 284 卷第 1007—1014 页（第九巡回法院，2002 年）（确认通过电子邮件送达文件的适当性）。虽然《联邦民事诉讼规则》第 4（f）（3）条赋予法院"制定其他送达方式"的自由裁量权，但这种方式仍然必须符合宪法关于正当程序的概念。（同上，第 1016 页）"为符合这项要求，地区法院制定的送达方式必须 '在任何情况下都经过合理计算，告知有关人士有关诉讼的未决期，并给予他们提出反对意见的机会'。"（同上，第 1016—1017 页；引用"穆莱恩诉中央汉诺威银行信托股份有限公司案"，《联邦最高法院判例》第 339 卷第 306—314 页）

本案中，威伦斯先生已经做了大量的努力来寻找和确认 Doe 1 的身份，但毫无效果。他已经就涉嫌违规的网站和博客注册的相关公司送达了 6 张传票，并提交了 3 份与滥用相关的起诉状，尽管他收到了一些答复信息，但这还不足以确定 Doe 1 的位置或确认其身份。威伦斯先生还采取了更多的非正式措施与那些涉嫌违规的网站和博客通信，虽然他已经通过电子邮件地址 jeffypetrov@mail. ru 与可能是 Doe 1 的人联系过，但此人没有将自己的位置或真实身份提供给威伦斯先生。

此外，假设 Doe 1 位于俄罗斯（根据提交的证据，这似乎是最有可能的位置），威伦斯先生和法院都不知道有什么国际条约会禁止威伦斯先生通过电子邮件向 Doe 1 送达起诉状或传票。（见动议，电子案例 第号档案第 45 号第 15 点）鉴于威伦斯先生已经通过 jeffypetrov@mail. ru 与那个人有信件往来。法院认为，在任何情况下电子邮件送达都是合理的方式，可以由此告知有关人士关于诉讼的未决期，并给予他们提出反对意见的机会。鉴于这一裁决，法院没有回应威伦斯先生关于支持通过公告送达起诉状和传票的论点。

结论

基于上述原因，本法庭批准威伦斯先生的动议。在 2015 年 2 月 20 日之前，[3] 他必须通过电子邮件将起诉状和传票通过 jeffypetrov@mail. ru, johnnytroll2@mail. ru, johnytroll2@gmail. com, 以 及 abuse@enom. com 等地址送达给 Doe 1。同样地，在 2015 年 2 月 20 日之前，他还必须在 www.

jeffreywilens. com, jeffreywilens. blogspot. com, lakeshorelawcenter. wordpress. com, attorneyjeffreywilens. wordpress. com, jeffreywilenslawyer. wordpress. com, unitedvictimsofjeffreywilens. wordpress. com 和 jeffreywilenslakeshorelaw. wordpress. com 等网站上发布评论，链接到起诉状和传票的副本。威伦斯先生必须提交送达证明或状态更新，解释其为何未能在 2015 年 2 月 20 日之前完成送达。

*6 作出如上判决。

所有引文

在《美国联邦法院判例集》副刊，2015 年 WL 498745 中未见报道。

脚注

1. 记录引用是指电子案例档案（"ECF"）中的文件；精确引文指文件顶部电子案例档案生成的页码。

2. 威伦斯先生除了提出通过电子邮件向 Doe 1 送达起诉状和传票的许可动议，还提出要求缩短其许可动议听证会时间的动议。（缩短时间动议，电子案例第 46 号档案）由于法院在裁决中认为没有必要举行听证会，所以批准了威伦斯先生通过电子邮件向 Doe 1 送达起诉状和传票的动议，驳回了缩短时间的动议，因为这份动议已无实际意义。

3. 目前，威伦斯先生向 Doe 1 送达起诉状和传票的截止日期是 2015 年 2 月 5 日。（2014 年 11 月 10 日裁决，电子案例第 44 号档案）根据该命令，法院特此将该截止日期延长至 2015 年 2 月 20 日。

United States District Court, E. D. Texas, Marshall Division.

VII MEMSMART SEMICONDUCTOR CORP., Plaintiff v. APPLE INC., Defendant.

CASE NO.2 : 13-cv-518-JRG
Signed 04/21/2014
Filed 04/22/2014

Attorneys and Law Firms

Deborah Jagai, Law Offices of Deborah Jagai, Decatur, TX, Winston Oliver Huff, W. O. Huff & Associates, PLLC, Dallas, TX, for Plaintiff.

Vincent J. Belusko, Alex S. Yap, Bita Rahebi, Morrison & Foerster LLP, Los Angeles, CA, Harry Lee Gillam, Jr., Melissa Richards Smith, Gillam & Smith, LLP, Marshall, TX, for Defendant.

ORDER

RODNEY GILSTRAP, UNITED STATES DISTRICT JUDGE

*1 Before the Court is Defendant Apple Inc.'s ("Apple's") Motion to Transfer Venue (Dkt. No.23). Apple moves the Court to transfer the above-styled action to the United States District Court for the Northern District of California pursuant to 28 U. S. C.§ 1404 (a) , contending that the Northern District of California is a clearly more convenient forum than the Eastern District of Texas. Having considered the parties' written submissions, the Court GRANTS the motion.

Section 1404 (a) provides that " [f] or the convenience of parties and witnesses, in the interest of justice, a district court may transfer any civil action to any other district or division where it might have been brought". *28 U. S. C.§ 1404 (a)*. The first inquiry when analyzing a case's eligibility for 1404 (a) transfer is "whether the judicial district to which transfer is sought would have been a district in which the claim could have been filed". *In re Volkswagen AG, 371 F.3d 201, 203 (5th Cir.2004)* ("In re Volkswagen I").

Once that threshold is met, the movant has the burden of proving that the transferee venue is "clearly more convenient" than the transferor venue. *In re Nintendo, 589 F.3d 1194, 1200 (Fed. Cir.2009)* ; *In re TS Tech, 551 F.3d 1315, 1319 (Fed. Cir.2008)* ; *In re Volkswagen of Am., Inc., 545 F.3d 304, 315 (5th Cir.2008)* ("In re Volkswagen II"). In this regard, courts analyze both public and private factors relating to the convenience of parties and witnesses as well as the interests of particular venues in hearing the case. See *In re Nintendo, 589 F.3d at 1198* ; *In re TS Tech, 551 F.3d at 1319.* The private factors include : (1) the relative ease of access to sources of proof ; (2) the availability of compulsory process to secure the attendance of witnesses ; (3) the cost of attendance for willing witnesses ; and (4) all other practical problems that make trial of a case easy, expeditious, and inexpensive. *In re Nintendo, 589 F.3d at 1198* ; *In re TS Tech, 551 F.3d at 1319* ; *In re Volkswagen I, 371 F.3d at 203.* The public factors include : (1) the administrative difficulties flowing from court congestion ; (2) the local interest in having localized interests decided at home ; (3) the familiarity of the forum with the law that will govern the case ; and (4) the avoidance of unnecessary problems of conflict of laws or in the application of foreign law. *In re Nintendo, 589 F.3d at 1198* ; *In re TS Tech, 551 F.3d at 1319* ; *In re Volkswagen I, 371 F.3d at 203.* Though the private and public factors apply to most transfer cases, "they are not necessarily exhaustive or exclusive", and no single factor is dispositive. *In re Volkswagen II, 545 F.3d at 314-15.*

Here, the Court has considered the motions, supporting declarations with exhibits, and related briefing. The parties do not dispute, and the Court expressly finds, that the action could have been filed in the Northern District of California. Such threshold having been crossed and having weighed the balance of public and private interest factors identified above, the Court finds that Apple has met its burden to show that the Northern District of California is clearly more convenient than the Eastern District of Texas. See *In re Nintendo Co., 589 F.3d 1194,*

1197-98 (Fed. Cir.2009)；*In re Genentech, Inc., 566 F.3d 1388, 1342 (Fed. Cir.2009)*；*In re TS Tech USA Corp., 551 F.3d 1315, 1319 (Fed. Cir.2008)*；*In re Volkswagen of Am., Inc. (Volkswagen II), 545 F.3d 304, 315 (5th Cir.2008)* (en banc). Accordingly, the Court hereby GRANTS Apple's Motion to Transfer Venue (Dkt. No.23).

*2 It is therefore ORDERED that the above-styled cause of action is hereby transferred to the United States District Court for the Northern District of California. The Clerk of the Court shall forthwith take such steps as are needed to effectuate the transfer.

So ORDERED and SIGNED this 21st day of April, 2014.

All Citations

Not Reported in Fed. Supp., 2014 WL 12707246.

美国得克萨斯州东部联邦地区法院，马歇尔分院。

7　Memsmart 半导体公司诉苹果公司

案件编号 2∶13-cv-518-JRG
签署时间：2014 年 4 月 21 日
提交时间：2014 年 4 月 22 日

律师及律师事务所

原告代理律师：得克萨斯州迪凯特市 Deborah Jagai 律师事务所的黛博拉·加盖；得克萨斯州达拉斯 W. O. Huff & Associates, PLLC 律师事务所的温斯顿·奥利弗·哈夫。

被告代理律师：加利福尼亚州洛杉矶美富律师事务所（有限责任合伙公司）的文森特·贝卢斯科、亚里克斯·亚普和比塔·拉赫比；得克萨斯州马歇尔 Gillam & Smith 律师事务所（有限责任合伙公司）的小哈里·李·吉勒姆和玛丽莎·理查兹·史密斯。

裁决

罗德尼·吉尔斯特拉普，美国联邦地区法官

*1 本法院审理的是被告苹果公司（简称"苹果"）关于诉讼地转移的动议（待审案件目录第 23 号）。苹果公司根据《美国法典》第 28 卷第 1404 节第 1 分节，请求法院将上述诉讼移交至加利福尼亚州北区联邦地区法院，理由是加利福尼亚州北区显然比得克萨斯州东区更便于诉讼。法院审查了双方当事人的书面陈述后批准了这项动议。

第 1404 节第 1 分节规定："为方便当事人及证人，维护司法公正，地区法院可将任何民事诉讼移交至其他可以审理民事诉讼的地区法院或分支法院。"《美国法典》第 28 卷第 1404 节第 1 分节。分析案件是否符合第 1404 节第 1 分节的移交条件，首先要调查的是"寻求移交的司法管辖区是不是可以提起本案诉讼的管辖区"。参见"德国大众汽车案"，《美国联邦法院判例集》第三辑第 371 卷第 201—203 页（第五巡回法院，2004 年）。（以下简称"大众汽车 I 案"）。

一旦符合这一条件，动议人就有责任证实接受转移的诉讼地比转移方诉讼地"明显更便利"。参见"任天堂案"，《美国联邦法院判例集》第三辑第 589 卷第 1194—1200 页（联邦巡回法院，2009 年）；"TS 科技公司案"，《美国联邦法院判例集》第三辑第 551 卷第 1315—1319 页（联邦巡回法院，2008 年）；"美国大众汽车公司案"，《美国联邦法院判例集》第三辑第 545 卷第 304—315 页（第五巡回法院，2008 年）（以下简称"大众汽车公司 II 案"）。为此，法院对涉及当事人、证人便利性以及特定诉讼地在案件审理中的利益相关的公、私因素进行了分析。参见"任天堂案"，《美国联邦法院判例集》第三辑第 589 卷第 1198 页；"TS 科技公司案"，《美国联邦法院判例集》第三辑第 551 卷第 1319 页。私人利益因素包括：（1）获取证据来源的相对难易度；（2）确保证人出庭的强制程序的可行性；（3）愿意作证的证人的出庭费用；（4）所有其他可以促使案件审判便利、快速和低成本的实际问题。参见"任天堂案"，《美国联邦法院判例集》第三辑第 589 卷第 1198 页；"TS 科技公司案"，《美国联邦法院判例集》第三辑第 551 卷第 1319 页；"大众汽车 I 案"，《美国联邦法院判例集》第三辑第 371 卷第 203 页。公共利益因素包括：（1）法院案件众多引发的行政管理困难；（2）在国内对当地利益进行裁决所涉及的地方利益；（3）法院对管辖案件适用法律的熟悉程度；（4）避免不必要的法律冲突问题或外国法律的适用问题。参见"任天堂案"，《美国联邦法院判例集》第三辑第 589 卷第 1198 页；TS 科技公司案，《美国联邦法院判例集》第三辑第 551 卷第 1319 页；"大众汽车 I 案"，《美国联邦法院判例集》第三辑第 371 卷第 203 页。虽然私人和公共利益因素适用于大多数管辖移交案件，但"这些因素未必是详尽的或唯一的因素"，而且没有哪一个因素能单独决定案件是否移交。参见"大众汽车 II 案"，《美国联邦法院判例集》第三辑第 545 卷第 314—315 页。

本案中，法院已经考虑了这些动议、附有证据的支持声明以及有关情况介绍。双方对于该诉讼本可以在加利福尼亚州北区提起没有争议，法院对此予以明确认可。在确认符合这一条件并权衡了上述公共和私人利益因素后，法院认定苹果公司已经履行了证明加利福尼亚州北区显然比得克萨斯州东区更具便利性的责任。参见"任天堂案"，《美国联邦法院判例集》第三辑第

589 卷第 1194 页，第 1197—1198 页（联邦巡回法院，2009 年）；"基因泰克公司案"，《美国联邦法院判例集》第三辑第 566 卷第 1388—1342 页（联邦巡回法院，2009 年）；"TS 科技公司案"，《美国联邦法院判例集》第三辑第 551 卷第 1315—1319 页（联邦巡回法院，2008 年）；"大众汽车 II 案"，《美国联邦法院判例集》第三辑第 545 卷第 304—315 页（第五巡回法院，2008 年）（全院庭审）。因此，法院特此批准苹果公司的诉讼地转移动议（待审案件目录第 23 号）。

*2 因此，法院裁定将上述案件移交至美国加利福尼亚州北区联邦地区法院。法院书记员应立即采取必要措施以促成案件移交。

于 2014 年 4 月 21 日裁决并签署。

所有引文

在《美国联邦法院判例集》副刊，2014 年 WL 12707246 中未见报道。

United States District Court, S. D. Texas, Brownsville Division.

VIII Uriel MARCUS, et al., Plaintiffs, v. APPLE INC., Defendant.

CIVIL NO.1 : 14-CV-82
Signed 08/21/2014

Attorneys and Law Firms

Omar Weaver Rosales, The Rosales Law Firm, LLC, Harlingen, TX, for Plaintiffs.

David M. Walsh, Kai S. Bartolomeo, Rose S. Lee, Morrison & Foerster LLP, Los Angeles, CA ; Edward Michael Rodriguez, Erin Hudson, Atlas Hall & Rodriguez LLP, Brownsville, TX ; William Michael Mills, Atlas Hall LLP, McAllen, TX ; for Defendant.

ORDER

Hilda Tagle, Senior United States District Judge

*1 BE IT REMEMBERED, that on August 21st, 2014, the Court GRANTED Defendant Apple Inc.'s ("Apple") Motion to Transfer Venue to the U. S. District Court for the Northern District of California. Dkt. No.8.

Plaintiffs brought this lawsuit in the U. S. District Court for the Southern District of Texas, Brownsville Division, alleging violations of the Magnuson-Moss Warranty Act, 15 U. S. C.§ 2310 (d) (1) , and California and Texas's consumer protection statutes. Dkt. No.1. Specifically, Plaintiffs allege that the Logic Board on Apple's MacBook, MacBook Pro, and MacBook Air (collectively

"MacBooks") are made with defective "Logic Boards". Dkt. No.1. Further, Plaintiffs allege that Apple had knowledge of this design defect and failed to warn Plaintiffs or other members of the Class. Dkt. No.1. Apple now seeks to transfer this case from the Southern District of Texas to the Northern District of California pursuant to 28 U. S. C.§ 1404 (a). Dkt. No.8. Plaintiffs do not oppose this motion. Dkt. No.12.

As a preliminary matter, a district court may transfer a civil action "to any other district or division where it might have been brought or to any district or division to which all parties have consented". 28 U. S. C.§ 1404 (a). Here, parties agree in their request to transfer venue. Dkt. Nos.8, 12.

Moreover, this Court finds that Plaintiffs could have originally brought this action in the Northern District of California. Venue is proper in "a judicial district in which any defendant resides, if all defendants are residents of the State in which the district is located". 28 U. S. C.§ 1391 (b) (1). As a defendant, an entity "reside [s] " in "any judicial district in which [it] is subject to the court's personal jurisdiction". Id.§ 1391 (c) (2). Apple maintains its principal place of business and corporate headquarters in Cupertino, California, Dkt. Nos.8, 12, and thus resides in the Northern District of California for the purpose of personal jurisdiction. As Apple is the sole defendant in this case, Dkt. No.8, Plaintiffs could have originally filed this action in the Northern District of California.

Next, Apple has the burden of showing good cause for the transfer. *In re Volkswagen of Am., Inc., 545 F.3d 304, 314 (5th Cir.2008)*. To show good cause, Apple must show that the Northern District of California is "clearly more convenient" than Plaintiffs' original venue choice. Id. at 315. This Court considers private and public interest factors in determining good cause. Id. The private interest factors are " (1) the relative ease of access to sources of proof ; (2) the availability of compulsory process to secure the attendance of witnesses ; (3) the cost of attendance for willing witnesses ; and (4) all other practical problems that make trial of a case easy, expeditious and inexpensive." Id. (quoting *In re Volkswagen AG, 371 F.3d 201, 203 (5th Cir.2004)*). The public interest factors are " (1) the administrative difficulties flowing from court congestion ; (2) the local interest in having localized interests decided at home ; (3) the familiarity of the forum with the law that will govern the case ; and (4) the avoidance of unnecessary problems of conflict of laws [or in] the application of foreign law". Id.

*2 The Court finds that this case should be transferred. The private-interest factors weigh in favor of transfer : the Court finds that most if not all of the sources of proof, including documents and witnesses, are likely located with Apple in Cupertino, California. Dkt. No.8 at 9-10. As witnesses are more likely to be already present in Northern California, the expenses associated with those witnesses will be significantly decreased following a transfer of venue. Dkt. No.8 at 11-12. The relevant public-interest factors also weigh in favor of the transfer. The Northern District of California has a strong connection to and interest in resolving this case, as Apple is based and operates there ; while members of the potential class might come from across the country, not just from the Southern District of Texas. Dkt. No.8 at 14-16.

Based on the foregoing, the Court GRANTS Defendant's Motion to Transfer Venue to the U. S. District Court for the Northern District of California. Dkt. No.8. Therefore, this case is hereby ORDERED to be transferred to the Northern District of California.

All Citations

Not Reported in Fed. Supp., 2014 WL 12770114.

2014 WL 2900129 (S. D. N. Y.) (Trial Pleading)

美国得克萨斯州南部联邦地区法院，布朗斯维尔分院。

8　乌列尔·马库斯等人诉苹果公司

案件编号 1 : 14-W-0082
签署日期 : 2014 年 8 月 21 日

律师及律师事务所

原告代理律师：得克萨斯州哈林根罗萨莱斯律师事务的奥马尔·韦弗·罗萨莱斯。

被告代理律师：加利福尼亚州洛杉矶莫里森福斯特律师事务所的大卫·沃尔什、凯·巴托洛米奥和罗斯·李；得克萨斯州布朗斯维尔市阿特拉斯·霍尔和罗德里格斯律师事务所的爱德华·迈克尔·罗德里格斯和艾琳·哈德森；得克萨斯州麦卡伦阿特拉斯霍尔律师事务所的威廉·迈克尔·米尔斯。

裁定书

希尔达·塔格尔，美国高级地方法官

*1 2014 年 8 月 21 日，法院批准了被告苹果公司的动议，将案件移交给美国加利福尼亚州北区联邦地区法院。（待审案件目录第 8 号）

原告在美国得克萨斯州南区联邦地区法院布朗斯维尔分院提起诉讼，指控被告违反了《美国法典》第 15 卷《马格努森 – 莫斯保修法》第 2310 节第 4 分节第 1 款，以及加利福尼亚州和得克萨斯州的消费者保护法规。（待审案件目录第 1 号）具言之，原告声称苹果公司 MacBook、MacBook Pro 和 MacBook Air（统称为 "MacBook"）上的逻辑电路板存在缺陷。（待审案件目录第 1 号）此外，原告还指控苹果公司明知存在前述设计缺陷，却未对原告或其他消费者作出警示。（待审案件目录第 1 号）苹果公司现在请求根据《美国法典》第 28 卷第 1404 节第 1 分节将本案从得克萨斯州南区法院转移到加

利福尼亚州北区法院。(待审案件目录第 8 号)原告并未反对这一动议。(待审案件目录第 12 号)

作为初步审理事项,联邦地区法院可以将民事诉讼"移交至其他可以审理民事诉讼的地区法院或分支法院,或者移交至所有当事方均认可的地区法院或分支法院"。(《美国法典》第 28 卷第 1404 节第 1 分节)本案中,各方都同意诉讼地转移的请求。(待审案件目录第 8 号、第 12 号)。

此外,法院认为原告原本可以在加利福尼亚州北区提起诉讼。根据《美国法典》第 28 卷第 1391 节第 2 分节第 1 款规定,"如果所有被告都是该地区法院所在州的居民,那么诉讼地应确立在所有被告居住的司法管辖区"。作为被告,实体"设立"在"受法院属人管辖权管辖的司法区"。(《美国法典》第 28 卷第 1391 节第 3 分节第 2 款)苹果公司的主要营业地和公司总部均位于加利福尼亚州库比蒂诺(待审案件目录第 8 号、第 12 号),因此为了适用属人管辖权,应将诉讼地确立在加利福尼亚州北区。由于苹果公司是本案的唯一被告(待审案件目录第 8 号),因此原告原本可以在加利福尼亚州北区提起诉讼。

另,苹果公司有义务证明诉讼地转移的正当理由。[引用"美国大众汽车公司案",《美国联邦法院判例集》第三辑第 545 卷第 304—314 页(第五巡回法院,2008 年)]为了证明理由正当,苹果公司必须证明加利福尼亚州北区"明显"比原告最初选择的诉讼地更方便。(同上,第 315 页)法院判断正当理由时考虑了私人和公共利益因素。私人利益因素包括:"(1)获取证据来源的相对难易度;(2)确保证人出庭的强制程序的可行性;(3)愿意作证的证人的出庭费用;(4)所有其他可以促使案件审判便利、快速和较低成本的实际问题。"[同上,引用"德国大众汽车案",《美国联邦法院判例集》第三辑第 371 卷第 201—203 页(第五巡回法院,2004 年)]公共利益因素主要表现为:"(1)法院案件众多导致的行政管理困难;(2)在国内对当地利益进行裁决涉及的地方利益;(3)法院对管辖案件适用法律的熟悉程度;(4)避免不必要的法律冲突问题或外国法律的适用问题。"(同上)

*2 法院裁定本案应当进行移交。私人利益因素有利于案件移交,大部分证据来源(包括文件和证人)很可能都位于加利福尼亚州库比蒂诺的苹果公司。(待审案件目录第 8 号第 9—10 点)由于证人很可能已经位于加利福尼亚州北区,诉讼地转移后,与这些证人相关的费用将大大减少。(待审案件目录第 8 号第 11—12 点)公共利益因素也有利于案件移交。加利福尼亚州北区与此案有着密切的联系,该地法院也希望解决此案,因为苹果公司的总部和业

务都在加利福尼亚州北区；而潜在的集体成员可能来自全国各地，不仅仅来自得克萨斯州南部地区。（待审案件目录第 8 号第 14—16 点）

基于上述情况，法院批准被告将诉讼地移交至美国加利福尼亚州北区地方法院的动议。（待审案件目录第 8 号）因此，现裁决将本案移交至加利福尼亚州北区。

所有引文

在《联邦判例补编》，2014 年 WL 127701146 中未见报道。

2014 WL 2900129 (S.D.N.Y.) (Trial Pleading)
United States District Court, S. D. New York.

IX CALLSOME SOLUTIONS, INC., Plaintiff, v. GOOGLE, INC., Defendant.

No.14 CV 04639.
June 25, 2014.

Complaint Jury Trial Demanded

Milberg LLP, Todd Kammerman, tkammerman@milberg. com, One Pennsylvania Plaza, 49th Floor, New York, New York 10119-0165, Telephone : (212) 594-5300, for Callsome Solutions, Inc.

Judge Keenan.

Plaintiff, Callsome Solutions, Inc. ("Callsome") , files its Complaint against Defendant, Google, Inc. ("Google") , and alleges the following :

NATURE OF THE CASE

1. This is an action against Google for intentionally misrepresenting to third parties and Callsome that Callsome's Post Call Manager ("PCM") Software Development Kit ("SDK") violated Google's ad policy as set forth in the "Google Play Developer Program Policies".

PARTIES AND JURISDICTION

2. Callsome Solutions, Inc., is a Delaware corporation, with its principal

office located at 839 West End Avenue, #4F, New York, NY 10025.

3. Google, Inc., is a publicly traded Delaware corporation, whose headquarters is located at 1600 Amphitheatre Parkway, Mountain View, CA 94043. Google also maintains an office at 76 Ninth Avenue, 4th Floor, New York, NY 10011.

4. This Court has jurisdiction pursuant to 28 U. S. C.§ 1332 (a) because the parties in this case are citizens of different states and the amount in controversy exceeds $75,000.

5. Venue is properly brought in this Court pursuant to 28 U. S. C.§ 1391.

GOOGLE

6. Google is a globally recognized technology leader that offers products and services to consumers. Although best known for its Google search engine, Google is also known for its Android operating system and its consumer products, which include its Google Nexus tablet, Google Glass and Chromecast.

7. Android is an open-source operating system software that is owned by Google, but is made available to the public for free. This open-source model allows anyone to view, modify and customize the Android operating system. The customizable nature of Android has resulted in manufacturers using it as their operating system in mobile phones, tablets, netbooks, televisions and even game consoles. Developers also use Android to create applications or "apps" for these devices. To begin using Android, a potential developer simply downloads the Android SDK.

8. The popularity of Android is manifest. As of September 2013, over a billion mobile devices had been activated that were running Android.[1] According to Google, "every day another million users power up their Android devices for the first time and start looking for apps, games, and other digital content". See http : //developer. android. com/about/index. html (last visited June 24, 2014).

9. Android users seeking to find, download and use apps, games and other digital content primarily turn to Google's digital entertainment store, Google Play. Google Play is the "premier market place for selling and distributing Android apps". Seehttp : //developer. android. com/about/index. html.

10. Although not the only app store available to Android users, Google utilizes two particularly effective methods to maintain the Google Play as the

premier market place : licensing agreements and user warnings.[2]

11. Most hardware manufacturers who install Android on their devices want the utility, recognition and goodwill associated with Google's apps, such as Maps, Search and YouTube. Accordingly, these manufacturers enter into licensing agreements with Google to preload its apps onto their devices. Google does not allow device manufacturers to pick and choose which Google apps to preload. Rather, under the licensing agreements, the device manufacturers must agree to offer a bundle of Google apps, including Google's Play Store, Gmail, Maps, YouTube and Calendar, among others. Device manufacturers must also agree to set Google's search engine as the default search provider for all web searches. Thus, device manufacturers who want to install Google's apps on their devices must install the Google Play Store.

12. Users who venture beyond Google Play and attempt to download an app or other digital content are confronted with Google's prominent warning that downloading apps from unknown sources could harm the user's device and the user is responsible for any damage caused by downloading apps outside of the Google Play store.

13. Google's actions to maintain the Google Play store as the premier market place for Android apps and digital content has been effective as "Android users download more than 1.5 billion apps and games from Google Play each month". Seehttp : //developer. android. com/about/index. html.

14. Although Google offers the Google Play store to Android users, it is not the primary developer of the over one million apps on its store. Rather, third parties develop the apps. Some of these developers are large corporations, such as Google, but the vast majority are individuals or small startup companies like Callsome. See Amy Cravens, A demographic and business model analysis of today's app developer (2012) (http : //research. gigaom. com/report/a-demographic-and-business-model-analysis-of-todays-app-developer/) (last visited June 24, 2014).

15. Google permits persons to develop and publish apps on the Google Play store by signing up for a developer account and agreeing to Google's "Developer Distribution Agreement" ("Developer Agreement") , a copy of which is attached as Exhibit A. A developer cannot distribute any apps on the Google Play Store without first agreeing to the Developer Agreement. As the Developer Agreement plainly

states, it "forms a legally binding contract" that governs the parties' relationship with respect to distributing apps on the Google Play store.

16. The Developer Agreement places the responsibility on the app developer to upload the app to the Google Play store, disclose all information required by Google to Android users, provide any necessary customer support and adhere to the "Google Play Developer Program Policies" ("Developer Policies"), a copy of which is attached as Exhibit B.

17. The Developer Agreement also includes a product takedown provision that permits Google to remove apps from the Google Play store. This provision, in relevant part, states :

While Google does not undertake an obligation to monitor the Products or their content, if Google is notified by you or otherwise becomes aware and determines in its sole discretion that a Product or any portion thereof or your Brand Features... (g) violates the terms of this Agreement or the Developer Program Policies for Developers...Google may remove the Product from the Market or reclassify the Product at its sole discretion. Google reserves the right to suspend and/or bar any Developer from the Market at its sole discretion.

See Developer Agreement at 17.2.

18. Google's Developer Policies set forth Google's policies with respect to content, promotion and advertising. Relevant to this case is Google's ad policy, which provides :

1. Developer Terms apply to the entire user experience of your app

Please be aware that Google's Developer Distribution Agreement and Developer Program Policies (together, "Developer Terms") apply to each app as well as any ads or third-party libraries bundled or made available through the app. Offer your users a consistent, policy compliant, and well communicated user experience.

Ads are considered part of your app for purposes of content review and compliance with the Developer Terms. Therefore all of the policies referenced above also apply. Please take care to use advertising which does not violate the Developer Terms.

Ads which are inconsistent with the app's content rating also violate our Developer Terms.

2. Ads Context

Ads must not simulate or impersonate the user interface of any app, or notification and warning elements of an operating system. It must be clear to the user which app each ad is associated with or implemented in.

3. Ad Walls and Interstitial Ads

Interstitial ads may only be displayed inside of the app they came with. Forcing the user to click on ads or submit personal information for advertising purposes in order to fully use an app is prohibited. A prominent and accessible target must be made available to users in any interstitial ad so they may dismiss the ad without penalty or inadvertent click-through.

4. Interfering with Apps and Third-Party Ads

Ads associated with your app must not interfere with other apps or their ads.

See Developer Policies at 5-6 (emphasis in original).

19. A developer that agrees to Google's Developer Agreement and Developer Policies may design, develop and publish apps to the Google Play store. This access is very desirable to developers because "Google Play is the premier market place for selling and distributing Android apps. When you publish an app on Google Play, you reach the huge installed base of Android". See http : // developer. android. com/about/index. html.

20. Google also promotes Google Play as being an "open marketplace" that gives developers the control to decide when to publish, who to publish to and what devices to focus on. Google represents to developers that they "can monetize in the way that works best for your business—priced or free, with in-app products or subscriptions—for highest engagement and revenues. You also have complete control of the pricing for your apps and in-app products and can set or change prices in any supported currency at any time". See http : // developer. android. com/about/index. html.

21. If developers want to use ads to monetize their apps, Google offers its Google Mobile Ads SDK which makes use of Google's AdMob, DoubleClick and AdSense publishers. Developers may also choose to use other mobile advertising SDKs, such as StartApp, Flurry, Tapjoy or InMobi.

22. The perceived control with which developers have to publish, promote and monetize their apps is facilitated by the fact that Google does not pre-screen

apps that are published on the Google Play store. Rather, users, developers or other persons may report apps that violate Google's policies. As set forth above, Google also voluntarily monitors apps that are published on the Google Play store for compliance and issues warning notices to developers whose apps it determines violate its Developer Agreement and Developer Policies. Google suspends apps whose developers do not bring their apps into compliance with Google's Developer Agreement or Developer Policies after receiving warning notices.

CALLSOME

23. Callsome is a startup company that designed and developed CallFlakes. CallFlakes is a free app that is offered to users of Android mobile phones and is published on the Google Play store.

24. CallFlakes is a utility app that enhances a user's productivity with respect to two of the most commonly used smartphone activities : telephone calls and text messages. Specifically, after ending a telephone call, CallFlakes opens a productivity board that allows users to call the person back, text the person back, send an email, set a meeting, set a reminder or search the internet for topics related to the call. Similarly, when a text message is received, CallFlakes opens a productivity board that allows the user to respond, call, set a meeting, set a reminder or search the web for topics related to the message. CallFlakes also has the added optional functionality of Facebook caller ID, which allows users to see Facebook friends' posts prior to starting a conversation with the Facebook friend.

25. After releasing CallFlakes, Callsome developed a win-win solution that would benefit app developers and their users alike : Post Call Manager ("PCM").

26. PCM is a "lite" version of CallFlakes that opens a productivity board, like the one in CallFlakes, after the user ends a telephone call.[3] Rather than use Google's search engine to power users' internet searches, PCM used Yahoo search which was powered by Microsoft's Bing search engine. PCM also shows a small banner advertisement along with the productivity board and provides a link that the user can press to see an app wall with other apps the user might be interested, but is not obligated to, in downloading.

27. To implement its win-win solution, Callsome partnered with Interchan, an app developer, and StartApp, a mobile advertising platform.

28. On April 24, 2013, Interchan agreed to integrate the PCM SDK as part of the apps it developed and published. In return for offering the additional functionality to Interchan's users, Callsome received 25% of the advertising revenue that was generated. Interchan used Google's AdMob as the ad server for its apps.

29. StartApp marketed the PCM SDK as an "ad unit" to entice app developers to integrate it into their apps. StartApp informed app developers that PCM would provide their users "an easy way to perform essential tasks once they end a call on their phone. The [PCM] allows users to quickly call back, reply via SMS, send an email, create a calendar event, search the web, and more. The [PCM] SDK is also based on our popular pay-per-download model". See http : // blog. startapp. com/announcing-suite-sdks/ (last visited June 24, 2014). Thus, developers who integrated the PCM SDK into their app provided their users the added functionality of PCM while also monetizing their app.

30. The additional functionality provided by PCM was not clandestinely installed onto users' phones. Rather, after downloading an app that integrated the PCM SDK, users were notified that they could also download PCM. The PCM widget and app would be installed and activated only with the user's acknowledgement and consent. If the user decided not to install PCM, the user would still be able to download the app without consequence.

31. Most users decided to install and retain the benefits offered by PCM. An example of a screenshot a user might see when interacting with PCM after a call is set forth below :

TABLE

32. The productivity board reveals that a user can dismiss it at any time by clicking on the "×" at the top right of the productivity board. The user can uninstall PCM at any time by clicking on "Disable" at the top left of the productivity board. The productivity board plainly notifies the user that the productivity board is powered by the app developer that integrated the PCM SDK into the app that was downloaded by the user. Finally, as noted above, the productivity board shows a small banner ad at the bottom of the screen and permits, but does not require, the user to download other free apps by clicking on the associated icon.

33. On or around April 2013, StartApp and Callsome test launched the PCM SDK.

Callsome offered the PCM SDK to a limited group of developers to gauge developer interest, evaluate the effectiveness of the monetization strategy and fix any software bugs or glitches.

34. Callsome and StartApp officially launched the PCM SDK on September 15, 2013. This method of distribution turned out to be beneficial and popular for Callsome, developers and users alike. By the end of September, Localytics, an analytics company, sent an email to Callsome which said that PCM was third in data points the previous week, just behind Tumblr and iHeart radio.

35. By late November 2013, developers had chosen to integrate the PCM SDK in over 800 apps. By the end of November 2013, less than three (3) months since its official launch, users had downloaded PCM more than 46 million times and logged approximately 1.3 billion user app sessions. Despite having the option to easily uninstall PCM, only a fraction of users chose to do so. Most users used PCM's added functionality on a daily basis to enhance their productivity.

36. The popularity of the PCM SDK among developers and users resulted in Callsome generating a profit from advertising revenue.

37. The growth, popularity and success of the PCM SDK was so tremendous that other companies sought to partner with Callsome to distribute its PCM SDK. Specifically, Callsome began negotiating with Ask Partner Network and Massive Impact to begin distributing the PCM SDK.

GOOGLE'S WARNING NOTICES

38. In November 2013, Google began sending suspension warning notices, via e-mail, to app developers who had integrated the PCM SDK into their apps.

39. Although the PCM SDK works the same no matter what app it is integrated into, Google gave different reasons for why the PCM SDK had to be removed.

40. One developer was told that his app violated section 4.3 of the Developer Agreement because it uploaded users' call logs to a service without informing and obtaining user consent. Google informed this developer that the app could be reinstated if it was brought into compliance with section 4.3 of the Developer Agreement. Subsequently, Google informed the developer that it would reinstate

the app if the developer removed "net. mz. callflakessdk". This is the PCM SDK. This reason was false because the PCM SDK does not upload or otherwise track users' call logs.

41. Other developers were told that their apps violated the ad policy in Google's Developer Policies : [4]

REASON FOR WARNING : Violation of the Ad-Policy :

• Ads associated with your app must not interfere with other apps or their ads.

After a regular review, we have determined that your app contains ad functionality which disrupts or interferes with the usage of other apps or their ads. This is in violation of the policy provision cited above.

Your application will be removed if you do not make modifications to bring it into compliance within 7 days of the issuance of this notification. If you have additional applications in your catalog, please also review them for compliance.

All violations are tracked. Serious or repeated violations of any nature will result in the termination of your developer account, and investigation and possible termination of related Google accounts. If your account is terminated, payments will cease and Google may recover the proceeds of any past sales and the cost of any associated fees (such as chargebacks and payment transaction fees) from you.

Before uploading or publishing any new applications, please review the Developer Distribution Agreement and Content Policy.

The Google Play Team

42. After receiving the suspension notices from Google, most of the app developers that integrated the PCM SDK into their apps removed it. The app developers who integrated the PCM SDK were primarily individuals or small startups and could not afford to have their apps suspended for even one day. Further, because Google tracks all violations of its Developer Agreement and Developer Policies, these developers cannot risk having their developer accounts terminated.

43. Accordingly, when Google sent the suspension notices, the developers who integrated the PCM SDK removed the PCM SDK from their apps and pushed the update to their users. Most Android users choose to have their apps update automatically and, consequently, once they received the update, PCM was removed from their phones. The developers did this to avoid suspension and future adverse action from Google.

44. As a result of Google's suspension notices, the download rate for PCM dropped by over 50% in December 2013, to approximately 9 million downloads from approximately 20 million downloads in November 2013. The download rate continued to drastically decrease to 4.7 million downloads in January 2014 and 2.3 million in February 2014.

45. Several developers contacted StartApp after receiving the suspension notices from Google. StartApp and Callsome then began investigating the basis of Google's suspension notices.

46. Following the issuance of these suspension notices, Callsome attempted to contact Google through its appeal and customer support process, as well as through individuals who worked for Google. There was never a response to these attempts. Subsequently, on December 6, 2013, Zach Sivan, Callsome's Director and co-founder, contacted Matthew Bye at Google to ask why app developers that implemented the PCM SDK received suspension notices. Mr. Sivan told Mr. Bye that the app developers "removed our program from their apps and the distributors of this program have ceased all distribution activities which basically stopped our business going forward completely". Mr. Sivan also informed Mr. Bye that " [m] ost of app developers [sic] are removing our program from their apps and none of the distributors we engaged is [sic] willing to take a risk and distribute an app that get such suspension notice [sic] from Google Play".

47. Having not received a response, Mr. Sivan contacted Mr. Bye again on December 12, 2013. Mr. Bye subsequently referred Mr. Sivan's concerns to Geoff Griffith, Google's senior counsel.

48. On December 18, 2013, Mr. Sivan wrote Mr. Griffith to determine why Google was sending suspension notices to app developers, providing examples of apps that were suspended.

49. On December 21, 2013, Mr. Griffith responded that the apps had not been suspended, but "received warnings for their implementation of another

SDK, Start App Post Call Manager..." On the same date, Mr. Sivan responded, informing Mr. Griffith that :

The StartApp Post Call Manager is a reduced version of CallFlakes promoted by our partner Start app to the developers I mentioned.

I will be happy to learn how this post call manager is violating the Google policy so we can make sure implementation is done in the right way.

None of our partners are willing to move ahead with CallFlakes until we can point out the problem with the post call manager.

50. On January 10, 2014, Mr. Griffith contacted Mr. Sivan, seeking clarification and additional information :

Hi Zach,

Sorry for the delay. It has taken me longer than expected to gather the information needed to respond, due to staff absences on holidays.

I am consulting with our removals team further about this case and should be able to respond early next week.

In the meantime, I'd like to confirm what we are discussing here : my understanding is that the third party apps that received warnings have implemented an SDK, PostCall Manager (PCM) developed by another third party, StartApp. You have said that StartApp is a partner of your business that markets PCM as a reduced version of your product CallFlakes. Can you provide more information on StartApp and its relation to your business ?

Thanks,

Geoff

51. On January 10, 2014, Mr. Sivan responded to Mr. Griffith's email, informing him that "PCM is a product developed by [Callsome] and it is a light version of CallFlakes. Startapp is a mobile advertising network who distribute our PCM SDK to their community of app developers".

52. On January 13, 2014, Mr. Griffith proffered the following explanation for the suspension notices :

Hi Zach,

Thanks for the information.

PCM is an SDK that can be implemented in a third party app to provide optional post-call functionality to the app if the user agrees to add it. However, PCM is marketed as an "ad unit" to developers (e. g. on the website here) to help monetize their apps. It also includes promotional content in the form of links to third party apps in the post-call screen. PCM as a whole is therefore considered an advertising service that has been added to an app, rather than being a Play store app itself. As such, PCM (and apps that implement it) are subject to our ad policy. That policy contains the restrictions below:

• Ads may not interfere with other apps and their apps. For the PCM ad unit implementation to be compliant, it must display itself inside of the app it came with. Today, it alters the functioning of the Phone app and the browser on the user's device. Policy provision:

• Interfering with Apps and Third-party Ads

Ads associated with your app must not interfere with other apps or their ads.

• The implementation is an interstitial ad service, since it contains commercial links to third party apps, is full screen and must be dismissed by the user before the user can use the default contacts/phone UI after a phone call.Policy provision:

• Ad Walls and Interstitial Ads

Interstitial ads may only be displayed inside of the app they came with.

This is why the apps implementing PCM received warnings.

Kind regards,

Geoff

53. Despite recognizing that PCM provided additional functionality to a user's mobile phone, Google took the position that PCM was an advertising service because it was marketed as an "ad unit". This position effectively precluded Callsome from distributing its PCM SDK to app developers and destroyed Callsome's business.

54. Callsome forwarded Mr. Griffith's e-mail to StartApp, who provided the following response:

We have learned this answer internally and it is our understanding that the post call manager cannot be distributed as an SDK to app developers through an ad funded model. Therefore, given the distribution cost involved, we will not be able to continue and distribute the Post Call Manager if it can't include an ad to support the business model.

I am really sorry that this is where things stand. As you know, we really liked your product and so did our app developers but we cannot distribute anything that is considered by Google as a violation of its ad policy.

55. In light of Google's position that the PCM SDK violated its ad policy, StartApp advised the developers who had integrated the PCM SDK to remove it from their apps.

56. Google's reasons for claiming the PCM SDK violated its ad policy were false.

57. PCM is not an "ad unit." PCM, as Google itself admitted, provides post-call functionality to users who agree to download it. All users who downloaded an app integrated with the PCM SDK were explicitly notified and agreed to download PCM. Thus, users agreed to download the additional functionality provided by PCM. The ads users see when using PCM are wholly contained within PCM and not outside of the app. In fact, the ads contained within PCM only take up about 1/16th of the user's screen. Consequently, PCM is neither an ad unit nor displays ads outside of PCM.

58. The PCM SDK does not alter the phone app or the user's web browser. PCM only appears after a call has ended and can easily be dismissed by the user. PCM does not interfere with the user's ability to use or interact with the phone app. PCM also does not change or alter the settings on the user's browser. Although users may enter searches after a phone call has ended, in a search box powered by Yahoo (not Google) contained within PCM, it does not change any of the settings contained on the phone's browser.

59. PCM is not an ad service and, as implemented, does not display interstitial ads.[5] As set forth above, Google's characterization of PCM as an ad unit or ad service is false because PCM provides additional functionality to increase productivity, which the user is expressly notified of and agrees to. In fact, 90% of the time users used the productivity features offered by PCM. Users only clicked the in-app ads 10% of the time, further demonstrating that users did not consider

PCM to be an ad unit or ad service. Accordingly, PCM's implementation and use of ads is consistent with Google's ad policy.

60. Google falsely told Callsome, StartApp and developers implementing the PCM SDK that they were not compliant with Google's Developer Agreement or Developer Policies.

61. Google's false statements to app developers who integrated the PCM SDK caused them to abandon and stop using the PCM SDK. The app developers were compelled to stop integrating the PCM SDK because their success is predicated on being able to publish apps on the Google Play store, the premiere Android marketplace. Simply put, app developers cannot afford to be suspended or banned from the Google Play store, even if the reason given by Google is false.

62. Google's false statements caused StartApp to stop offering the PCM SDK to app developers and affirmatively advise app developers that they should remove it from their apps. StartApp was compelled to stop offering the PCM SDK because its success as a mobile advertising platform is dependent on being able to offer app developers monetization solutions that comply with Google's Developer Policies so the app developers can publish on the Google Play store, the premiere Android marketplace. Simply put, StartApp cannot afford to offer monetization solutions that will result in app developers being warned or suspended by Google, even if the basis for the warning or suspension is false.

63. After StartApp stopped offering the PCM SDK, Interchan decided that it would no longer integrate the PCM SDK into any of the new apps it was developing and would be releasing. Rather than remove the PCM SDK from its existing apps, Interchan simply left it integrated into the apps knowing that it would stop supporting and promoting these apps after releasing its new apps.

64. Google's false statements have materially harmed Callsome. StartApp and app developers have terminated their relationship with Callsome as a result of Google's false statements. Google's false statements have greatly diminished Callsome's ability to earn income from Interchan and have otherwise foreclosed its ability to earn any income from its PCM SDK with StartApp even though it is fully compliant with Google's Developer Agreement and Developer Policies. Callsome's relationships with third parties that wanted to offer the PCM SDK to app developers have also been terminated. Google's false statements have practically destroyed Callsome's business.

65. Google's false statements have assured that Callsome can no longer develop, distribute, market or receive any benefit from its fully compliant PCM SDK, which was beneficial to users and profitable for Callsome.

COUNT I—TORTIOUS INTERFERENCE WITH CALLSOME'S CONTRACT WITH STARTAPP

66. Callsome re-alleges paragraphs 1-65 as if fully set forth herein.

67. On March 18, 2013, Callsome entered into a contract with StartApp to develop and deliver the PCM SDK in return for StartApp offering the PCM SDK "as a new monetization solution for mobile applications developers". As amended on August 1, 2013, Callsome and StartApp's contract would have expired on July 31, 2015, with automatic 24 month extensions unless either party provided written notice of its desire to terminate.

68. Callsome delivered the PCM SDK to StartApp and StartApp offered it to its developers. As set forth above, the PCM SDK was very popular amongst StartApp's developers with over 200 developers implementing the PCM SDK in 1902 apps.

69. By virtue of Mr. Sivan's e-mail dated December 21, 2013, and Mr. Griffith's e-mail dated January 10, 2014, Google knew that Callsome had a contractual relationship with StartApp to distribute the PCM SDK.

70. Google falsely informed Callsome, StartApp and developers that the PCM SDK violated its ad policy. Google knew that StartApp would not continue offering the PCM SDK if it violated Google's ad policy. Google also knew that Callsome could not bring the PCM SDK into compliance based on the false reasons it gave and the manner in which the PCM SDK was being distributed.

71. Upon learning that Google believed the PCM SDK was an advertising service that violated its ad policy, StartApp terminated its contract with Callsome.

72. Google's tortious conduct has resulted in Callsome's inability to market, sell or otherwise profit from the PCM SDK as no advertiser, advertising service, advertising platform or developer will distribute or integrate an app or SDK that Google claims violates its Developer Agreement or Developer Policies.

73. Wherefore, Callsome requests judgment be entered against Google for compensatory damages, punitive damages and any such further and other relief

the Court deems proper.

COUNT II – TORTIOUS INTERFERENCE WITH CALLSOME'S CONTRACTS WITH APP DEVELOPERS

74. Callsome re-alleges paragraph 1-65 as if fully set forth herein.

75. On September 15, 2013, Callsome and StartApp began offering the PCM SDK to developers.

76. During the short period that the PCM SDK was offered, 247 developers integrated the PCM SDK into over 1900 apps. Some of these developers include Wait What and Nikhil Kulria.

77. By integrating the PCM SDK into the apps they developed and offered on the Google Play store, the developers were paid every time a user downloaded PCM along with their app. Developers who integrated the PCM SDK into their apps were not bound to continue using it and could decide to use a different SDK offered by Start app or any other competitor at any time.

78. Google knows which developers use its advertising SDKs as such developers must sign up to use these SDKs. In testing or reviewing the developers' apps who integrated the PCM SDK for compliance with the Developer Agreement or Developer Policies, Google knew that these developers were not using Google's advertising SDKs, but were using a competing advertising SDK, in this case StartApp. Google sent these developers suspension notices.

79. The developers who integrated the PCM SDK removed the PCM SDK after receiving suspension warning notices from Google. But for these suspension notices, the developers would have continued using the PCM SDK.

80. Google's suspension notices informed the developers who integrated the PCM SDK into their apps that the PCM SDK violated Google's ad policy or uploaded users' call logs without notifying and obtaining user consent. As set forth above, these reasons were knowingly false because the PCM SDK does not violate Google's ad policy or upload users' call logs.

81. The developers who received these suspension notices were compelled to remove the PCM SDK from their apps because their success is contingent on being able to offer their apps on the Google Play store and maintain good standing with Google as a developer. These developers simply cannot afford to have Google

suspend their apps and, as a result, simply capitulate when Google asserts their apps violate Google's policies.

82. In fact, once it became clear Callsome could not bring the PCM SDK into compliance with Google's purported ad policy violation, StartApp e-mailed all of the developers who integrated the PCM SDK to remove it. StartApp was required to take this action to maintain credibility with its developers and because StartApp's success is contingent on being able to offer developers SDKs that are compliant with Google's Developer Agreement and Developer Policies.

83. Google's tortious conduct has resulted in Callsome's inability to market, sell or otherwise profit from the PCM SDK as no advertiser, advertising service, advertising platform or developer will distribute or integrate an app or SDK that Google claims violates its Developer Agreement or Developer Policies.

84. Wherefore, Callsome requests judgment be entered against Google for compensatory damages, punitive damages and any such further and other relief the Court deems proper.

COUNT III-TORTIOUS INTERFERENCE WITH CALLSOME'S PROSPECTIVE RELATIONSHIP WITH ASK PARTNER NETWORK AND MASSIVE IMPACT

85. Callsome re-alleges paragraphs 1-65 as if fully set forth herein.

86. On September 15, 2013, Callsome and StartApp began offering the PCM SDK to developers.

87. During the short period that the PCM SDK was offered, 247 developers integrated the PCM SDK into over 1900 apps. Some of these developers included Escape Mobile, Wait What and Nikhil Kulria.

88. As a result of the PCM SDK's popularity, Callsome began negotiating with Ask Partner Network and Massive Impact to distribute its PCM SDK.

89. Callsome had an agreement in principle with Ask Partner Network to distribute the PCM SDK to app developers.

90. Callsome was also negotiating with Massive Impact to distribute its PCM SDK.

91. In November 2013, Google began sending suspension notices to developers that had integrated the PCM SDK.

92. Ask Partner Network learned that StartApp removed the PCM SDK from

its site and was notifying its developers to remove the PCM SDK from their apps. Accordingly, Ask Partner Network contacted Callsome to determine why the PCM SDK was not compliant with Google's policies.

93. As set forth above, Callsome contacted Google to obtain an explanation for the suspension warning notices.

94. In the numerous e-mails sent to obtain an explanation, Callsome informed Google that " [m] ost of app developers [sic] are removing our program from their apps and none of the distributors we engaged is [sic] willing to take a risk and distribute an app that get such suspension notice [sic] from Google Play". Callsome also told Google that since it began sending suspension warning notices that "all our distributors stopped working with us, an investment deal that was about to sign [sic] has been backed off and basically there is a huge decline in download rate". Thus, Callsome informed Google that the distributors Callsome had engaged had stopped working with it due to Google's suspension warning notices.

95. As set forth above, Google falsely told Mr. Sivan that the PCM SDK was an ad unit and advertising service that did not comply with Google's ad policy. Callsome relayed Google's response to Ask Partner Network and Massive Impact. Both subsequently declined to work any further with Callsome.

96. Google's tortious conduct terminated the potential contractual relationships Callsome was negotiating with Ask Partner Network and Massive Impact. Despite knowing of these relationships, Google falsely stated that the PCM SDK was not compliant with its ad policy. Google's tortious actions have resulted in Callsome's inability to market, sell or otherwise profit from the PCM SDK as no advertiser, advertising service, advertising platform or developer will distribute or integrate an app or SDK that Google claims violates its Developer Agreement or Developer Policies.

97. Wherefore, Callsome requests judgment be entered against Google for compensatory damages, punitive damages and any such further and other relief the Court deems proper.

COUNT IV-TRADE LIBEL

98. Callsome re-alleges paragraphs 1-65 as if fully set forth herein.

99. Google told app developers, StartApp and Callsome that apps which integrated the PCM SDK violated its Developer Policies.

100. Contrary to Google's statements, the PCM SDK is fully compliant with Google's Developer Policies.

101. Google's false statements of non-compliance were intended to prevent app developers from integrating the PCM SDK into their apps.

102. Google's false statements of non-compliance resulted in app developers and StartApp terminating their relationships with Callsome.

103. Google's false statements of non-compliance resulted in Interchan deciding not to integrate the PCM SDK into any of the new apps it offered.

104. As a result of Google's false statements, Callsome has suffered the following damages :

a.$32,700,000 in estimated lost advertising revenue from StartApp abandoning the PCM SDK and being forced to stop offering the PCM SDK to app developers ;

b.$19,525,000 in estimated lost advertising revenue from Ask Partner Network who refused to contract with Callsome after learning of Google's suspension notices ;

c.$19,525,000 in estimated lost advertising revenue from Massive Impact who refused to contract with Callsome after learning of Google's suspension notices ; and

d. Attorney's fees and costs.

105. Wherefore, Callsome requests judgment be entered against Google for compensatory damages, punitive damages and any such further and other relief the Court deems proper.

Dated : June 25, 2014

Respectfully submitted,

MILBERG LLP

By : <<signature>>

Todd Kammermah

tkammerman@milberg. com

One Pennsylvania Plaza

49th Floor

New York, New York 10119-0165

Telephone : (212) 594-5300

Attorneys for Callsome Solutions, Inc.

Appendix not available.

Footnotes

1 See https : //www. sec. gov/Archives/edgar/data/1288776/000128877614 000020/goog2013123110-k. htm #sD639E991EBB55393BBAF2E71A87E5ECB.

2 Google Play is not the only app store available for Android devices as Amazon and Samsung, among others, offer app stores.

3 PCM is a lite or reduced version of CallFlakes because it does not open the productivity board after a text message is received or offer the Facebook caller ID functionality.

4 Inconsistently, not every app developer received a suspension warning notice from Google. For example, Interchan, which was using Google's AdMob ad server, never received warning notices from Google.

5 Interstitial ads are full screen ads that a user can close with a close button. Seehttps : //support. google. com/webdesigner/answer/32504157hHen (last visited May 2014).

美国纽约南区联邦地区法院。

9　CALLSOME SOLUTIONS 公司诉谷歌公司

案件编号：民诉 14 号 04639
签署日期：2014 年 6 月 25 日

申诉要求陪审团审判

　　原告代理律师：托德·卡默曼，米尔贝格律师事务所，邮箱：tkammerman@milberg. com，地址：纽约宾夕法尼亚广场一号 49 楼，邮编：NY 10119–0165，电话：（212）594–5300。

　　基南法官。

　　原告 Callsome Solutions,Inc.(以下简称"Callsome")对被告 Google,Inc.(以下简称"谷歌"）提起诉讼，并指控如下：

案件性质

　　1. 本次诉讼针对谷歌提起，因为谷歌故意向第三方和 Callsome 作出误述，声称 Callsome 的呼叫后管理器（"PCM"）的软件开发工具包（"SDK"）违反了《谷歌商城开发者程序政策》以下简称《开发者政策》中规定的谷歌广告政策。

当事人和司法管辖权

　　2. Callsome 是一家特拉华州的公司，其总部位于纽约西区大街 839 号 4 号楼 F 座，邮箱：NY 10025。

　　3. 谷歌是一家特拉华州的上市公司，其总部位于加利福尼亚州山景城剧场路 1600 号,邮编:CA94043。谷歌在纽约第九大道 4 楼 76 号同样设有办事处,邮编：NY 10011。

4. 根据《美国法典》第 28 卷第 1332（a）节，由于案件当事方是来自不同州的居民，且争议金额超过 75000 美元，本院对本案具有管辖权。

5. 根据《美国法典》第 28 卷第 1391 节，本法院审慎选择了诉讼地。

谷歌

6. 谷歌是全球公认的向消费者提供产品和服务的技术领域领军企业。虽然谷歌最著名的是其谷歌搜索引擎，但该公司也以其安卓操作系统和包括谷歌 Nexus 平板电脑、谷歌眼镜和谷歌电视棒 [①] 在内的消费产品而闻名。

7. 安卓是谷歌旗下一款免费向公众开放的开源操作系统的软件，这种开源模式使得所有人都可以访问、修改和定制安卓操作系统。由于安卓系统具有可定制性，制造商将其用于手机、平板电脑、上网本、电视机，甚至游戏机的操作系统中。开发者也使用安卓系统为以上这些设备创建应用程序（"apps"）。用户只需下载安卓工具包，即可使用安卓系统。

8. 安卓系统的普及显而易见。截至 2013 年 9 月，已累计激活了超过 10 亿台运行安卓系统的移动设备。[1]据谷歌称："每天都有数百万用户首次启动安卓设备，并开始搜索应用、游戏和其他数字信息。"（详见 http：//developer. android. com/about/index. html，最后一次访问：2014 年 6 月 24 日）

9. 安卓用户可以使用谷歌的数字娱乐商店，即谷歌商城，来搜索、下载和使用应用程序、游戏和其他数字信息。谷歌商城是"销售和分销安卓应用程序的主要市场"。（详见 http：//developer. android. com/about/index. html）

10. 虽然谷歌并不是安卓用户唯一可用的应用程序商店，但它利用两种特别有效的方法保住了谷歌商城作为主要市场的地位：特许权协议和用户警告。[2]

11. 大多数在设备上安装安卓系统的硬件制造商都希望能够获得谷歌应用程序（如地图、搜索引擎和 YouTube 视频网站）所带来的实用性、认可度和好口碑。这些制造商会与谷歌签订特许权协议，以在其设备上预装谷歌的应用程序。谷歌不允许设备制造商自行选择预装哪些谷歌应用程序。相反，根据特许权协议，设备制造商必须同意提供绑定的谷歌应用程序，包括谷歌商城、谷歌邮箱、地图、YouTube 视频网站和日历等。设备制造商还必须同意将谷歌的搜索引擎设置为所有网络搜索的默认搜索引擎。因此，设备制造商如果想在设备上安装谷歌的应用程序，则必须安装谷歌商城。

---

① 译者注：谷歌电视棒指迷你电视投影配件。

12. 用户如果想在谷歌商城之外下载应用程序或其他数字信息，将面临谷歌的特别警告，提醒他们从未知来源下载应用程序可能会损害用户的设备，在谷歌商城之外下载应用程序所造成的任何损害需用户自行负责。

13. 从"安卓用户每月从谷歌商城下载了超过 15 亿个应用程序和游戏"这一数据中可以看出，谷歌为维护谷歌商城作为安卓应用程序和数字信息主要市场的地位而采取的措施是行之有效的。（详见 http：//developer. android. com/about/index. html）

14. 虽然谷歌向安卓用户提供了谷歌商城，但它并非谷歌商城上 100 多万个应用程序的主要开发者。事实上，这些应用程序均由第三方开发。这些开发者中有些是类似谷歌的大公司，但绝大多数是类似 Callsome 的个人或小型初创公司。（详见艾米·克雷文斯：《现今应用程序开发者人口结构和商业模式分析》，2012，http：//research. gigaom. com/report/a-demographic-and-business-model-analysis-of-todays-app-developer/，最后访问时间：2014 年 6 月 24 日）

15. 谷歌允许个人通过注册开发者账户并同意谷歌的《开发者分销协议》（以下简称《开发者协议》，该协议的副本见附件 A），在谷歌商城上开发和发布应用程序。在未同意《开发者协议》之前，开发者不得在谷歌商城发布任何应用程序。《开发者协议》中明确指出，该协议"形成了一份具有法律约束力的合同"，约束各方关于在谷歌商城发布应用程序的关系。

16. 《开发者协议》规定，应用程序开发者有责任将应用程序上传到谷歌商城，向安卓用户披露谷歌所要求的全部信息，提供所有必要的客户支持，并遵守《开发者政策》（该政策副本见附件 B[①]）

17. 《开发者协议》还包括一项产品下架条款，该条款允许谷歌从谷歌商城中下架应用程序。该条款在相关部分中声明：

> 虽然谷歌不承担监控产品本身或产品内容的义务，但如果谷歌接到通知，或以其他方式知悉某产品或该产品任一部分或品牌特色……（g）违反了本协议的条款或针对开发者的《开发者程序政策》……谷歌可自行决定将该产品从谷歌商城中下架或重新分类。谷歌保留自行决定暂停和 / 或禁止任何开发者进入谷歌商城的权利。（详见《开发者协议》第 17.2 条）

18. 谷歌的《开发者政策》规定了谷歌关于内容、推广和广告方面的政策。与本案相关的是谷歌的广告政策，其中规定：

---

① 译者注：附件 B 因属于案件判决之外的附加材料，所以此处译者既未翻译也没有附加该材料。

（1）开发者条款适用于应用程序的全部用户体验过程

请注意，谷歌的《开发者分销协议》和《开发者程序政策》（合称"开发者条款"）适用于所有应用程序以及通过应用程序绑定或提供的全部广告或第三方平台。可为用户提供始终如一的、符合政策的和具备良好沟通性的体验。

为了完成内容审查和遵守"开发者条款"，广告同样被视为应用程序的一部分。因此，上述所有政策均适用。请注意使用不违反"开发者条款"的广告。

与应用程序内容评级不一致的广告同样违反我方的"开发者条款"。

（2）广告语境

广告不得模仿或模拟其他应用程序的用户界面，或操作系统的通知和操作系统的提醒要素。用户必须清楚地知道每个广告与哪个应用相关或在哪个应用中运行。

（3）广告墙和插播广告

插播广告只能在其自带的应用程序内显示。禁止以广告为目的强迫用户点击广告或者强迫用户在提交个人信息后才能完整使用应用程序。所有插播广告必须向用户提供显眼且可点击的标识，从而使用户可以在不受任何损失的情况下关闭广告，或避免用户无意点击。

（4）干扰应用程序和第三方广告

与应用程序相关的广告不得干扰其他应用程序或其广告。

［详见《开发者政策》第5—6页（原版］

19. 所有同意谷歌的《开发者协议》和《开发者政策》的开发者都可以在谷歌商城中设计、开发并发布应用程序。这种权限吸引了许多开发者，因为"谷歌商城是销售和分销安卓应用程序的主要市场。只要在谷歌商城上发布应用程序，就能接触到安卓背后巨大的安装基量"。（详见 http：// developer. android. com/about/index. html。）

20. 谷歌还将谷歌商城推广为一个"开放市场"，开发者有权决定何时发布、向谁发布以及重点发布于哪些设备。谷歌向开发者表示，他们"可以用最适合业务发展的方式来盈利——无论是收费还是免费，无论是通过应用程序内部产品还是订阅——以获得最高的参与度和收入。同时，开发者对于应用程序和应用程序内产品的定价，以及何时设置或更改价格（只要是支持的货币形式）都享有绝对的自由"。（详见 http：// developer. android. com/about/

index. html）

21. 如果开发者想通过广告来为自己的应用程序盈利，谷歌提供了谷歌移动广告工具包，该工具包包含谷歌的 AdMob、DoubleClick 和 AdSense 等发布商。开发者也可以选择使用其他移动广告工具包，如 StartApp、Flurry、Tapjoy 或 InMobi。

22. 由于谷歌不会预先筛选发布在谷歌商城中的应用程序，因此，开发者能够更好地控制应用程序的发布、推广和盈利。但是，用户、开发者或其他人员可以举报违反谷歌政策的应用程序。如上所述，谷歌也会主动监控在谷歌商城上发布的应用程序是否符合规定，并向其认定的违反其《开发者协议》和《开发者政策》的应用程序开发者发出警告通知。如果开发者在收到警告通知后仍然没有调整应用程序使其符合谷歌的《开发者协议》或《开发者政策》，谷歌将暂停该应用程序的使用。

CALLSOME

23. Callsome 是一家负责设计和开发 CallFlakes 的初创公司。CallFlakes 是一款发布于谷歌商城中面向安卓手机用户的免费应用。

24. CallFlakes 是一款实用的应用程序，可以提高用户在打电话和发短信这两项最常用的智能手机活动方面的工作效率。具体而言，结束通话后，CallFlakes 会开启任务面板，允许用户给对方回电话、回短信、发送电子邮件、安排会面、设置提醒或在互联网上搜索与通话内容相关的主题。同样，收到短信后，CallFlakes 也会开启任务面板，允许用户回复、打电话、安排会面、设置提醒或在网上搜索与信息内容相关的主题。CallFlakes 还增加了可选择的脸书来电显示功能，用户在与脸书好友开始对话之前，可以看到脸书好友的帖子。

25. 在发布 CallFlakes 之后，Callsome 公司制定了一个双赢方案，能同时兼顾应用开发者和用户的利益，这一方案就是呼叫后管理器（"PCM"）。

26. PCM 是"精简版"的 CallFlakes。与 CallFlakes 一样，用户结束电话通话后，该程序会开启任务面板。[3] 但 PCM 没有使用谷歌的搜索引擎来帮助用户进行互联网搜索，而是使用了由微软必应搜索引擎提供技术支持的雅虎搜索。同时，PCM 还在任务面板上设置了一个小横幅广告，并附上了链接，点击链接后可以看到一个应用墙，上面有用户可能感兴趣但还未下载的其他应用程序。

27. 为了实施双赢方案，Callsome 与应用开发商 Interchan 和移动广告平台 StartApp 合作。

28. 2013 年 4 月 24 日，Interchan 同意将 PCM SDK 集成到其开发和发布的应用程序上。作为向 Interchan 的用户提供额外功能的回报，Callsome 获得了广告收入的 25%。Interchan 使用谷歌的 AdMob 作为其应用程序的广告服务器。

29. StartApp 将 PCM SDK 作为"广告单元"进行销售，以吸引应用程序开发者将其嵌套到应用程序中。StartApp 会告知应用开发者，PCM 将为用户提供"一种在结束通话之后执行基本任务的简便方法。PCM 允许用户快速回拨电话、回复短信、发送电子邮件、创建日历事件、搜索网络等。PCM SDK 实行的付费模式也是现在流行的按次付费下载模式。"（详见 http：// blog. startapp. com/announcing–suite–sdks，最后访问时间：2014 年 6 月 24 日）因此，开发者将 PCM SDK 嵌套到应用程序中，既能为用户提供 PCM 的附加功能，也能使应用程序盈利。

30. PCM 提供的附加功能并非秘密地被安装到用户手机上。恰恰相反，下载嵌套了 PCM SDK 的应用程序后，用户会收到通知，告知他们也可以下载 PCM。用户只有在确认和同意后，才能安装和激活 PCM 的小工具和应用程序。如果用户不愿安装 PCM，仍然可以不受任何影响地下载该应用程序。

31. 大多数用户都会选择安装 PCM 以便享受其带来的便捷（原判决中在此处列举了用户在通话结束后与 PCM 交互时可能看到的屏幕截图）。

示例（内容略）

32. 任务面板显示,用户可以随时点击任务面板右上方的"×"将其关闭。用户也可以随时点击任务面板左上方的"停用"来卸载 PCM。任务面板会明确地告知用户其运行是通过开发人员将 PCM SDK 集成到用户下载的应用程序中。最后，如上所述，任务面板在屏幕底部设置有一个小横幅广告，并允许（不强制要求）用户通过点击相关图标下载其他免费应用程序。

33. 2013 年 4 月前后,StartApp 和 Callsome 测试推出了 PCM SDK 测试版。Callsome 仅向少数开发者提供 PCM SDK，以评估开发者对该产品的兴趣和盈利战略的效率，并修复软件错误或故障。

34. 2013 年 9 月 15 日,Callsome 和 StartApp 正式推出 PCM SDK。事实证明，这种发布方式无论是对 Callsome、开发者还是用户都大有益处，因此广受欢迎。到了 9 月底，分析公司 Localytics 给 Callsome 发了一封邮件，邮件中说，PCM 在上一周的数据点中排名第三，仅次于 Tumblr 和 iHeart radio。

35. 在 2013 年 11 月底前，开发者决定在 800 多个应用程序中嵌套 PCM SDK。截至 2013 年 11 月底，也就是 PCM 正式推出后不到 3 个月的时间内，用户下载 PCM 的次数已超过 4 600 万次，系统记录了约 13 亿次用户应用程序会话。尽管用户可以自行选择卸载 PCM，但只有一小部分用户最后选择了卸载。大多数用户为了提升工作效率，每天都在使用 PCM 的新增功能。

36. PCM SDK 在开发者和用户中的大受欢迎，为 Callsome 在广告收入方面创造了丰厚利润。

37. PCM SDK 的增长、普及和成功广为人知，其他公司也试图与 Callsome 合作并从 PCM SDK 中分一杯羹。具体而言，Callsome 开始与 Ask Partner Network 和 Massive Impact 谈判，着手准备分销 PCM SDK 的业务。

谷歌的警告通知

38. 2013 年 11 月，谷歌开始通过电子邮件向嵌套 PCM SDK 的应用程序开发者发送暂停使用的警告通知。

39. 虽然 PCM SDK 无论嵌套到何种应用程序中工作原理都是一样的，但是谷歌仍就下架 PCM SDK 一事给出许多理由。

40. 一名开发者收到通知称，他的应用程序违反了《开发者协议》第 4.3 节规定，因为该程序在没有通知用户并征得用户同意的情况下，将用户的通话记录上传到服务器中。谷歌告知这名开发者，如果该应用程序符合《开发者协议》第 4.3 节规定就可以恢复使用。此外，谷歌还表示只有开发者删除"net. mz. callflakessdk"（即 PCM SDK），该应用程序才可恢复使用。这个理由毫无根据，因为 PCM SDK 并未上传或以其他任何方式追踪用户的通话记录。

41. 其他开发者则收到如下通知称，他们的应用程序违反了谷歌《开发者政策》中的广告政策：[4]

警告理由：违反广告政策

• 与应用程序相关的广告不得干扰其他应用程序或其广告。

经过定期审查，可以确定贵方的应用程序所包含的广告功能会干扰或妨碍其他应用程序或其广告的使用，这违反了上述政策规定。

如果贵方在本通知发出后 7 天内未进行修改，使其符合规定，我方将下架贵方的应用程序。如果您的产品目录中还有其他的应用程序，请一并审查它们是否符合规定。

我方会追踪所有的违规行为。任何性质严重或重复的违规行为都将导致您的开发者账户终止。我方还将对相关的谷歌账户进行调查，并最终可能终止您的谷歌账户。一旦账户终止，付款也将停止，并且谷歌可能收回过去销售所产生的收益和相关费用（如退单拒付和支付交易费用）。

上传或发布新应用程序之前，请查看《开发者分销协议》和《内容政策》。

谷歌商城团队

42. 收到谷歌方的暂停通知后，大多数将 PCM SDK 嵌套进应用程序的开发者都已将其删除。整合 PCM SDK 的应用程序开发者主要是个人或小型初创企业，其无力承担应用程序被暂停的后果。此外，由于谷歌会追踪所有违反了《开发者协议》和《开发者政策》的行为，这些开发者无法承担开发者账户被终止的风险。

43. 因此，谷歌的暂停通知一经发出，整合了 PCM SDK 的开发者就把 PCM SDK 从应用程序中进行删除，并向用户推送了软件更新。大多数安卓用户会选择自动更新应用程序，因此，一旦用户接受更新，PCM 就会从他们的手机中删除。开发者通过这种做法避免了业务暂停及谷歌将来可能会采取的不利行动。

44. 由于谷歌的暂停通知，2013 年 12 月，PCM 的下载率下降了 50% 以上，从 2013 年 11 月的约 2000 万次下载降至约 900 万次。而且，下载率仍在急剧下降，截至 2014 年 1 月，下载量为 470 万次，而 2014 年 2 月仅为 230 万次。

45. 一些开发者在收到谷歌的暂停通知后与 StartApp 联系。StartApp 和 Callsome 随后开始调查谷歌暂停通知的依据。

46. 这些暂停通知发出后，Callsome 试图通过申诉、客户支持程序以及为谷歌工作的个人与谷歌取得联系。但这些努力均未得到任何回应。2013 年 12 月 6 日，Callsome 的董事兼联合创始人扎克·希文联系到了谷歌的马修·拜伊，询问安装 PCM SDK 的应用程序开发者均收到暂停通知的原因。希文告诉拜伊，这些应用开发者"从应用程序中卸载了我方的程序，而这个程序的分销商也停止了所有的分销活动，这基本上完全阻碍了我方的业务发展"。希文还告诉拜伊："大多数应用开发商都从应用程序中删除了我方的程序，而本来与我方合作的分销商也没有一个愿意冒险分销收到过谷歌商城发出暂停通知的应用程序。"

47. 由于没有收到答复，2013 年 12 月 12 日，希文再次联系拜伊。随后，拜伊将希文的问题转达给谷歌的高级顾问杰夫·格里菲斯。

48. 2013 年 12 月 18 日，希文致函格里菲斯，询问谷歌为何要向应用程序开发者发送暂停通知，并附上了被暂停的应用程序名称。

49. 2013 年 12 月 21 日，格里菲斯答复说这些应用程序并未被叫停，只是"由于安装了另一个 SDK（StartApp 呼叫后管理器）而受到警告……"同日，希文在回复中告知格里菲斯：

StartApp 呼叫后管理器是我方的合作伙伴 StartApp 向前述的开发者推广的 CallFlakes 的精简版本。

我方想了解呼叫后管理器是如何违反谷歌政策的，以便我方确保能够以正确的方式来实施这一程序。

在明确呼叫后管理器存在的问题之前，没有一个合作伙伴愿意继续使用 CallFlakes。

50. 2014 年 1 月 10 日，格里菲斯与希文联系，尝试进一步说明并补充信息：

扎克，你好。

未能及时回复，我深感抱歉。由于节假日工作人员不在，我收集答复所需资料的时间比预期要长。

就此次事件，我与谷歌的下架团队进行了进一步协商，应该可以在下周早些时候作出答复。

同时，我想确认一下我们所讨论的问题：我的理解是，收到警告的第三方应用程序安装了另一个第三方（StartApp）所开发的 SDK，即收到警告的第三方应用程序运行了一个由另一第三方应用程序（StartApp）开发的呼叫后管理器（PCM）SDK。呼叫后管理器（PCM）。您曾说过，StartApp 是贵公司的合作伙伴，该公司将 PCM 作为贵公司产品 CallFlakes 的精简版进行销售。您能提供更多关于 Start App 及其与贵公司业务关系的信息吗？

非常感谢

杰夫

51. 2014 年 1 月 10 日，希文回复了格里菲斯的电子邮件，表示"PCM 是 Callsome 开发的产品，属于 CallFlakes 的精简版。StartApp 是一个移动广告网络，负责将我们的 PCM SDK 分销到其应用程序开发社区中"。

52. 2014 年 1 月 13 日，格里菲斯对暂停通知作出如下解释：

扎克，你好。

感谢你所提供的信息。

PCM 是一种可以在第三方应用中实现的 SDK，以在用户同意添加的情况下为应用程序提供可选的通话后功能。然而，PCM 是作为"广告单元"向开发者进行销售的（如在这个网站上），并以此来为这些应用程序盈利。PCM 还包括在通话后屏幕中以第三方应用程序链接的形式推广广告内容。因此，整体看来，PCM 可以视为添加到应用程序中的广告服务，而不是谷歌商城的应用程序本身。所以，PCM（以及安装它的应用程序）受到谷歌广告政策约束。该政策包含以下限制：

• 广告不得干扰其他应用程序及其相关应用程序的运行。为了使 PCM 广告单元的运行符合要求，必须在其自带的应用程序内进行显示，而它改变了手机应用程序和用户设备上的浏览器的功能。相关政策规定如下：

• 应用程序和第三方广告

与应用程序相关联的广告不得干扰其他应用程序或其广告。

• 由于含有第三方应用的商业链接，并全屏显示，且在用户结束通话后，必须先关闭页面，才能使用默认的联系人 / 电话用户界面，因此，安装 PCM 属于插播广告服务。相关政策规定如下：

• 广告墙和插播广告

插播广告只能在其自带的应用内显示。

这就是安装了 PCM 的应用程序收到警告的原因。

谨致问候

杰夫

53. 尽管谷歌承认 PCM 为用户的移动电话提供了额外功能，但 PCM 因为作为"广告单元"进行销售而被认为是一种广告服务。这一观点实际上阻碍了 Callsome 向应用程序开发者分销 PCM SDK，并对 Callsome 的业务造成了毁灭性打击。

54. Callsome 将格里菲斯的电子邮件转发给 StartApp，StartApp 作出如下答复：

经过内部讨论，目前我们的观点是，呼叫后管理器不能作为 SDK 来通过广告资助的模式向应用程序开发者分销。因此，考虑到分销成本，如果不能包含广告来支持这一商业模式，我们将无法继续分销呼叫后管理器。

事情发展到这一步，我深表歉意。如您所知，本公司以及我们的应用程序开发者都很青睐贵方的产品，但如果谷歌认为这项产品违反了广告政策，我们将无法继续对其进行分销。

55. 鉴于谷歌方认为 PCM SDK 违反了其广告政策，StartApp 建议已嵌套 PCM SDK 的开发者从应用程序中删除该程序。

56. 谷歌方声称 PCM SDK 违反其广告政策的理由是错误的。

57. PCM 不是一个"广告单元"。正如谷歌自己所承认的那样,PCM 向同意下载的用户提供呼叫后功能。所有下载已嵌套 PCM SDK 应用程序的用户都收到了明确通知,并同意下载 PCM。因此,用户同意下载 PCM 所提供的附加功能。用户在使用 PCM 时看到的广告完全被包含在 PCM 中,而非在应用程序之外。实际上,PCM 内包含的广告只占用户屏幕的 1/16 左右。因此,PCM 不是广告单元,也不会在 PCM 之外显示广告。

58. PCM SDK 不会改变手机应用程序或用户的网络浏览器。PCM 只在通话结束后才会出现,而且用户可以轻易关闭页面。PCM 不会影响用户使用手机应用程序或与手机应用程序之间交互的能力。同样的,PCM 也不会改变或更改用户浏览器上的设置。虽然用户可以在电话结束后,在 PCM 中包含的由雅虎(而非谷歌)提供技术支持的搜索框中输入搜索,但并不会改变用户手机浏览器上的任何设置。

59. PCM 不是广告服务,安装后不会显示插播广告。[5] 如上所述,谷歌将 PCM 定性为广告单元或广告服务这一判断是错误的,因为对于 PCM 为提高工作效率提供的附加功能,用户均已收到明确通知并表示同意。事实上,用户 90% 的时间都在使用 PCM 提供的提高工作效率的功能。用户只有 10% 的时间点击了应用内广告,这进一步表明用户并未把 PCM 看作广告单元或广告服务。因此,PCM 对广告的执行和使用符合谷歌的广告政策。

60. 谷歌认为 Callsome、StartApp 和安装 PCM SDK 的开发者不遵守谷歌的《开发者协议》或《开发者政策》属于误述。

61. 谷歌对已嵌套 PCM SDK 的应用程序开发者作出了误述,导致他们放弃并停用 PCM SDK。应用程序开发者被迫停止嵌套 PCM SDK,因为其应用程序的成功完全建立在是否能够在谷歌商城这个最早的安卓应用市场上发布该应用程序。简单来说,应用程序开发者无法承担在谷歌商城上被暂停或禁用应用程序的后果,即使谷歌给出的理由是错误的。

62. 谷歌的误述导致 StartApp 停止向应用程序开发者提供 PCM SDK,并明确建议应用程序开发者从应用程序中删除 PCM SDK。StartApp 被迫停止提供 PCM SDK,因为要想作为移动广告平台存活下去取决于能否向应用程序开发者提供符合谷歌《开发者政策》的盈利方案,从而使应用程序开发者能够在谷歌商城这一主要安卓市场上发布。简单地说,如果 StartApp 所提供的盈利策略导致应用程序开发者受到谷歌的警告或暂停,StartApp 将无力承担这样的后果,即使警告或暂停的依据是错误的。

63. StartApp 停止提供 PCM SDK 之后,Interchan 决定不再将 PCM SDK

嵌套纳入正在开发和即将发布的新应用程序中。Interchan 并没有将 PCM SDK 从现有的应用程序中卸载，而是任其继续嵌套在这些应用程序中，因为一旦发布新的应用程序后，这些现有的应用程序将不再得到技术支持和产品推广。

64. 谷歌的误述对 Callsome 造成了实质性损害。由于谷歌的误述，StartApp 和应用程序开发者都已终止了与 Callsome 的合作。谷歌的误述极大地削弱了 Callsome 从 Interchan 方获利的能力，并以其他方式损害了 Callsome 利用 PCM SDK 与 StartApp 合作所产生的收益，即使 Callsome 完全符合谷歌的《开发者协议》和《开发者政策》。与此同时，Callsome 与有意愿向应用程序开发人员提供 PCM SDK 的第三方的合作关系也被终止。谷歌的误述对 Callsome 的业务造成毁灭性打击。

65. 尽管 PCM SDK 有利于用户，也能为 Callsome 创造收益，但谷歌的误述导致 Callsome 无力再开发、销售完全合规的 PCM SDK 或以其他方式利用其获利。

诉因 I 对 CALLSOME 与 STARTAPP 合同的侵权干预

66. 正如所列，Callsome 在此重新诉称了第 1~65 段。

67. 2013 年 3 月 18 日，Callsome 与 StartApp 签订合同，规定 Callsome 负责开发和交付 PCM SDK，以换取 StartApp 将 PCM SDK "作为移动应用程序开发者的新型盈利方案"。经 2013 年 8 月 1 日修订后的合同规定，Callsome 和 StartApp 的合同将于 2015 年 7 月 31 日到期，除非任何一方提供希望终止合同的书面通知，否则合同将自动延长 24 个月。

68. Callsome 将 PCM SDK 交付给 StartApp，StartApp 又把 PCM SDK 提供给其开发者。如上所述，PCM SDK 在 StartApp 的开发者中大受欢迎，有超过 200 名开发者选择了 PCM SDK，并将其安装于多达 1902 个应用程序中。

69. 根据希文 2013 年 12 月 21 日的电子邮件和格里菲斯 2014 年 1 月 10 日的电子邮件，谷歌已知晓了 Callsome 与 StartApp 有分销 PCM SDK 的合同关系。

70. 谷歌向 Callsome、StartApp 和开发者提供虚假信息，声称 PCM SDK 违反了谷歌的广告政策。谷歌知晓，如果 PCM SDK 违反了谷歌的广告政策，StartApp 将停止对 PCM SDK 的供应。谷歌同样知晓，根据其给出的虚假理由和 PCM SDK 分销的方式，Callsome 无法使 PCM SDK 符合规定。

71. 在得知谷歌认为 PCM SDK 属于违反广告政策的广告服务后，

StartApp 终止了与 Callsome 的合同。

72. 谷歌的侵权行为使得 Callsome 无法营销、售卖或以其他方式从 PCM SDK 中获利，因为没有任何广告商、广告服务、广告平台或开发者愿意分销或嵌套这种被判定违反谷歌《开发者协议》或《开发者政策》的应用程序或 SDK。

73. 因此，Callsome 请求判决谷歌败诉，并支付补偿性损害赔偿金、惩罚性损害赔偿金，以及法院认为适当的进一步救济及其他救济。

诉因 II 对 CALLSOME 与应用程序开发者合同的侵权干预

74. 正如所列，Callsome 在此重新诉称了第 1~65 段。

75. 2013 年 9 月 15 日，Callsome 和 StartApp 开始向开发者提供 PCM SDK。

76. 在提供 PCM SDK 的短短几个月时间内，有 247 名开发者将 PCM SDK 集成到 1 900 多项应用程序中。这些开发者中包括 Wait What 和 Nikhil Kulria。

77. 这些嵌套了 PCM SDK 的应用程序最终上架谷歌商城，每次用户下载 PCM 和应用程序，开发者都能得到报酬。将 PCM SDK 嵌套入应用程序中的开发者不一定要继续使用它，他们可以随时决定使用 StartApp 或任何其他竞争对手所提供的不同 SDK。

78. 谷歌知道哪些开发者使用谷歌的广告 SDKs，因为开发者必须注册才能使用这些 SDK 测试或审查已嵌套 PCM SDK 的应用程序是否符合《开发者协议》或《开发者政策》后，谷歌知道哪些开发者没有使用谷歌的广告 SDKs，而是使用了竞争对手的广告 SDK，如本案中的 StartApp。谷歌向这些开发者发出了暂停使用通知。

79. 已嵌套 PCM SDK 的开发者在收到谷歌的暂停使用警告通知后删除了 PCM SDK。但如果没有这些暂停通知，这些开发者本会选择继续使用 PCM SDK。

80. 谷歌在暂停通知中告知了将 PCM SDK 嵌套入应用程序的开发者，PCM SDK 违反了谷歌的广告政策，或在没有通知用户并征得用户同意的情况下上传了用户的通话记录。如上所述，这些理由是明显的误述，因为 PCM SDK 既没有违反谷歌的广告政策，也没有上传用户的通话记录。

81. 收到这些暂停通知的开发者被迫从应用程序中删除了 PCM SDK，因为他们的成功取决于能否在谷歌商城上架其应用程序，以及能否维持与谷歌的良好合作关系。这些开发者根本无法承担谷歌暂停其应用程序的后果，因此，谷歌一宣称这些应用程序违反谷歌政策，他们便只能屈服。

82. 实际上，一旦发现 Callsome 无法使 PCM SDK 符合谷歌声称的广告政策，StartApp 就向所有嵌套了 PCM SDK 的开发者发送了电子邮件，要求他们删除 PCM SDK。StartApp 这样做是为了维护对开发者的信誉，也是因为 StartApp 的成功取决于能否为开发者提供符合谷歌《开发者协议》和《开发者政策》的 SDKs。

83. 谷歌的侵权行为使得 Callsome 无法营销、售卖或以其他方式从 PCM SDK 中获利，因为没有任何广告商、广告服务机构、广告平台或开发者愿意分销或嵌套这种谷歌声称违反其《开发者协议》或《开发者政策》的应用程序或 SDK。

84. 因此，Callsome 请求判决谷歌败诉，并支付补偿性损害赔偿金、惩罚性损害赔偿金，以及法院认为适当的进一步救济及其他救济。

诉因 III　对 CALLSOME 与 ASK PARTNER NETWORK 和 MASSIVE IMPACT 业务关系的侵权干预

85. 正如所列，Callsome 在此重新诉称了第 1—65 段。

86. 2013 年 9 月 15 日，Callsome 和 StartApp 开始向开发者提供 PCM SDK。

87. 在提供 PCM SDK 的短短几个月时间内，有 247 名开发者将 PCM SDK 嵌套到 1900 多项应用程序中。这些开发者包括 Escape Mobile、Wait What 和 Nikhil Kulria。

88. 由于 PCM SDK 大受欢迎，Callsome 开始与 Ask Partner Network 和 Massive Impact 谈判，准备着手分销 PCM SDK。

89. Callsome 与 Ask Partner Network 签订原则性协议，向应用程序开发者分销 PCM SDK。

90. Callsome 与 Massive Impact 就分销 PCM SDK 一事尚处于谈判阶段。

91. 2013 年 11 月，谷歌开始向已嵌套 PCM SDK 的开发者发送暂停通知。

92. Ask Partner Network 获悉，StartApp 从网站上删除了 PCM SDK，并通知开发者在应用程序中卸载 PCM SDK。因此，Ask Partner Network 与 Callsome 取得联系，询问 PCM SDK 为何不符合谷歌的政策。

93. 如上所述，Callsome 与谷歌联系，希望谷歌就暂停警告通知一事作出解释。

94. 在数封询问解释的电子邮件中，Callsome 告知谷歌，"大多数应用开发者都从应用程序中卸载了我方的程序，而本来与我方合作的分销商也没人愿意冒险分销一个收到过谷歌商城暂停通知的应用程序"。Callsome 还告诉谷歌，由于谷歌发送暂停警告通知，"所有分销商都停止了与我方的合作，一项即将签署的投资协议被取消，下载率也出现了大幅下降"。因此，Callsome 告知谷歌，由于谷歌的暂停警告通知，与 Callsome 合作的分销商都已与其终止了合作关系。

95. 如上所述，谷歌向希文所称 PCM SDK 是一个广告单元和广告服务，不符合谷歌的广告政策，这是误述。Callsome 将谷歌的答复转达给了 Ask Partner Network 和 Massive Impact，随后两者都拒绝与 Callsome 进一步合作。

96. 谷歌的侵权行为阻断了 Callsome 与 Ask Partner Network 和 Massive Impact 经谈判后可能达成的合同关系。谷歌尽管知晓这种关系，但仍作出误述，称 PCM SDK 不符合谷歌的广告政策。谷歌的侵权行为使得 Callsome 无法继续营销、售卖或以其他方式从 PCM SDK 中获利，因为没有任何广告商、广告服务、广告平台或开发者愿意分销或嵌套被判定违反谷歌《开发者协议》或《开发者政策》的应用程序或 SDK。

97. 因此，Callsome 请求判决谷歌败诉，并支付补偿性损害赔偿金、惩罚性损害赔偿金，以及法院认为适当的进一步救济及其他救济。

诉因 IV　商业诽谤

98. 正如所列，Callsome 在此重新诉称了第 1—65 段。

99. 谷歌告知应用程序开发者、StartApp 以及 Callsome，集成 PCM SDK 的应用程序违反了谷歌的《开发者政策》。

100. 与谷歌的声明相反，PCM SDK 完全符合谷歌的《开发者政策》。

101. 谷歌关于 PCM SDK 不符合政策的误述意在阻止应用程序开发者将 PCM SDK 嵌套到应用程序中。

102. 谷歌关于 PCM SDK 不符合政策的误述导致应用程序开发者和 StartApp 终止了与 Callsome 的合作关系。

103. 谷歌关于 PCM SDK 不符合政策的误述导致 Interchan 公司决定不再将 PCM SDK 嵌套入其提供的新应用程序中。

104. 由于谷歌的误述，Callsome 遭受了以下损失：

a. 由于 StartApp 放弃 PCM SDK，并被迫停止向应用程序开发者提供 PCM SDK，估计将损失广告收入 32700000 美元；

　　b. Ask Partner Network 在得知谷歌的暂停通知后拒绝与 Callsome 签约，估计将损失广告收入 19525000 美元；

　　c. Massive Impact 在得知谷歌的暂停通知后拒绝与 Callsome 签约，估计将损失广告收入 19525000 美元；

　　d. 律师费和诉讼费。

　　105. 因此，Callsome 请求判决谷歌败诉，并支付补偿性损害赔偿金、惩罚性损害赔偿金，以及法院认为适当的进一步救济及其他救济。

　　日期：2014 年 6 月 25 日

　　特此函达

　　米尔贝格律师事务所

　　（签名）

　　托德·卡默曼

　　tkammerman@milberg. com

　　宾夕法尼亚广场一号

　　49 楼

　　纽约，邮编：NY 10119–0165

　　电话：（212）594–5300

　　Callsome Solutions 公司代理律师

附录不详

脚注

　　1. 详见 https://www. sec. gov/Archives/edgar/data/1288776/000128877614000020/goog2013123110–k. htm #sD639E991EBB55393BBAF2E71A87E5ECB.

　　2. 谷歌商城并不是安卓设备唯一可用的应用商城，亚马逊和三星等也都提供相关应用商城。

　　3. PCM 是 CallFlakes 的精简版或缩小版，它在收到短信后不会打开任务面板，也不提供脸书的来电显示功能。

　　4. 不同的是，并不是每个应用程序开发者都收到了谷歌的暂停警告通知。例如，使用谷歌 AdMob 广告服务器的 Interchan 就从未收到过谷歌的警告通知。

　　5. 插播广告属于全屏广告，用户可以通过关闭按钮进行关闭。（详见 https://support. google. com/webdesigner/answer/32504157hHen，最后访问时间：2014 年 5 月）

United States District Court, D. New Mexico.

X   RRIO REAL ESTATE INVESTMENT OPPORTUNITIES, LLC, Plaintiff, v. TESTLA MOTORS, INC., Defendant.

Civ. No.12-758 JP/ACT
Filed 02/28/2013

Attorneys and Law Firms

Christopher M. Pacheco, Leeann Werbelow, Lastrapes, Spangler & Pacheco, PA, Rio Rancho, NM, for Plaintiff.

Andrew G. Schultz, Rodey, Dickason, Sloan, Akin & Robb, P. A., Albuquerque, NM ; Nicholas M. Sydow, New Mexico Attorney General, Santa Fe, NM, for Defendant.

MEMORANDUM OPINION AND ORDER

JAMES A. PARKER, SENIOR UNITED STATES DISTRICT COURT JUDGE

*1 This lawsuit concerns a contract dispute involving a Development Agreement between Tesla Motors, Inc., and Rio Real Estate Investment Opportunities, LLC (Development Agreement) entered into by the parties on February 19, 2007. On May 24, 2012, Plaintiff Rio Real Estate Investment Opportunities, LLC (Developer) filed a COMPLAINT FOR BREACH OF CONTRACT, NEGLIGENT MISREPRESENTATION, FRAUD AND BREACH

OF THE COVENANT OF GOOD FAITH AND FAIR DEALING (Doc. No.1-1) (Complaint) with a copy of the Development Agreement attached to it. Developer alleges in the Complaint that Defendant Tesla Motors, Inc. (Tesla) breached the Development Agreement (Count I) , engaged in negligent misrepresentation (Count II) , committed fraud (Count III) , and breached the covenant of good faith and fair dealing (Count IV).

Tesla now moves under Fed. R. Civ. P.12 (b) (6) to dismiss Counts I, III, and IV for "failure to state a claim upon which relief can be granted". See DEFENDANT TESLA MOTIORS [sic], INC.'S MOTION FOR PARTIAL DISMISSAL (Doc. No.14) (Motion to Dismiss) , filed Oct.16, 2012. Developer opposes the Motion to Dismiss and, if the Court denies the Motion to Dismiss, Developer seeks an award of the attorney's fees and costs it incurred in responding to the Motion to Dismiss. See RESPONSE TO DEFENDANT'S MOTION TO DISMISS AND MEMORANDUM OF POINTS AND AUTHORITIES IN SUPPORT (Doc. No.15) , filed Oct.29, 2012. Tesla also filed DEFENDANT TESLA MOTORS, INC.'S REPLY IN SUPPORT OF ITS MOTION FOR PARTIAL DISMISSAL (Doc. No.17) on November 15, 2012.

On February 14, 2013, the Court held a hearing on the Motion to Dismiss. Attorneys Christopher Pacheco and LeeAnn Werbelow represented Developer, and Attorneys Andrew Schultz and Nicholas Sydow represented Tesla. Counsel agreed to strike a document entitled "Position Paper on Tesla Motors" (Doc. No.1-1) at 16-17 which is appended to Attachment "A" of the Development Agreement. Consequently, the Court will disregard the "Position Paper on Tesla Motors" in its consideration of the Motion to Dismiss. Mr. Pacheco also clarified that Count IV, the breach of the covenant of good faith and fair dealing claim, arises solely from the Development Agreement and is only a contract claim, not also a tort claim. Moreover, the Court determined that it will dismiss Count III, the fraud claim, without prejudice and give Developer until March 5, 2013 to amend the Complaint, consistent with Rule 1-009 (B) NMRA 1998, Fed. R. Civ. P.9 (b) and Fed. R. Civ. P.11, to re-allege the fraud claim with sufficient particularity. Although the Court has decided to dismiss Count III without prejudice, the Court will, nonetheless, discuss the fraud claim in this MEMORANDUM OPINION AND ORDER so that the parties clearly understand the Court's reasoning in dismissing the fraud claim without prejudice. Furthermore, the Court will consider the arguments counsel made at the February 14, 2013 at the hearing, as well as the briefs, the Complaint, and the Development Agreement, in deciding the remainder of the Motion to Dismiss[1].

A. Background

1. The Development Agreement

*2 According to Developer, Tesla owns property in Bernalillo County, New Mexico known as the Cordero Mesa Business Park (Park). Complaint at ¶ 6. Developer agreed to build a 150, 000 square foot facility at the Park so Tesla could manufacture electric vehicles on that property. In exchange for Developer building the facility, Tesla stated it would enter into a lease agreement with Developer for use of the facility. Additionally, Developer intended to obtain various economic incentives to benefit Tesla.

The Development Agreement "contains the principal terms with respect to the relationship between" the parties. Ex. A (Doc. No.1-1) at 1 (attached to Complaint). The Development Agreement more specifically "establishes a relationship between Tesla and Developer whereby Tesla will conduct certain of its operations at a facility located in [the Park], in exchange for certain economic incentives that have been outlined in a separate agreement between Tesla and the State of New Mexico…" Id. Moreover, the Development Agreement provides that " [t] he parties contemplate that successor agreements will be drafted between Developer and Tesla that reflect the following terms and effect the relationship contemplated in the Development Agreement". Id. Nonetheless, the parties agreed "that unless and until such agreement is signed, this [Development] Agreement represents the spirit of the overall agreement and a good faith commitment by the parties to perform the obligations described herein". Id.

Those obligations include that Tesla would enter into a lease agreement with Developer to rent the 150, 000 square foot facility for at least ten years with rent beginning "at \$1,350,000 per year, increasing at 2% per year, based on Facility requirements provided by Tesla to Developer…" Id. Also, " [t] he first year's lease payments will be reduced by 50% each month. This is a NNN lease where Tesla pays all expenses. The lease term begins upon certificate of occupancy". Id.

Any changes to the facility could result in modifications to the lease terms.

Developer further agreed to "finalize an agreement with SunCal to convey, at no charge to Tesla, up to 75 acres of land which abuts the proposed site in Cordero Mesa. The conveyance of this land is contingent upon a decision by Tesla to make a significant expansion onto the site". Id. at 1-2. In addition, " [t] he intention of the parties is that various public entities and Developer (s) will pay for and, provide utilities and infrastructure to the site at no cost to Tesla". Id. at 2. As of the date of the Development Agreement, the parties had "no authority to obligate future local and state governments to any future commitments and expense". Id.

Next, Developer agreed to pay Tesla signing bonuses totaling $8,700,000 "conditional upon Tesla meeting certain financial requirements to be agreed upon by the parties...and conditional upon Bernalillo County's successful negotiation and implementation of a project participation agreement under the terms of [the Local Economic Development Act] ..." Id. The New Mexico State Legislature would contribute a total of $7,000,000 towards the signing bonuses by appropriating funds during the 2007 and 2008 legislative sessions. The Development Agreement contains a schedule for paying the signing bonuses and restricts Tesla's use of the signing bonuses to the manufacturing of electric vehicles. Moreover, the Development Agreement establishes that the signing bonuses are "contingent upon sufficient funding" from local and state entities, and that the state's contribution "will be further described in agreements between the applicable parties..." Id. at 3. Finally, " [e] xecution of the signing bonus will be subject to review by Developer of Tesla's financial documents, including business plans and forecasts, as reasonably required by Developer". Id.

*3 The Development Agreement also states that the Developer will provide Tesla with written statements from local or state governments "that the proposed uses by Tesla of the Facility have been approved and are consistent with any applicable development plan, zoning, or any other restrictions in use". Id. Additionally, the Developer will ensure that "the site will be fully served with infrastructure" and will provide Tesla with a written statement from Bernalillo County "confirming that, to its knowledge, no additional public infrastructure or service is required to operate the Facility as contemplated by the parties". Id. at 4.

Furthermore, the Development Agreement provides :

Each of the parties represent and warrant that any commitments made herein are made in good faith with the express and sincere intention to follow through as outlined herein. The State and other local governments will use their best efforts to provide any permits necessary for Tesla's intended use of the Facility and will use their best efforts to assist with approval of any applicable special needs variances. The State and other local governments will work with Tesla to ensure that Tesla is in compliance of applicable environmental laws or regulations.

Id. at 3.

2. Counts I, III, and IV of the Complaint

Developer alleges that in 2007 it "began taking the actions necessary to complete its obligations under the Development Agreement" and that it has "otherwise satisfied its obligations under the Development Agreement". Complaint at ¶ 12 and ¶ 14. Developer further alleges that Tesla has "refused to enter into a lease and otherwise abandoned the Project". Id. at ¶ 15. Developer asserts in its Count I breach of contract claim that Tesla's failure to enter into a lease agreement and abandonment of the Project constitutes breach of the Development Agreement. In Count III, Developer maintains that Tesla committed fraud by "intentionally concealing [its] intent to abandon the Project after over a year of perpetual preparation..." Id. at ¶ 32. Finally, Developer alleges in Count IV that Tesla breached the covenant of good faith and fair dealing "by purposely failing to enter into the Lease, failing to complete the Project, and abandoning the Project". Id. at ¶ 38.

B. Standard of Review

In ruling on a Rule 12 (b) (6) motion to dismiss for "failure to state a claim upon which relief can be granted", the Court must accept all well-pleaded allegations as true and must view them in the light most favorable to the plaintiff. See *Zinermon v. Burch*, *494 U. S.113, 118 (1990)*; *Swanson v. Bixler*, *750 F.2d 810, 813 (10th Cir.1984)*. Rule 12 (b) (6) requires that a complaint set forth the grounds of a plaintiff's entitlement to relief through more than labels, conclusions and a formulaic recitation of the elements of a cause of action. See *Bell Atl. Corp. v. Twombly*, *550 U. S.544, 555 (2007)*. While a complaint does not need to include detailed factual allegations, "factual allegations must be enough to raise a right to relief above the speculative level". Id. In other words, dismissal of a complaint under Rule 12 (b) (6) is proper only where it is obvious that the plaintiff failed to set forth "enough facts to state a claim to relief that is plausible on its face". Id. at 570.

A claim has facial plausibility when the plaintiff pleads factual content that allows the court to draw the reasonable inference that the defendant is liable for the misconduct alleged. The plausibility standard is not akin to a "probability requirement", but it asks for more than a sheer possibility that a defendant has acted unlawfully. Where a complaint pleads facts that are "merely consistent with" a defendant's liability, it "stops short of the line between possibility and plausibility of 'entitlement to relief'".

*4 *Ashcroft v. Iqbal, 556 U. S.662, 678 (2009)* (citations omitted). Courts must draw on their "judicial experience and common sense" to assess a claim's plausibility. Id. at 679.

C. Discussion

1. Breach of Contract Claim (Count I)

Tesla argues that Developer cannot plausibly assert that Tesla breached the Development Agreement because the Development Agreement is not an enforceable contract. To state a claim of breach of contract in New Mexico, a plaintiff "must allege : (1) the existence of a valid and binding contract ; (2) the plaintiff's compliance with the contract and his performance of the obligations under it ; (3) a general averment of the performance of any condition precedent ; and (4) damages suffered as a result of defendant's breach". *McCasland v. Prather, 92 N. M.192, 194, 585 P.2d 336, 338 (Ct. App.1978)*. Tesla asserts that Developer has not plausibly shown that the Development Agreement is a valid and binding contract because the Development Agreement does not set forth the essential and material elements of a deal. Tesla further asserts that Developer does not allege in the Complaint that all of the contingencies set forth in the Development Agreement have been met and that Developer "nowhere alleges that any of the conditions or necessary actions to be completed by any of the other entities, agencies or governments were undertaken, let alone completed". Motion to Dismiss at 9.

In New Mexico, it is "the well settled rule that a contract to enter into a future contract will not be enforced unless the essential and material terms have been agreed upon". *Stites v. Yelverton, 60 N. M.190, 200, 289 P.2d 628, 635 (1955)*. Moreover, an agreement will not be enforced as a contract if the essential and material terms of the agreement are vague, indefinite, or uncertain. *Hyder v. Brenton*, *93 N. M.378*, *384*, *600 P.2d 830*, *836 (Ct. App.)* , cert. quashed, No.12, 620 (1979) (Walters, J., dissenting in part, concurring in part) (citation omitted). See also *7A Am. Jur.2d Contracts § 39 (updated Nov.2012)* (" [A] n agreement to agree to do a certain specified thing is valid if all the conditions and terms of the postponed agreement are specified."). There is authority in New Mexico to support the proposition that contingencies in an agreement together with lack of a completion time can make an agreement "so indefinite as to render it unenforceable". See *Hyder*, *93 N. M. at 384-85*, *600 P.2d at 836-87* (Walters, J., dissenting in part, concurring in part). Even so, "'a written contract need not detail every term' , but 'essential terms must be expressly provided or necessarily implied by construction for a court to find the contract unambiguous on its face'". *Randles v. Hanson*, *2011-NMCA-059 ¶ 32*, *150 N. M.362* (citation omitted). In other words, contract terms must be reasonably certain. *Padilla v. RRA*, *Inc.*, *1997-NMCA-104 ¶ 8*, *124 N. M.111*. "Contract terms are reasonably certain 'if they provide a basis for determining the existence of a breach and for giving an appropriate remedy'". Id. (citation omitted).

Having examined the Development Agreement in the light most favorable to Developer, the Court finds that it lacks many essential and material terms. Although the lease terms appear rather specific, the Development Agreement does not specify (1) a time frame for completing the commitments described in the Development Agreement, (2) who will build the facility, (3) the cost of building the facility, (4) the method of financing the entire project, (5) when construction of the facility would begin and end, (6) what would happen if the legislative appropriations were not passed, and (7) performance benchmarks. Additionally, several material and essential terms are simply left to future negotiations.

*5 Many of the terms of the Development Agreement are also unduly vague or indefinite, i. e., not reasonably certain, because they involve contingencies, additional tasks to be performed by third parties, and unresolved negotiations. Developer argues, however, that contingencies in an agreement do not limit a contract's enforceability. Developer cites to *Republic Nat. Life Ins. Co. v. Red Lion Homes*, *Inc.*, *704 F.2d 484 (10th Cir.1983)* , a case wherein the Tenth Circuit Court of Appeals specifically relied on two Colorado cases which held that "when [a] contract is contingent on obtaining additional financing, purchaser must make reasonable efforts to secure it". Id. at 486. However, in New Mexico, the

Honorable New Mexico Court of Appeals Judge Mary Walters, in an opinion dissenting in part and concurring in part with the majority of the New Mexico Court of Appeals, discussed an agreement in which property was conveyed with the limitation that the property have a home built on it. Two contingencies were expressed prior to construction of the home : (1) construction could not start until the spring ; and (2) construction of the home was contingent on the sale of the purchaser's home. Judge Walters concluded that these "contingencies, together with the fact that no time for completion of the project was ever decided upon, or even discussed, make [purchaser's] 'promise' to build so indefinite as to render it unenforceable". *Hyder, 93 N. M. at 384-85, 600 P.2d at 836-37*. Judge Walter's opinion demonstrates that in New Mexico contingencies can indicate an indefinite agreement and thus an unenforceable contract.

Moreover, generally, "the question is whether the indefinite promise is so essential to the bargain that inability to enforce that promise strictly according to its terms makes it also unfair to enforce the remainder of the agreement. The more important the subject matter to be agreed upon, the more likely it is that the uncertainty will prevent or hinder enforcement". Richard A. Lord, 1 Williston on Contracts 4 : 31 (4th ed.) (updated May 2012). In other words, "if the undetermined matter does not preclude performance of the remainder of the contract and is of comparatively little importance, the uncertain promise may be left entirely unperformed and the remainder of the contract enforced". Id. In this case, viewing the Development Agreement in the light most favorable to Developer, the Court concludes that the contingent provisions of the Development Agreement, like the contingencies in Hyder, are not minor or fairly unimportant provisions. Tesla would need for these contingencies to be met before it could occupy and lease the Developer's facility and begin manufacturing electric vehicles. Put another way, the contingencies are so essential to the deal that it would be unfair to enforce the remainder of the Development Agreement without the contingencies having been met first.

Developer also argues that the questions of whether a contract exists and whether the contingencies have actually been met are fact questions for a jury to determine. In deciding a Rule 12 (b) (6) motion to dismiss, the Court is only obligated to examine the Complaint and the attached Development Agreement to determine if Developer has alleged a plausible breach of contract claim. To state a plausible breach of contract, Developer must show that, on its face, the Development Agreement is a valid and Binding contract. Only after Developer has plausibly demonstrated that the Development Agreement is a valid and binding contract, does the Court need to address whether Developer has plausibly alleged that it has performed its obligations under the Development Agreement. Since the Court believes that Developer has not plausibly demonstrated that the Development Agreement is a valid and binding contract, the Court need not decide if Developer has plausibly alleged that it has fulfilled its obligations under the Development Agreement. In sum, the Court cannot draw a reasonable inference from the Complaint and the Development Agreement that Tesla is liable for breach of contract. At most, the Development Agreement is an unenforceable agreement to agree. Hence, the breach of contract claim is subject to dismissal with prejudice under Rule 12 (b) (6).

2. Breach of the Covenant of Good Faith and Fair Dealing (Count IV)

If there is no enforceable contract, one cannot bring a claim for breach of the covenant of good faith and fair dealing sounding in contract law. See, e. g., *Rennick v. O. P. T. I. O. N. Care, Inc.*, *77 F.3d 309, 317 (9th Cir.)*, *cert. denied, 519 U. S.865 (1996)*. Because Developer has not stated a plausible breach of contract claim, Developer cannot state a plausible claim for breach of the covenant of good faith and fair dealing. That claim is, therefore, subject to dismissal with prejudice under Rule 12 (b) (6).

3. Fraud (Count III)

*6 Tesla argues that the fraud claim should be dismissed under Rule 12 (b) (6) because Developer has not pled that claim with the required particularity. Rule 1-009 (B) states : "In all averments of fraud or mistake, the circumstances constituting fraud or mistake shall be stated with particularity. Malice, intent, knowledge and other condition of mind of a person may be averred generally". Rule 1-009 (B) is similar to Fed. R. Civ. P.9 (b) which also requires "particularity" in stating a claim of fraud. In New Mexico, " [a] pleading of fraud is sufficient if the facts alleged are facts from which fraud will necessarily be implied ; in addition, the allegations should leave no doubt in defendants' minds as to the claim asserted". *Delgado v. Costello*, *91 N. M.732, 734, 580 P.2d 500, 502 (Ct. App.1978)*. The federal courts have explained that "an allegation of fraud must 'set forth the time, place, and contents of the false representation, the identity of the party making the false statements and the consequences thereof'". *Midgley v. Rayrock Mines, Inc., 374 F. Supp.2d 1039, 1047 (D. N. M.2005)* (quoting *Schwartz v. Celestial Seasonings, Inc., 124 F.3d 1246, 1252 (10th Cir.1997)*). Although "[R] ule 9 (b) does not require specific knowledge regarding the defendant's state of mind", like Rule 1-009 (B), speculative and conclusory allegations of fraud will not suffice. See id.

Here, Developer makes only a bare-bones allegation of fraud in the Complaint at ¶ 32 : "The actions of Defendant in intentionally concealing their intent to abandon the Project after over a year of perpetual preparation constitutes fraud". Developer does not allege specific times, places, actions, or even identities of the persons who allegedly committed the fraud. Without those allegations, the Court cannot determine that Developer has stated a plausible fraud claim. Consequently, the fraud claim should be dismissed without prejudice at this time under Rule 12 (b) (6). Nevertheless, the Court will give Developer until March 5, 2013 to amend the Complaint, if Developer can do so consistent with Rule 1-009 (B) NMRA 1998, Fed. R. Civ.9 (b) and Fed. R. Civ. P.11, to re-allege the fraud claim with sufficient particularity.

4. Developer's Request for an Award of Attorney's Fees and Costs

Since the Court will grant Tesla's Motion to Dismiss, the Court will deny Developer's request for an award of the attorney's fees and costs it incurred in responding to the Motion to Dismiss.

IT IS ORDERED that :

(1) DEFENDANT TESLA MOTIORS [sic], INC.'S MOTION FOR PARTIAL DISMISSAL (Doc. No.14) is granted ;

(2) Counts I and IV will be dismissed with prejudice ;

(3) Count III will be dismissed without prejudice ;

(4) Developer has until March 5, 2013 to amend the Complaint, if it can do so consistent with Rule 1-009 (B) NMRA 1998, Fed. R Civ. P.9 (b) and Fed. R Civ. P.11, to re-allege the fraud claim with sufficient particularity ; and

(5) Developer's request for an award of attorney's fees and costs is denied

All Citations

Not Reported in Fed. Supp., 2013 WL 12136382.

Footnotes

1 In deciding a Rule 12 (b) (6) Motion to Dismiss, courts "may look at the complaint, the attached exhibits and any documents incorporated into the complaint by reference that is filed with the defendant's 12 (b) (6) motion". Commonwealth Property Advocates, LLC v. Mortgage Electronic Registration Systems, Inc., 680 F.3d 1194, 1203 n.10 (10th Cir.2011).

美国新墨西哥联邦地区法院。

10 RIO 房地产投资有限责任公司诉 特斯拉汽车公司

案件编号：12-758 JP/ACT
提交日期：2013 年 2 月 28 日

律师和律师事务所

原告代理律师：新墨西哥州里奥兰珠市拉斯特拉普斯、斯潘格勒和帕切科律师事务所的克里斯托弗·M. 帕切科和利安·韦尔贝娄。

被告代理律师：新墨西哥州阿尔伯克基市阿金和罗布律师事务所的安德鲁·G. 舒尔茨、罗迪、迪卡森和斯隆；新墨西哥州圣达菲市总检察长，尼科尔斯·M. 赛多。

备忘意见书与裁定

詹姆斯·帕克，美国联邦地区法院高级法官

*1 本诉讼涉及特斯拉汽车公司（以下简称"特斯拉"）与 RIO 房地产投资有限责任公司（以下简称"开发商"）于 2007 年 2 月 19 日签订的《开发协议》所产生的合同纠纷。

2012 年 5 月 24 日，原告开发商提交了一份关于违反合同、过失性误述、欺诈、违反诚信和公平交易契约的起诉状（文件 1-1），并附有《开发协议》的副本。开发商在起诉状中指控，被告特斯拉违反了《开发协议》（诉因一），作出了过失性误述（诉因二），实施了欺诈行为（诉因三），并违反了诚信和公平交易契约（诉因四）。

特斯拉现根据《联邦民事诉讼规则》第 12 节第 2 分节第 6 款，以"未能提出可以给予救济的权利要求"为由，请求驳回开发商第一、第三和第四项诉因［见《被告特斯拉公司要求驳回部分起诉的动议》（部分），（文件14，2012年10月16日提交）开发商对此表示反对，如果法院拒绝支持这份驳回起诉的动议，开发商将请求法院判予其因答复该动议而产生的律师费及相关费用。（见《对被告驳回起诉的动议的答复和支持要点及授权备忘录》，文件15，2015年10月29日提交）特斯拉还于2012年11月15日提交了该公司的《支持部分驳回起诉的动议的答辩状》（文件17）。

2013年2月14日，法院举行了驳回起诉的动议听证会。律师克里斯托弗·帕切科和利安·韦尔贝娄代表辩护律师开发商，律师安德鲁·舒尔茨和总检查长尼科尔斯·赛多代表特斯拉出席听证会。辩护律师同意将（文件号1-1）第16页至17页中一份题为"关于特斯拉汽车的意见书"的文件撤回，将文件附在《开发协议》附加文件"A"中。因此，法院在审议"驳回起诉的动议"时将不考虑"关于特斯拉汽车的立场文件"。帕切科先生澄清，诉因四，即违反诚信和公平交易契约的主张，完全是由《开发协议》引起的，是合同诉讼，而非侵权诉讼。此外，法院决定将在不影响诉讼结果的情况下驳回诉因三，即欺诈诉讼，并根据《1998年NMRA规则》第1–009节第2分节、《联邦民事诉讼规则》第9节第2分节以及第11节之规定给予开发商在2013年3月5日之前修改起诉状的权利，使其有机会以足够具体的方式重新提出欺诈指控。虽然法院已决定在不影响诉讼结果的情况下驳回诉因三，但法院仍将在本备忘录意见和命令中讨论欺诈诉因，以便各方清楚地了解法院在不影响诉讼结果的情况下驳回欺诈诉因的理由。此外，法院将考虑律师在2013年2月14日的听证会上提出的论点，以及案情摘要、起诉状和《开发协议》，以决定如何处理其余的驳回起诉的动议。[1]

A. 案件背景

1. 关于《开发协议》

*2 据开发商介绍，特斯拉在新墨西哥州贝纳里洛县拥有名为Cordero Mesa商业园（以下简称"园区"）的房产。（见起诉状第6段）开发商同意在园区建设一个15万平方英尺的设施，以便特斯拉在该园区生产电动汽车。特斯拉表示，作为开发商建造该设施的交换条件，其将与开发商就该设施的使用订立租赁协议。此外，开发商还计划获得有利于特斯拉的各种经济激励。

《开发协议》包含了有关双方关系的主要条款。［附件A（文件号1-1）第1页（附于起诉状）］。《开发协议》亦具体地明确了"特斯拉与开发商之间的关系，根据这一关系，特斯拉将在位于园区的设施中开展某些业务，以换取特斯拉与新墨西哥州之间的单独协议中概述的某些经济激励措施……"（同上）此外，《开发协议》规定，"双方预期开发商和特斯拉将起草反映下述条款及影响《开发协议》项下拟议关系的后续协议"。（同上）尽管如此，双方同意"只有签署此类协议，本开发协议才代表整体协议的精神及双方履行本协议所述义务的诚信承诺"。

这些义务包括，特斯拉将与开发商签订租赁协议，至少租用 15 万平方英尺的设施 10 年，租金"起始价为每年 1350000 美元，根据特斯拉向开发商提供的设施，要求每年递增 2%……"（同上）另外，"第一年的租金付款额将每月减少 50%。这是一项三净租赁 ᵃ，特斯拉支付所有费用。租期自占用证签发放之日起开始"。（同上）对设施的任何改变都可能导致对租赁条款的修改。

开发商还同意"与 SunCal 达成协议，向特斯拉免费出让 Cordero Mesa 拟建场地附近不超过 75 英亩的土地。这块土地的出让取决于特斯拉是否决定对该地块进行重大扩建"。（同上，第 1—2 页）此外，"双方表示，各公共实体和开发商将为该站点免费提供公用设施和基础设备，而特斯拉不需要支付任何费用"。（同上，第 2 页）截至《开发协议》签署之日，双方"无权要求未来的地方和州政府承担任何未来的承诺和费用"。（同上）

接下来，开发商同意向特斯拉支付总额为 8700000 美元的签约奖金，"条件是，特斯拉需满足双方商定的某些财务要求……且贝纳里洛县根据《地方经济发展法》的条款进行成功谈判并执行项目参与协议……"（同上）新墨西哥州议会将在 2007 年和 2008 年立法会议期间通过拨款总额为 7000000 美元的资金作为签约奖金。《开发协议》中包含了支付签约奖金的时间表，并限制特斯拉只能将签约奖金用于电动汽车制造。此外，《开发协议》规定，签约奖金取决于地方和州实体"提供的充足资金"，而州的贡献"将在适用各方的协议中进一步说明……"（同上，第 3 页）最后，"签约奖金的支付将受限于开发商对特斯拉财务文件的审查，包括开发商合理要求的业务计划和前景展望"。（同上）

*3《开发协议》还规定，开发商将向特斯拉提供地方或州政府的书面声明，说明"特斯拉对该设施的拟议使用已获批准，并符合适用的开发计划、规划或其他使用限制"。（同上）此外，开发商将确保"该场地将拥有全面的基础设施服务"，并将向特斯拉提供贝纳里洛县的书面声明，"确认据其所知，

---

① 译者注：NNN Lease（Triple Net Lease）是美国商业地产中最常见的一种租约，又称"房东免责"租约／"债券"租约。3N 分别代表：地税（Net of Property Tax）、保险费（Net of Insurance）、房屋维护费（Net of maintenance costs）。

无须订约方拟议的其他公共基础设施或服务来运营设施"。（同上，第 4 页）

此外，《开发协议》规定："各方均声明并保证，此协议中的所有承诺均本着遵守本协议所述的明示意思表示及真诚善意而作出。州政府和其他地方政府将尽最大努力为特斯拉拟使用该设施提供必要许可，并将尽最大努力协助批准可能适用的特殊需求变更。国家和其他地方政府将与特斯拉合作，确保特斯拉遵守适用的环境法律或法规。"（同上，第 3 页）

2. 起诉状第一、第三和第四项诉因

开发商称，其在 2007 年"开始采取必要行动，完成《开发协议》规定的义务"，并"以其他方式履行了《开发协议》规定的义务"。（起诉状第 12 段、第 14 段）开发商还称，特斯拉"拒绝签订租赁合同，并以其他方式放弃该项目"。（同上，第 15 段）开发商在第一项诉因，即违约指控中称，特斯拉未能签订租约并放弃该项目的行为构成对《开发协议》的违约。在第三项诉因中，开发商认为，特斯拉"故意隐瞒其在经过一年多的长期准备后放弃该项目的意图……"这一行为构成欺诈。（同上，第 32 段）最后，开发商在第四项诉因中称，特斯拉"故意不签订租赁合同，不完成项目，并放弃项目，违反了诚信和公平交易契约"。（同上，第 38 段）

B. 上诉审查标准

在依据《联邦民事诉讼规则》第 12 节第 2 分节第 6 款驳回原告"未能陈述可以给予救济的请求"的动议时，法院必须接受所有证据的充分指控，并从对原告最有利的角度审视这些指控。参见"泽尼蒙诉伯奇案"，《联邦最高法院判例》第 494 卷第 113—118 页（1990 年）；"斯旺森诉比克斯勒案"，《美国联邦法院判例集》第二辑第 750 卷第 810—813 页（第十巡回法院，1984 年）。《联邦民事诉讼规则》第 12 节第 2 分节第 6 款要求，起诉状中除了标示、总结和公式化地叙述诉因，还要说明原告有权获得救济的理由。参见"贝尔大西洋公司诉托姆布雷案"，《联邦最高法院判例》第 550 卷第 544—555 页（2007 年）。虽然起诉状不需要包括详细的事实指控，但"事实陈述必须足以使救济的权利高于推定的水平"。（同上）换言之，只有在原告明显未能以"充分的事实陈述表面上似乎合理的救济请求"的情况下，根据《联邦民事诉讼规则》第 12 节第 2 分节第 6 款驳回起诉才是适当的。（同上，第 570 页）

原告提出的基于事实的内容使法院能够合理地推断出被告应对所指控的不当行为负责时，该请求就具有表面上的合理性。合理性标准不同于"盖然性要求"，它要求的不仅仅是表明被告存在违法行为的可能性，还需要明确证明被告作出了违法行为。如果起诉状列明的事实"仅仅符合"被告的责任，则其"并未区分'救济权'的可能性和合理性之间的界限"。

*4 "阿什克罗夫特诉伊克巴尔案",《联邦最高法院判例》第 556 卷第 662—678 页（2009 年）（引文省略）。法院必须利用其"司法经验和常识"来评估一项请求的合理性。（同上，第 679 页）

C. 讨论

1. 违约请求（诉因一）

特斯拉认为，由于《开发协议》不是强制性合同，开发商不能断言特斯拉违反了《开发协议》。在新墨西哥州，要提出违约诉讼，原告必须证明：（1）存在具有约束力的有效合同;（2）原告遵守合同并履行了合同规定的义务;（3）对先决条件的履行情况进行一般陈述 ;（4）因被告违约而遭受损失。参见"麦卡斯兰诉普拉瑟案",《新墨西哥州判例汇编》第 92 卷第 192—194 页;《太平洋地区判例汇编》第二辑第 585 卷第 336—338 页（联邦上诉法院,1978 年）。特斯拉称，开发商没有合理地证明《开发协议》是具有约束力的有效合同，因为《开发协议》并未载明交易的基本要素和实质要素。特斯拉还称，开发商在起诉状中并没有指控《开发协议》中规定的所有条款要得到满足，开发商"在任何地方均未声称任何其他实体、机构或政府完成了任何条件或采取了必要行动，更遑论完成了该等必要行动"。（驳回起诉的动议第 9 页）

在新墨西哥州，"根据合同既定原则，除非双方就必要及实质性条款已达成一致，否则双方缔结的远期合约将不具有可执行性"。参见 "斯蒂茨诉耶尔弗顿案",《新墨西哥州判例汇编》第 60 卷第 190—200 页 ;《太平洋地区判例汇编》第二辑第 289 卷第 628—635 页（1995 年）。此外，如果协议的必要及实质性条款语义模糊，或者具有不确定性，协议将不会作为合同被执行。参见 "海德诉布伦顿案",《新墨西哥州判例汇编》第 93 卷第 378—384 页 ;《太平洋地区判例汇编》第二辑第 600 卷第 830—836 页（联邦上诉法院）,调卷令撤销,案号:12, 620（1979 年）（沃尔特斯法官,部分驳回、部分支持）（引文省略）。另见 "7A Am. 朱尔案",《美国合同法第二次重述》第 39 条（2012 年 11 月更新）（"若经延期协议约定的所有条件及条款均已列明，则就某一特定事项达成的协议有效"）。新墨西哥州的司法判例支持这一主张，即协议中预期事项完成期限不定，可使协议因 "不明确而无法执行"。参见 "海德案",《新墨西哥州判例汇编》第 93 卷第 384—385 页 ;《太平洋地区判例汇编》第二辑第 600 卷第 836—837 页（沃尔特斯法官,部分驳回、部分支持）即使如此，"'一份书面合同不需要详细说明每项条款'，但 '实质条款必须得到明确规定，或者能够通过解释而成为必然的默示条款，法院才会判定合同表面上清楚明确'"。参见"兰德尔斯诉汉森案",2011-NMCA-059第32段,《新墨西哥州判例汇编》第150卷第362页(引文省略)。换句话说,合同条款必须合理明确。参见"帕迪利亚诉RRA公司案",1997-NMCA-104第8段,《新墨西哥州判例汇编》第124卷第111页。"'如果合同条款为确定违约行为和提供适当的补救措施提供了依据',那么这些条款就是合理明确的。"(引文省略)

法院从最有利于开发商的角度审查了《开发协议》,认为该协议缺乏许多必要和实质性条款。虽然租赁条款看似具体,但《开发协议》并没有具体规定:(1)完成《开发协议》所述承诺的时间框架;(2)由谁来建设该设施;(3)建设该设施的费用;(4)整个项目的融资方式;(5)建设设施开始和结束的时间;(6)如果立法拨款未获通过会怎样;(7)业绩基准。此外,部分必要和实质性条款留待今后谈判解决。

*5《开发协议》中的许多条款也过于模糊或不确定,即缺乏合理明确性,因为这些条款涉及预期事项、需由第三方履行的额外任务和悬而未决的谈判。但开发商认为,协议中的或有事项并不影响合同的可执行性。开发商援引了Republic Nat. Life Ins公司诉红狮房屋公司案,《美国联邦法院判例集》第二辑第704卷第484页(第十巡回法院,1983年),在该案中,第十巡回上诉法院特别依据科罗拉多州的两个案例,认为"如果合同是否成立取决于能否获得额外的融资,买方必须努力确保获得融资"。(同上,第486页)然而,新墨西哥州上诉法院法官玛丽·沃尔特斯在一份部分驳回、部分支持新墨西哥州上诉法院多数意见的意见书中,讨论了一项财产转让协议,其中房地产转让的条件是该房地产上必须建有房屋。建造房屋之前,存在两种或有事项:(1)春季之前不能开工;(2)房屋的建造取决于买方的房屋销售情况。沃尔特斯法官的结论是,这些"或有事项,加上从未决定或甚至从未讨论过项目完成时间的这一事实,使得买方对建造的'承诺'变得相当不确定,以至于无法强制执行"。参见"海德案",《新墨西哥州判例汇编》第93卷第384—385页;《太平洋地区判例汇编》第二辑第600卷第836—837页。根据沃尔特斯法官的意见,在新墨西哥州,预期事项可以被视为不确定协议,因此该协议是不可执行的合同。

此外,一般来说,"问题在于不确定的承诺对交易是否非常重要,以至于无法严格按照其条款执行该承诺将使得执行协议的其余部分也不公平。越是需要明确约定的重要标的物,其不确定性就越有可能阻止或阻碍协议的执行"。参见理查德·A·洛德,《威利斯顿合同》第1卷第4节第31页(第4版)(2012年5月更新)。换句话说,"如果未确定的事项不妨碍合同剩余部分的履行,而且相对来说不那么重要,则可以完全不履行不确定的承诺,直接执行合同的剩余部分"。（同上）。在本案中，从对开发商最有利的角度看待《开发协议》，法院认为，《开发协议》的预期条款与海德案中的预期条款一样，并非是次要的或无关紧要的条款。特斯拉需要满足这些预期事项，才能占用和租赁开发商的设施，并开始生产电动汽车。换句话说，这些预期事项对交易非常重要，如果不首先满足这些预期事项就强制执行《开发协议》的其余部分是不公平的。

开发商还认为，合同是否存在以及预期事项是否实际得到满足，是由陪审团裁定的事实问题。在裁定根据《联邦民事诉讼规则》第 12 节第 2 分节第 6 款的驳回起诉的动议时，法院只需审查起诉状和所附的《开发协议》，以确定开发商是否提出了看似合理的违约指控。要说明违约行为的合理性，开发商必须证明，《开发协议》表面上是一份具有约束力的有效合同。只有开发商能够合理地证明《开发协议》是具有约束力的有效合同，法院才需要处理开发商诉称其已履行了《开发协议》规定的义务是否合理这一问题。由于法院认为，开发商未能合理地证明《开发协议》是具有约束力的有效合同，因此，法院不需要裁定开发商声称其已履行了《开发协议》规定的义务是否合理。综上所述，法院不能从起诉状和《开发协议》中合理推断出特斯拉应承担违约责任。《开发协议》至多只是一个无法强制执行的协议约定。因此，根据《联邦民事诉讼规则》第 12 节第 2 分节第 6 款，开发商的违约指控应接受法院的有偏见驳回[a]。

2. 违反诚信和公平交易契约（诉因四）

如果没有可执行的合同，任何人都不能提出违反合同法规定的诚信和公平交易契约的主张。参见"瑞尼克诉 O. P. T. I. O. N. 护理公司案"，《美国联邦法院判例集》第三辑第 77 卷第 309—317 页（第九巡回法院），调卷令被拒绝，《联邦最高法院判例》第 519 卷第 865 页（1996 年）。由于开发商没有提出合理的违约指控，故其也不能提出合理的违反诚信和公平交易契约的指控。因此，根据《联邦民事诉讼规则》第 12 节第 2 分节第 6 款，该指控应接受法院的有偏见驳回。

3. 欺诈（诉因三）

*6 开发商提出的指控未包含所要求的详情叙述，因此特斯拉认为，根据《联邦民事诉讼规则》第 12 节第 2 分节第 6 款规定，开发商的欺诈指控应予以驳回。《联邦民事诉讼规则》第 1–009 节第 2 分节规定："所有关于欺诈或

---

① 译者注："有偏见驳回"是指在作出判决后，根据案情驳回民事诉讼。如果一个案件因偏见而被驳回，原告将被禁止以后就同一问题提起诉讼。

错误的指控中，应详尽叙述构成欺诈或错误的情况。恶意、故意、知情和一个人的其他心态状况可以笼统地加以说明。"《联邦民事诉讼规则》第1-009节第2分节和《联邦民事诉讼规则》第9节第2分节一样，要求在陈述欺诈指控时要有"详尽叙述"。在新墨西哥州，"如果所指控的事实中必然隐含欺诈，则对欺诈的指控是充分的；此外，这些主张不应使被告对其声称的主张产生任何怀疑"。参见"德尔加多诉科斯特洛案"，《新墨西哥州判例汇编》第91卷第732—734页；《太平洋地区判例汇编》第二辑第580卷第500—502页（联邦上诉法院，1978年）。联邦法院对此解释道："关于欺诈的指控必须'说明误述的时间、地点和内容，以及作出误述一方的身份及其后果'。"参见"米奇利诉雷罗克矿山公司案"，《联邦判例补编》第二辑第374卷第1039—1047页（新墨西哥州地区法院，2005年）[引用"施瓦茨诉诗尚草本公司案"，《美国联邦法院判例集》第三辑第124卷第1246—1252页（第十巡回法院，1997年）]。尽管"《联邦民事诉讼规则》第9节第2分节并不要求具体了解被告的心理状态"，这正如《联邦民事诉讼规则》第1-009节第2分节的规定，即推测性和结论性的欺诈指控是不充分的。（同上）

　　此案中，开发商在起诉状第32段中只提出了最基本的欺诈指控："被告故意隐瞒其在超过一年的长期准备后企图放弃该项目的行为构成欺诈。"开发商并没有指称具体的时间、地点、行为，甚至没有指称实施欺诈的人的身份。在没有这些指控的情况下，法院无法判定开发商是否提出了可信的欺诈指控。因此，根据《联邦民事诉讼规则》第12节第2分节第6款规定，欺诈指控应接受法院的有偏见驳回。不过，如果开发商能够按照《联邦民事诉讼规则》第1-009节第2分节、《联邦民事诉讼规则》第9节第2分节和《联邦民事诉讼规则》第11节的规定，在2013年3月5日之前重新提出包含详情叙述的欺诈指控，法院将给予开发商修改起诉状的机会。

　　4. 开发商请求赔偿律师费和诉讼费用的请求书

　　由于法院将批准特斯拉"驳回起诉的动议"，因此法院将拒绝开发商要求支付其因答复"驳回起诉的动议"而产生的律师费和诉讼费用的请求。

　　现裁决如下：

　　（1）批准被告特斯拉汽车公司提出的部分驳回起诉的动议（案卷编号：14）；

　　（2）第一项和第四项诉因将因偏见而被驳回；

　　（3）第三项诉因将毫无偏见地被驳回；

　　（4）如果开发商能够按照《联邦民事诉讼规则》第1-009节第2分节、《联邦民事诉讼规则》第9节第2分节和《联邦民事诉讼规则》第11节规定，在2013年3月5日之前重新提出包含详情叙述的欺诈指控，法院将给予开发商修改起诉状的机会；并且

（5）开发商要求判给其律师费和其他相关费用的请求予以驳回。

所有引文：

在《联邦判例补编》副刊，2013年WL 12136382中未见报道。

脚注

1. 在对《联邦民事诉讼规则》第12节第2分节第6款规定的驳回起诉的动议作出裁决时，法院"可以审查起诉状、所附的证物以及与被告提交的《联邦民事诉讼规则》第12节第2分节第6款动议中一起提交的、经援引纳入答辩状的任何文件。"参见英联邦财产律师事务所诉按揭电子登记系统公司案，《美国联邦法院判例集》第三辑第680卷第1194页至1203页（第十巡回法院，2011年）。